The BROTHERHOOD *of* FREEMASON SISTERS

The

BROTHERHOOD

of

FREEMASON SISTERS

———— ✳ ————

Gender, Secrecy, and Fraternity in Italian Masonic Lodges

Lilith Mahmud

THE UNIVERSITY OF CHICAGO PRESS   ∴   Chicago and London

LILITH MAHMUD is assistant professor of women's studies
and anthropology at the University of California, Irvine.

The University of Chicago Press, Chicago 60637
The University of Chicago Press, Ltd., London
© 2014 by The University of Chicago
All rights reserved. Published 2014.
Printed in the United States of America

23 22 21 20 19 18 17 16 15 14 · 1 2 3 4 5

ISBN-13: 978-0-226-09572-1 (cloth)
ISBN-13: 978-0-226-09586-8 (paper)
ISBN-13: 978-0-226-09605-6 (e-book)

DOI: 10.7208/chicago/9780226096056.001.0001

Library of Congress Cataloging-in-Publication Data

Mahmud, Lilith, author.
The brotherhood of Freemason sisters : gender, secrecy,
and fraternity in Italian Masonic lodges / Lilith Mahmud.
pages cm
Includes bibliographical references and index.
ISBN 978-0-226-09572-1 (cloth : alk. paper) — ISBN 978-0-226-09586-8
(pbk. : alk. paper) — ISBN 978-0-226-09605-6 (e-book)
1. Freemasons—Italy.   I. Title.
HS447.I8M345 2014
366'.10820945—dc23
2013022932

⊗ This paper meets the requirements of ANSI/NISO z39.48—1992
(Permanence of Paper).

A mia Nonna.

A Posy, Ismaele, Tellal, Maggie, Sittel, Santippe, Mucci.

And to Dido.

Well, of course, anthropologists have studied every primitive
society in the world. We were the only ones missing!

‹ FELLOW FREEMASON, Grand Lodge of Italy, Rome, March 2006›

CONTENTS

ACKNOWLEDGMENTS

Like the Masonic initiation path, which is walked in the company of others, the writing of this book was no solitary endeavor. For their extraordinary gifts of talent, wisdom, energy, love, and friendship, I must acknowledge here, however partially or inadequately, those who walked alongside me in the writing path.

I would like to begin by thanking my mentors. Michael Herzfeld was a true maestro. He taught me by example how to embrace anthropology as a way of being rather than a profession. His confidence in me and in this improbable project never wavered, and words do not suffice to express my gratitude to him for being a guide, an interlocutor, an advocate, and a friend for so many years. I hope to pay it forward one day. Arthur Kleinman reminded me always to empathize with the suffering of all people, even the powerful, and I am grateful for our many conversations over the years. Mary Steedly taught me how to write with fairness and sensibility even about those with whom I disagree the most, and her love of writing and storytelling continues to be an inspiration to me. Kath Weston's piercing intellectual critique was matched only by the exemplary generosity with which she lives her politics and theories every day, and I am so very grateful for her ongoing friendship.

This book would not have seen the light of day without the solidarity and the intellectual and affective bonds forged with all the graduate students and the administrative staff who walked the halls of the Department of Anthropology at Harvard University. I also thank the Minda de Gunzburg Center for European Studies at Harvard University for supporting this study. Fieldwork research was generously funded by the Social Science Research Council IDRF Program and the Wenner-Gren Foundation for Anthropological Research.

At the University of California, Irvine, I thank my wonderfully brilliant colleagues in the Department of Women's Studies for their support both personally and institutionally, and for making our department a place where I could always look forward to going to work: Laura Kang, Jeanne Scheper, Jennifer Terry, Mary Underwood, Bindya Baliga, Liz Sanchez and Jonathan Alexander have been a veritable dream team, and I am honored to call them my comrades in academia. I also thank my colleagues in the Department of Anthropology for the collegiality with which they have provided me a second intellectual home in Irvine, and especially Victoria Bernal, Julia Elyachar, Karen Leonard, and Bill Maurer for all their support. Tom Boellstorff has been a generous interlocutor, an attentive reader, and the most extraordinary ally I could have dreamed to have. I am thankful to him and Bill Maurer for welcoming me into their lives with open arms. To George Marcus I owe a debt of gratitude not only for his gracious reading of this entire manuscript but also for the many visionary conversations we have had over lunch, which have reframed in profound ways my writing and my thinking about ethnography and academic exchange.

Many other colleagues have commented on parts of this manuscript in one of its many versions, and their generative insights have been a testament to the power of interdisciplinary dialogue: Maylei Blackwell, Claudia Castañeda, Cornelia Mayer Herzfeld, Miriam Shakow, and also Kris Peterson, in whose company I sat at coffee shops and wrote most of this book. My writing group, the "Suspicious Minds," nurtured the development of both content and prose with grace, devotion, and good humor: Erika Hayasaki, Arlene Keizer, Rodrigo Lazo. I am also grateful to my students, whose questions are often the most enlightening, and to the audiences who heard some of this material presented at the American Anthropological Association, the National Women's Studies Association, UC Irvine, UCLA, the University of California Humanities Research Institute, the University of Konstanz, and the University of Leiden.

Much of this book is about fraternity, and if I know what it feels like to cherish an intersubjective bond that transcends the limits of time, space, and words, I owe it to Antonia Forni, Laura Martelli, Soheila Soflai Sohee, and Patrick Stacchini. Silvia Silvestro, who left us before this project was over, will always be with us. Urvashi Chakravarty, Rusaslina Idrus, and Miriam Shakow have been family and a home base through the good times and the bad, wherever we might be on this planet.

I thank the many friends who have come into my life, and whose loving presence alone has sustained me through the writing process: Kate Bronstad, Julia Bryan-Wilson, Mel Chen, Samantha Franklin, Jean Fromm, Rose Hiu, Nancy Megli, Kris Peterson, Michele Po, Sarah Rodriguez, Shireen Roshanravan, Priya Shah, Tushabe wa Tushabe, Deb Vargas, Tiffany Willoughby-Herard. My cousins, aunts, and uncles in Orange County are by far too many to enumerate or to fit in a kinship chart, but they know who they are and they helped me get settled and start anew in Southern California. Raja Bhattar and Arlene Keizer have been my lifelines and my sunshine; we are kindred spirits, and I am very grateful for their gift of friendship. I am especially thankful to Beneka Bali, my self-appointed "book manager," for the military discipline with which she oversaw every step of the reconstruction of this book from the fragments and debris of earlier drafts.

At the University of Chicago Press, I am deeply grateful to T. David Brent for believing in this book long before it was a book. His indefatigable assistant, Priya Nelson, and my manuscript editor, Carol Fisher Saller, have made the production process a pleasure. The two anonymous reviewers critiqued my manuscript with such a degree of care, dedication, and intellectual generosity that even the greatest cynics could regain faith in academia. Some parts of chapter 1 have previously appeared in my article "'The World Is a Forest of Symbols': Italian Freemasonry and the Practice of Discretion," published in *American Ethnologist* 39.2 (2012): 425–438. Portions of chapter 5 originally appeared in my article "In the Name of Transparency: Gender, Terrorism, and Masonic Conspiracies in Italy," published in *Anthropological Quarterly* 85.4 (2012): 1177–1207.

In Italy many people have made this research possible. Elena Berhane and Giuseppe Seganti first inspired me to dream of this project. I cannot even begin to thank the former Grand Maestra of the Grand Women's Masonic Lodge of Italy, Paola Foggi, for introducing me to her world and for trusting this profane ethnographer with a subject so dear to her. In thanking her, I also want to acknowledge all the women and men Freemasons who opened up their homes to me and told me their life stories. To respect their privacy, I cannot name them here, *ma sapete chi siete*. Thanks also go to Stephanie Daddi and to the Cartei family (Stefano, Monica, Stella, and Andrea) for making me feel welcome in Florence.

I say *grazie* to my great-aunt Maria Ertola, whom I have always loved as another grandmother, and who gave me care and hospitality whenever I went to Rome. From my parents I learned to love to travel, to think critically and intellectually, and to have a healthy distrust of authority. Little did they know I would use their example to become a feminist anthropologist.

Finally, I thank my grandmother Nur, who raised me since birth and who died before this book was finished. She was born in Eritrea in 1925 under the violence of the Italian Fascist colonial regime, whose racial laws had both ripped apart her family and prevented black and mixed Eritrean children like her to study beyond the fifth grade. She could not fulfill her life dream of being a teacher, but she spent her life reading books of history and literature and ensuring that her daughter and granddaughter would pursue the highest degrees of education. I loved my *nonna* for all she did in raising me as her own child, but especially for the urgency with which she taught me how to read and write when I was only two and a half years old.

This book is dedicated to her and to all of my cats. Although she pretended to detest them, she always treated them with love, care, and acceptance because she knew they were my family of choice. On that note, I must also thank Dido for making my day every day.

Introduction to the Path

The things that the novel does not say are necessarily more
numerous than those it does say, and only a special halo around
what is written can give the illusion that you are reading also what is
unwritten. ‹ITALO CALVINO, *If on a Winter's Night a Traveler*›

This introduction is my attempt to share with the reader some of the intellectual itineraries along which this project came into existence. The convention in anthropological writing is to start from the *field*, beginning with a description of the landscape—social, historical, or geopolitical—on which all the action will play out. As Bronislaw Malinowski famously wrote of the ethnographer's entry into the field a century ago, "Imagine yourself suddenly set down surrounded by all your gear, alone on a tropical beach close to a native village, while the launch or dinghy which has brought you sails away out of sight" (1984: 4). Anthropologists have since taken apart Malinoswki's prescription, questioning his colonialist assumptions, Orientalist eroticism, and gender and racial positioning in the course of epistemological and methodological reformulations of our discipline. One of Malinowski's tropes, however, would seem to have survived the test of time, persisting in the genre of ethnographic writing into the present: "Imagine yourself *suddenly*."

Suddenly, the ethnographer appears *in medium campum*—and while the *field* has undoubtedly acquired new meanings, implied new recognitions of ethnographic relationships, and expanded to a variety of peoples and locales, it continues to carry a powerful "mystique" as the grounds upon which anthropological research is founded (Gupta and Ferguson 1997a). If we believe the ethnographies, the field is simply there, waiting steadily for the arrival of an anthropologist by dinghy, car, airplane, or parachute. Beginning in the first page, the field is usually presented as the given, passive backdrop on which fieldwork unfolds. The story begins with the anthropologist's arrival to *his* or *her* field site—a narrative convention that sets as time zero the moment of that particular spatial encounter.

Since by convention the field was always already there, the ethnographer's project can also appear as a neatly bounded, inevitable task. Given the field, *voilà* fieldwork. The "ethnographer's magic" has pulled a field out of the anthropologist's hat, and the work that followed, the story that came out after years of revisions, was apparently always there, waiting to be discovered and narrated—six characters in search of an author, as the Italian playwright Luigi Pirandello put it, six informants in search of an anthropologist. The trope of the ethnographer "suddenly set down surrounded by all your gear" hides the months and years of preparation that precede fieldwork research. From graduate studies and grants applications to early reconnaissance research, personal histories, and the economic, social, and political currents that contribute to shaping intellectual desires for "interesting" topics, very little is sudden about the ethnographer's arrival to that mythical field that he or she has territorially claimed for him- or herself.

An attentive reader knows of course to read between the lines, in footnotes, endnotes, acknowledgements, and bibliographies, to find clues of the story behind the story. What would happen to ethnographic writing, though, if those hidden clues—hidden in places where they are in fact meant to be found by those in the know—were simply integrated into the story, explicitly recognized as essential to it? In other words, what would happen to ethnography if we were to recognize the entry into the field as only one step along the path, instead of its starting point?

To borrow a metaphor from my own fieldwork, ethnography too is a knowledge path for initiates, and it is somewhere along the path and usually only in hindsight that its meanings can be appreciated. It is a knowledge path that many people can walk, but every walk is different, and our movements shape the landscape at the same time as they allow us to see it. The following is a fragmentary, equally arbitrary, yet alternative possible beginning to my own fieldwork path.

Incipit

One could say that this project came to life on a rainy and cold afternoon in a historic café in Rome. It was January 2004, and I had flown to Italy over winter break to trace the sources of a very different project I had in mind at the time on charismatic Catholic churches. My aunt, who has long lived in Rome, had mentioned that she might be able to give me some good contacts at Vatican Radio. Since my father and stepmother happened to be in Rome for work as well, we all decided to meet at a café near the Colosseum. It had been many years since I had last seen my aunt and her husband. She and my father had grown up together in Eritrea, and their families had been close for a couple of generations back, before the war between Ethiopia and Eritrea produced diasporic migrations and mass displacements. That is why I had always referred to her as an "aunt," in a shared sense of social relatedness beyond biological kinship. Her husband, who effectively became my "uncle" over the course of this research, I knew very little at the time, having met him only once before. He was a retired lawyer with a great sense of humor and very kind manners. He was also the only white person at our table, something quite remarkable in Italy in 2004. As we sipped our coffees and teas, there was a lot to catch up on—relatives, jobs, and some of my research ideas. It turned out that my aunt and uncle did in fact have some helpful tips for me, but the more they heard about my research interests, the more they seemed to grow perplexed. All of a sudden—I do not recall how it happened exactly—my uncle turned to me and asked, "Why not Freemasonry?"

I remember vividly my confusion at his question, and thinking that I must have forgotten to breathe for too long. It was a sensorial experience that I later reflected upon many times as I carried out research in Italy and I observed the extraordinary power that a single utterance of that word, *Massoneria*, would have over people. His question sounded so lighthearted—why not Freemasonry?—and yet it carried a heavy weight of political history. For what felt like an interminable moment, our whole table fell silent. My uncle kindly repeated his question, only more slowly the second time. Would I be interested in studying Freemasonry? Given my broader theoretical interests, he offered, it would seem like a rather appropriate fit.

I found myself at a loss for words. At the time, I only knew Freemasonry as an elite secret society. In Italy it was usually talked about in relation to very powerful conspiracies, right-wing terrorist acts, and even attempted coups. Freemasons were supposed to control political appointments, university jobs, medical careers in all leading hospitals, and to have tentacles reaching well into the mafia. The political scandal of the secret lodge P2, which brought together members of the upper echelons of the Italian government's executive, legislative, and judiciary branches as well as secret services, financial tycoons, and the military, had reverberated across mass media all over Europe through the

1980s and 1990s. I pictured secret gatherings of men in black hooded robes, and the thought of me studying them seemed, quite frankly, ludicrous. Perhaps, I thought, I had not made myself clear as to what anthropologists do. Perhaps my uncle had assumed that I could merely do archival research on the history of the lodges—and indeed, I could not imagine how else one could possibly study Freemasons in Italy.

I was just about to explain what ethnography is, when my father awoke from his silence and asked my uncle the direct question I had not dared to ask.

"Are you a Freemason?"

What happened next was an epistemological rupture of sort. It was less my uncle's affirmative answer and more the confident tone of his admission, without the slightest hesitation, that left the rest of us stunned. My uncle showed us his hand. Next to his wedding band, he wore a thicker, golden ring, with a compass and a square engraved on top. Although it was unnecessary, he explained to us that the compass and the square are the most famous Masonic symbols.

"But Freemasonry is a secret society?" I blurted out a statement but then raised my intonation at the very end to turn it into a question, as Romance languages allow one to do. It was astounding to hear somebody, to hear my own aunt's husband, talking about it so openly in Italy.

At that question, my uncle turned very serious. No, absolutely not, he insisted. *La Massoneria non è una società segreta.* Freemasonry is not a secret society. It is an esoteric society, he clarified, founded upon humanistic principles, but it is not secret. In fact, he told us he wished that all Freemasons were more open about it, more willing to speak about it like he was doing, so that people would realize that Freemasons have nothing to hide.

"In fact," he added pointing to my aunt, "even *she* is in Freemasonry."

As three sets of eyes all turned to stare at my aunt in disbelief, I thought for sure I must have misheard him, but she quickly dispelled any doubts. "Yes, yes, I'm part of the women's group." She said it in the most casual tone, just as she added nonfat sweetener to her coffee. As disconcerting as it was to speak openly about Freemasonry, and to discover that family friends close enough to be considered relatives could be members of one of Italy's most infamous secret societies, the real shock was another.

"Do you mean to say," I asked in a whisper, "that there are *women* in Freemasonry?"

"Of course there are women in Freemasonry!" My uncle looked like he had explained this before to other audiences. "Although it's true," he conceded, "that many people think there are only men."

That was an understatement. Women have been virtually invisible in representations of the Masonic brotherhood for the last three centuries. Throughout the time of my fieldwork, long after I recovered from my own initial shock, I continued to run into other people's disbelief at the notion that there are women Freemasons, too.

"Yes, dear," my aunt began to correct her husband. "But, see, the women have to be relatives of the men: wives, daughters, nieces, *et cetera*." They explained to us that he belonged to the Grand Orient of Italy (GOI), a Masonic group for men only. She belonged to the Order of the Eastern Star (ES), an auxiliary para-Masonic group for female relatives of GOI men. They told us that the ES was actually an international organization, headquartered in Washington, D.C. "That's why we use a lot of English terms," my aunt informed me in Italian, the language we spoke together. "For example, in every chapter there are a 'Worthy Matron' and a 'Worthy Patron' in charge."

That afternoon we learned some of the background of the GOI and the ES. It was only later that I learned that in addition to auxiliary groups (technically called "adoption lodges") like the ES, there are also both women-only and mixed-gender Masonic lodges in which women receive a full Masonic ritual initiation—something that the ES do not have. My aunt and uncle seemed very happy to share their experiences with us. Before we left, I asked them if they were serious when they suggested that I study Freemasonry. They said they would help me in any way they could. "Do you think you could come back in April?" my uncle asked. "Every year the GOI has a big convention. Brothers come from all over Italy to attend, and foreign delegations come too. You would meet a lot of people there." Indeed, the convention turned out to be an invaluable entry point to the social world of Freemasons in Italy.

We said our good-byes quickly out in the rain that day, trying to stay clear of scooters splashing puddle water onto the sidewalk as they sped by and promising to stay in touch more often. As my aunt and her husband disappeared from sight among a sea of thick, dark coats and colorful umbrellas in the distance, my father, who also seemed to have just recovered from the shock, looked toward them and said something to me that I came to hear time and time again from non-Masons in Italy. "Her husband is such a good person. If all Masons were like him, I would join them tomorrow."

One could say that this project came to life serendipitously that afternoon in a Roman café when my aunt and her husband planted an idea in my mind that at the time sounded foolish. Why don't I study Freemasons? Or perhaps one could say that it began a couple of days later, in the back of a different Roman café, where according to academic hierarchies I went to seek approval from my then advisor, Michael Herzfeld, to proceed, and the two of us found ourselves whispering with excitement our plots for what this profane ethnography of Italian Freemasons could look like. Or perhaps one could say that this project only really began months later, after early reconnaissance trips, after IRB approval, after fieldwork grants awarded for this "rare ethnographic opportunity," and only after I landed in Florence in 2005 to start the requisite fifteen continuous months of ethnographic research, calculated summer to summer, in northern-hemisphere academic standard time.

In the months that followed that first mention of Freemasonry in a Roman café, I was back in the United States learning as much as I could about the lodges from books and websites, realizing in the process that I had a lot to catch up on. Discussing my newly found project with friends and colleagues, I soon realized that Freemasonry had very different connotations in the States, where temples stand proud on Main Streets throughout the country and Masons are generally viewed as members of a benign, small-town organization. Almost everyone I talked to back in the States seemed to have a grandfather who was a Freemason and at least one happy childhood memory of attending a barbeque at the local lodge. I had to evoke the Ku Klux Klan, or the figure of the "commie" in the McCarthy era, or perhaps the Mafia, to conjure for an American audience an image comparable to that of Freemasonry in Italy and to elicit that sensorial, visceral discomfort that Italian audiences so often experience, half fright and half repugnance. Above all, however, I had to reconsider my own commonsense notions of what Freemasonry meant in Italy.

The Secret Society That Isn't One

Freemasonry is the quintessential Western secret society, one that since its foundations has been mythologized in countless works of fiction and in the collective imaginary. Depictions of the brothers performing esoteric rituals in their black robes and conspiring to bring about a new world order have inspired not only best-selling books and movies but also journalistic and police investigations that, in countries like Italy, have attributed to the lodges a virtually unlimited power to infiltrate the highest levels of government. And yet, the women and men Freemasons I came to know over the course of eighteen combined months of fieldwork were adamant about one thing: Freemasonry is not a secret society.

To write about the subject of Freemasonry therefore poses a critical problem of representation. Most audiences, including myself before the start of this project, believe they already know what Freemasonry is, whether through their childhood memories of the lodge on Main Street, or through political scandals attributing to Freemasons antidemocratic criminal acts. That assumption of prior knowledge also carries with it a disavowal, an admission that as much as I believe I know about Freemasonry, I nonetheless don't know what Free-masons *really* do, since they are supposed to be, after all, members of a secret society (or aren't they?). Knowledge of Freemasonry follows a conspiratorial logic, and it tends to reify Freemasonry as a secret society, both known and unknowable, familiar and yet understudied; and regardless of how critical or sympathetic an account it offers, women are usually absent from depictions of the brotherhood.

To better understand the problem of secrecy as it came to define the Masonic experiences that are the topic of this book, we need to locate Italian Freemasonry within particular historical, political, and social contexts. To put it simply, Freemasonry is an esoteric society whose members receive a ritual initiation and then pursue a life-long self-cultivation path. The goal of Freemasonry is to better society by bettering individuals, who are supposed to develop their full potential through the Masonic path in accordance with humanist values, such as liberty, fraternity, and equality, and by practicing rituals with their lodge brothers or sisters.

The history of Freemasonry is somewhat controversial. Freemasons themselves draw a lineage that often dates back to the Temple of Solomon. Most scholars, however, agree that Freemasonry found its roots in medieval guilds of "operative" stonemasons, united in what might anachronistically be defined as labor unions, and that modern "speculative" Freemasonry emerged at the turn of the eighteenth century, partly in relation to the Enlightenment and as the continuation of several pre-existing secret societies (Stevenson 1988). The year 1717 is when most Freemasons claim that the first speculative lodge was established in England, despite the fact that historiographic research has dated the first lodges back to the late seventeenth century (Jacob 1991). It was in 1723 that a pastor by the name of James Anderson published the first edition of the *Constitutions of the Free-Masons*, which codified a history of the brotherhood, as well as its tenets, principles, and rules. Anderson's *Constitutions*, as they became known, continue to serve as foundational texts for lodges worldwide (Anderson, Vibert, and Freemasons 1924).[1]

Throughout the eighteenth century, Freemasonry played a significant role in the shaping of democratic ideals, including the very notion of the "public" on which democracy is based. Reviewing the post-Enlightenment shift toward democratic politics, several scholars have suggested that it was precisely in the secrecy of Masonic lodges that modern ideals of republicanism and publicity could find a safe ground to blossom against the absolutist authority of the sovereign (Dean 2002; Habermas 1989; Jacob 1991). Jürgen Habermas (1989) has famously argued that Masonic lodges gave rise to a political and intellectual public sphere that was specifically modern and bourgeois in character. Paradoxically, the public conjured inside the lodges—bourgeois, democratic, literate—needed to rely on its own secrecy to challenge the obscurantism of the monarch. As Habermas (1989) wrote, "Social equality was possible at first only as an equality outside the state. The coming together of private people into a public was therefore anticipated in secret, as a public sphere still existing largely behind closed doors" (35). With their emphasis on enlightened rationality and equality, secret Masonic lodges functioned according to Habermas as "proto-publics" in an era of absolute monarchy.

Historians of Freemasonry have further suggested that wherever they were in the world, Masonic lodges of the eighteenth and nineteenth centuries were directly involved in nation-building projects. Many the founding fathers of the United States, for instance, were Freemasons, as were many founding fathers of the Italian nation-state (Ciuffoletti and Moravia 2004; Clawson 1989; Mola 1992). Bringing together a rationalist political philosophy and a nondenominational spirituality, the lodges became secret sites for the harboring of liberal and secular democratic visions that threatened monarchic and religious authority.

The development of Freemasonry in Italy began a little later than in Northern Europe. Although there were some traces of Masonic activity as early as the mid-eighteenth century, the precursor of the major and oldest Masonic Order in Italy, the men-only Grand Orient of Italy–Palazzo Giustiniani (GOI), was founded in 1805, and it was only after Italian unification in 1860 that it gained more prominence.[2] In the years that led to the unification of the country, many secret societies of intellectuals, aristocrats, and politicians plotted a nationalist project. Among these, perhaps one of the most renowned is Giuseppe Garibaldi's *carboneria*, a secret society whose ultimate goal was the unification of the peninsula under the rule of the Savoy king. Several historians have pointed out the overlapping of membership between the *carboneria* and Freemasonry, and Giuseppe Garibaldi himself became Grand Master of the GOI (Dito 1905; Esposito 1956).

The list of Grand Masters of the GOI in the decades following Italian unification included illustrious members of the ruling parties and the aristocracy. Masonic elitism is not unique to the Italian experience, but whereas in countries such as the United States the legacy of Freemasons like George Washington or Benjamin Franklin has faded over time (Clawson 1989), in Italy Freemasonry has remained largely an upper-class phenomenon to the present.

Antonio Gramsci famously defined Freemasonry as the party of the bourgeoisie (Gramsci, Gerratana, and Istituto Gramsci 1975: 2146). While commentators have since debated the extent to which Freemasonry represents a form of association comparable to that of a political party, most have agreed that Italian Freemasonry had essentially a bourgeois and urban basis at the turn of the twentieth century (Conti 2003: 321–351). Perhaps this elitism, reinforced by a vow of secrecy, has contributed to the negative portrayals of Freemasonry in Italian mass media, and to the general sense of mistrust with which most ordinary people in Italy refer to it.

An important center of anti-Masonic sentiment has been the Roman Catholic Church, which, since the eighteenth century, has repeatedly excommunicated anyone initiated into Freemasonry. In nineteenth-century Italy, Catholic opposition to Freemasonry was understandable in political terms, as the new secular country literally had to wage war against the Vatican to conquer territory for the nation-state, including its capital city of Rome. During the Risorgimento, Italy's nation-building decades in the middle of the nineteenth century, while many politicized Italian Catholics remained faithful to the pope and refused to bear arms for the Italian state against the Vatican, others chose to embrace the nationalist project, as did Freemasons, who advocated a strong separation of church and state. Long after diplomatic relations between Italy and the Vatican had been fully restored in the post-Fascist era, Catholic loathing for Freemasonry continued in the form of accusations of heresy and Satanism, fomented by the esoteric rituals that the initiated are known to perform.

During fieldwork, I found that my interlocutors were often dismissive of their excommunication. They seemed to be under the impression that because the excommunication had been issued in past centuries it was only a historical event, a sign of its times, and that it would no longer apply. Mostly, they seemed uncomfortable with the topic and were quick to change the subject. I followed their lead, and did not push or pursue it any further. Nonetheless, as recently as 1983, Cardinal Joseph Ratzinger, who later became Pope Benedict XVI, issued a declaration on behalf of the Vatican Sacred Congregation for the Doctrine of the Faith, in which he reminded the faithful that the papal ban against Freemasonry was still very much in effect, and that all Catholics initiated to Freemasonry were forbidden from receiving Holy Communion in a Catholic church as a result of their "grave sin" (Mola 1992: 959–962; Ratzinger 1983).

Religion occupies indeed a central, if ambivalent, place in Freemasonry. Masonic rules forbid lodge members from discussing politics or religion inside the temple, and Freemasons have long denied the accusation that they are a cult or an organized religion. Anderson's *Constitutions*, however, prescribe that "a Mason is oblig'd by his tenure, to obey the moral Law; and if he rightly understands the Art, he will never be a stupid *Atheist*, nor an irreligious *Libertine*" (Anderson, Vibert, and Freemasons 1924). A prospective apprentice must profess a belief in a higher being, or what they refer to as the "Great Architect" of the universe—a metaphor in line with the actual masonic origins of the lodges. In everyday practice within Masonic temples, this belief translates into highly elaborate rituals in ceremonial garments, through which the members, purportedly from different faiths, celebrate this nondenominational higher being. Freemasons are therefore required to be believers, and the lodges do practice esoteric rituals, but they typically do not ascribe to the dogmatic truths of any one organized religion in particular.[3]

The question of belief has been central to anthropological studies of ritual, as Evans-Pritchard (1976 [1937]) established in his own work on magic (Asad 1993; Luhrmann 1989; but cf. Needham 1972). Anthropologists have often attempted to make sense of seemingly irrational belief systems, as a way to familiarize the exotic and to provincialize Eurocentric assumptions about logic and rationality. The case of Italian Freemasons poses a challenge to this common paradigm not only because my subjects were European, and thus eschew simplistic cultural explanations of difference, but also because, as Freemasons, they embodied the very Enlightenment ideals that gave rise to a rationalist and progressive modernity. Those ideals have engendered the notion of the "secular," which was never a denial of spirituality (Jakobsen and Pellegrini 2008). Several Enlightenment philosophers who were also Freemasons, such as brother Voltaire, were not atheists but rather believers in a nondenominational and universal deism. As heirs to that philosophical tradition, the Freemasons I met in Italy still held faith in a higher being as an eligibility requirement for prospective members. While rationality and secularism have been exalted to demarcate the "West" in contrast to the presumed traditionalism and religiosity of other peoples, multiple belief systems continue to coexist in the global North, alongside its scientific episteme and modernist discourse (Good 1994; Tambiah 1990). In line with their Enlightenment heritage, the Freemasons I met approached their spirituality with intellectualism, studying assiduously ancient forms of worship, symbolism, and philosophy. Many of them were well versed in Latin, Greek, and all that constitutes the "high culture" of the Italian nation-state. From their perspective, they were human beings who followed the revolutionary credo of liberty, fraternity, and equality, believing in cultivation of the intellect as a necessary means to self-improvement, and combining spirituality with intellectual inquiry to produce good citizens.

Despite Italian Freemasonry's strong nationalism, it was during Benito Mussolini's Fascist dictatorship that the lodges were most persecuted, as their secret gatherings and their liberal political philosophies were viewed as a threat by the regime (Isastia 2004). Mussolini's attack against the lodges, which he eventually banned and dismantled, was the beginning of a Fascist politics of systematic repression of social organizations and labor unions hostile to the regime. Interestingly, when Mussolini presented his anti-Masonic bill to the Italian parliament for debate in 1925, before his rule turned into a full-fledged dictatorship, the representative who stood up in defense of Freemasonry was Antonio Gramsci. Although Gramsci was a Communist and a hardened critic of Freemasonry, which he viewed as the party of the bourgeoisie, the transcript of that parliamentary debate between him and prime minister Mussolini shows that Gramsci foresaw the effects that a Fascist law against Masonic lodges was sure to have on labor unions and on other political parties (Gramsci and Mussolini 1997).

In the post-1946 democracy, the new constitution, while guaranteeing the right of citizens to associate freely, nonetheless forbade all secret societies. As a result, the second half of the twentieth century saw many attempts, more or less successful, by the press, by Catholic forces, and by left-wing parties to accuse Freemasons of being members of a secret society that must be eradicated. The public's right to transparency has battled in court against Freemasons' right to privacy (Mazzocchi 1994).

The height of anti-Masonic sentiments in the second half of the twentieth century came in the 1970s and 1980s, during the period known as the "Lead Years," when Italy was the site of a string of deadly terrorist acts—bombings, assassinations, shootings—attributed to far-right and far-left paramilitary organizations. Freemasons were the prime suspects behind most of the right-wing terrorist attacks of those years. Moreover, the political scandal of the deviated Masonic lodge P2, which was accused of plotting a coup and of being at the center of a massive embezzlement of public funds, put the final nail in the coffin of Freemasonry's reputation in Italy.

The Freemasons I met were painfully aware of their reputation, and in the beginning of the twenty-first century many of the lodges had come to embrace the rhetoric and practice of transparency precisely to counter dominant narratives against them. Although my interlocutors vehemently denied that Freemasonry is a secret society in the legal and political sense of the term, their esoteric practices and the organizational structure of the lodges are so steeped in ritual secrecy that it is easy to see why Freemasonry has historically been a hiding ground for groups and individuals viewed as subversive by the rulers of the times, whether in times of dictatorship or in times of democracy.[4]

Masonic Architecture and Membership

Freemasonry is an esoteric organization with a pyramidal structure. Upon receiving a ritual initiation, a neophyte becomes an Apprentice and enters a path that progressively leads to higher degrees of initiation, often requiring years of esoteric studies and frequentation of a lodge to advance from one level to the next. There are three degrees in the Masonic path: first degree or Apprentice; second degree or Fellow; and third degree or Master (*Maestra/o* in Italian).[5] These first three degrees constitute what is known as a Masonic Order, or blue Freemasonry, and that is what most people think of when they think of Freemasonry. In many cases, upon reaching the third degree of the Order, a Maestro or Maestra might choose to continue his or her initiation path through the advanced degrees of a Rite, or red Freemasonry.[6] Ranging from the fourth to the thirty-third degree or even beyond, Rites are especially esoteric pursuits, inspired by a variety of magical, alchemical, or chivalrous groups, such as the Knights Templar or Rosicrucians, and they are far more secretive than the Orders.

Most countries have at least one if not more national Masonic groups (*Obbedienze*). Each of these national organizations has multiple local chapters, known as *lodges*, which usually include seven to fifteen members who meet regularly to perform rituals. In large cities, such as Rome or Florence, there might be several lodges belonging to the same national group. In my research I worked closely with four separate Masonic organizations in Italy. The Grande Oriente d'Italia–Palazzo Giustiniani (Grand Orient of Italy or GOI) was a men-only group and the oldest and largest Masonic organization in Italy, with a membership of approximately fifteen thousand. The Ordine della Stella d'Oriente (Order of the Eastern Star or ES) was an auxiliary para-Masonic group open to female relatives of GOI men. Headquartered in Washington, D.C., this international organization was technically a mixed-gender adoption lodge, including both women and some GOI brothers who fulfill a supervisory role in ES chapters. The only admission requirement for prospective female initiates to the ES was to prove kinship ties to a man of the GOI. Each local chapter of the ES was presided over by an elected Worthy Matron and an elected Worthy Patron, and the organization worked directly under the leadership of the GOI. Another organization with which I worked was the mixed-gender Gran Loggia d'Italia degli Antichi Liberi Accettati Muratori–Obbedienza di Piazza del Gesù, Palazzo Vitelleschi (Grand Lodge of Italy of Ancient Free and Accepted Masons or GLDI). Born out of a split within the GOI at the beginning of the twentieth century, the GLDI had begun initiating women in the 1950s. With a membership of approximately nine thousand, the GLDI was the second-largest Masonic organization in Italy. Finally, the fourth group I studied was the Gran Loggia Massonica Femminile d'Italia (Grand Women's Masonic Lodge of Italy or GLMFI). Headquartered in Florence, and with a few local lodges in other major Italian cities, this small national organization with only a few hundred members had the honor of being the only women-only Masonic group in Italy. It was also significantly younger than the others, having been formally established in 1990 from the ashes of a women's lodge that had been operative in Italy since the late 1970s under the auspices of a French Grand Lodge for women.

Each of these four groups reflected a different Masonic path and was characterized by particular understandings of gender and esotericism. For instance, the mixed-gender GLDI and the women-only GLMFI had friendship treaties with each other. Neither organization, however, recognized the legitimacy of the men-only GOI, nor did the GOI recognize them. Moreover, the ES, which was administratively a subsidiary of the GOI, was not recognized as a Masonic Order by any of the other three groups. The complex topography of recognition, formal treaties, and strategic alliances among lodges spanned far beyond the borders of Italy. International connections were just as important to affirm the status of a particular Masonic organization, whose legitimacy depended on the quantity (and quality) of the formal recognitions it could secure from lodges worldwide. In addition to treaties with each other, lodges also relied on particular historical narratives to reinforce their own legitimacy. For instance, the GOI considered itself to be the only legitimate (*regolare*) Masonic lodge operating in Italy because it had long held the endorsement of the United Grand Lodge of England (UGLE), which asserts its hegemony over universal Freemasonry by virtue of its status as the first and oldest Masonic lodge in the world.[7] The GLMFI and the GLDI, however, refused to grant to the UGLE ultimate authority over the development of Freemasonry throughout the world. Instead, the women-only and mixed-gender groups based their claims to legitimacy on the dozens of treaties of mutual recognition they had signed with lodges all over the world.[8]

Despite their philosophical differences, all of these groups shared fundamental beliefs about the Masonic path that shaped their daily lives in interestingly similar ways. Moreover, members of each group often had ties of kinship and personal friendship with members of other groups. Not only were ES women related to GOI brothers, as required by their Order's membership rules but, more often than not, family members could be found in the mixed-gender and women-only lodges as well. Therefore, and despite the lodges' official policies, members of each Masonic organization I studied were sure to be found at the dinner parties and even ritual celebrations hosted by members of the other lodges.

The composition of Masonic lodges has diversified over the years and in different parts of the world to include members of lower socioeconomic status, people of color, and women (Clawson 1989). Despite such changes, however, the lodges I studied largely maintained their elitism, and the issue of women's initiation was still highly controversial in the early twenty-first century. The appearance of elitism is sometimes a direct result of an organization's secrecy. As Georg Simmel argued, "Secrecy and pretense of secrecy are means of building higher the wall of separation, and therein a reinforcement of the aristocratic nature of the group" (1906: 486–487). Moreover, Italian Freemasonry has continued to draw its members from the highest ranks of society, including those from aristocratic, intellectual, political, and corporate backgrounds. This is not to say that every Freemason I met necessarily belonged at the top of social hierarchies. Despite hefty annual membership fees, it would be foolish to suggest that only lawyers, physicians, architects, university professors, or journalists belonged to Masonic lodges—though certainly those professions seemed to be overrepresented. Clerical workers, administrators, and government officials whose jobs for the state's bureaucratic machine may not have been as prestigious or financially rewarding were nonetheless able to become Freemasons, often through personal contacts. Individual economic differences could also be seen across gender. Older women in particular often held middle-level jobs in teaching, in accounting, or within small family firms, reflecting the uneven employment prospects available to them when they came of age in the 1960s. While Masons in Italy certainly had different income levels—most falling within an upper-middle to upper-class range—each of the Masonic groups I worked with was typically viewed overall as an "elite" organization, whose members were imagined to enjoy a great deal of cultural and social capital. They thus provided apt entry points to the study of gender mobilization among the upper classes in Italy.

The very question of what makes an elite, and of how to study social class ethnographically, has increasingly preoccupied anthropologists and other researchers attempting to broaden the field of social scientific inquiry on relations of power (see Bourdieu 1984; Marcus and Hall 1992; Nader 1972; Ortner 2003; Pina-Cabral and Lima 2000; Shore and Nugent 2002). Whereas some defining characteristics have been outlined in the literature on elites—their ability to command respect, to ensure succession, to control resources or make claims to history—the category is erratic nonetheless, immediately familiar yet uncannily ephemeral. When I use the word *elite* throughout this book, I do not mean to pin down any one set of traits in an effort to provide an operational definition. My goal is not to offer an illusory conquest of a fleeting identity category but rather to recognize that the experiential reality of such a category, in its rhetorical and material consequences, is itself the product of a discursive reification.

By approaching the study of elites ethnographically, in the intimacy of the fieldwork encounter, I could hope to examine the complexities not of a static class ideology or worldview but, rather, in Raymond Williams's sense, of a "structure of feeling" that meshes aesthetic and social experiences irreducible to fixed class positions (Williams 1977: 128–135). I therefore take the elite not to be a static position on a class ladder but, rather, a set of relations, desires, and aesthetics performed within and beyond class lines to conjure a collective identity category, which is then reproduced as if effortlessly through a labor of accumulation and gatekeeping (see Bourdieu 1977; Bourdieu 1984; Bourdieu 1990; Butler 1990; Butler 1999; Ortner 2006). Through the ethnographic interrogation of the analytical category of elite, it is then possible to "discommode the received images we currently entertain of what constitutes an elite" (Herzfeld 2000: 227).

In addition to the lodges' elitism, the old question of women's initiation into Freemasonry remained one of the major ongoing debates within Masonic circles at the time of my fieldwork, and it had the effect of further policing the boundaries of membership into the brotherhood (Calzolari and Vanni 2001; Caracciolo 2004; Vigni and Vigni 1997). Even though three of the four Masonic groups I studied included women, the historical predominance of the men-only GOI over Italian Freemasonry and women's overall invisibility in mainstream representations of the lodges have meant that the question of women's inclusion into the brotherhood remained central to my interlocutors' lives and to my research as well. Throughout this book, I will therefore return to women's presence in and exclusion from this fraternal society as a way to make sense of my interlocutors' paradoxical subject positions, which inspired the title of this book, and to understand Freemasons' project of self-cultivation as also a gender project.

A Brotherhood of Sisters

What is it that still makes the words *women Freemasons* sound inherently oxymoronic to most, even at a time when women have arguably entered all kinds of masculine spaces, albeit with great difficulty and amid ongoing sexism? Why is the subject position of a woman Freemason beyond recognition? This is the question that will haunt every chapter of this book, and which I will address with reference to Masonic practices and to my interlocutors' complex relationships with the rest of Italian society. To be clear, my purpose in asking this question is not to dwell on a victimizing narrative of sexism, which, however true it might be, would also nonetheless reify a binary essentialism of gender, positing generic women versus generic men, and anyway would be unlikely to reveal anything that we do not already know about gender-based discrimination. Yes, there is undoubtedly sexism, but that is only for starters. What pervades Freemasonry is a universalizing claim of acceptance and inclusivity. Liberty, fraternity, and equality *for all* are guiding Masonic principles that also became the slogan of the French revolution. When the Freemasons I met through the course of this research insisted with a straight face that they "accept anybody," despite the overwhelmingly white, male, and upper-class composition of most lodges, it was clear that they really meant it. By taking seriously Masonic claims of inclusivity, even from the standpoint of women Freemasons who espoused those claims while simultaneously fighting for a seat at the table, in the following chapters I will explore further the meaning of "anybody" that is at the heart of Freemasonry's self-cultivation project and also at the heart of the liberal political beliefs that characterize European democracies. What the two have in common is a shared history, a coproduction of Masonic values and of liberal political philosophies inside Masonic lodges of the Enlightenment, where intellectuals and revolutionaries of the time met (in secret) to theorize a new society and a new form of liberal democratic governance *for all* free from the tyranny of absolute monarchy (Dean 2002; Habermas 1989; Jacob 2006). The Freemasons with whom I worked in Italy positioned themselves as heirs to the intellectual and philosophical contributions of the Enlightenment, and even claimed with pride that the Enlightenment had been made by Freemasons. Twenty-first-century lodges were therefore not only sites where an anthropologist of Europe could analyze contemporary practices of gender and citizenship, but they were also central sites for the reproduction of beliefs about gender, citizenship, and humanity that have become hegemonic in liberal countries of the global North. The pervasive exclusion of women (and of many other subject categories) from Freemasonry's imaginary of "anybody" is therefore a case of sexism that is also, and more fundamentally, a case of humanism.

The paradox of a group of sisters reconstituting themselves into a brotherhood is an illustration of humanism's formidable capacity to inspire social imaginaries that are rooted in an abstract notion of a political subject. Through a life-long esoteric self-cultivation path, my women and men informants aimed to refashion their subjectivities into an abstract, cosmopolitan, liberal, secular subject, a person of good character endowed with reason and wisdom, who believed in the democratic principles of liberty, equality, and fraternity as much as in the benevolent presence of a higher being guiding us all. Such lofty goals, however, were caught in the treacherous web of liberal humanism's failed promises as much as in the specific context of Italy's violent political history. The experiences of women Freemasons in particular expose both the enduring appeal of liberal humanism and its inherent failures, even within the geopolitical boundaries of Europe.

There are two lines of inquiry woven throughout these chapters. The first one is about secrecy. The second one is about fraternity. They are not so much two separate lines as two sides of the same coin. As Jacques Derrida wrote in his reflections on the politics of friendship, a meditation on fraternity is inseparable from a meditation on secrecy because it is the sharing of secrets that makes friends (2005: 145). Secrecy, as a foundational sociological principle (Simmel 1906), builds relationships and communities, and that is why anthropologists have long been in the business of studying secret societies (see Bellman 1984; Evans-Pritchard 1976 [1937]; Gable 1997; Little 1951; MacCormack 1980; Murphy 1980; Turner 1967).

Freemasonry is a fraternal society, and although my interlocutors denied the title of a secret society, secrecy nonetheless permeated their rituals, their sociality, and their relationship to the rest of Italy. As I analyze Freemasons' secretiveness, I focus on *discretion*, the term that they preferred to use when they had to explain why, for instance, they would not advertise their public events, or why they would not disclose even to their loved ones their identities as Freemasons. Being discreet was for my interlocutors an embodied disposition that allowed them to assert their belonging in a community of initiates at the same time as it shielded them from the intrusive gaze of Italian media and law enforcement. Freemasons were not secret, but they were very discreet, and their discretion mediated their ability to thrive in a fraternal society that was also highly suspect.

Chapter 1, "Spaces of Discretion," situates Freemasonry in the Italian social and architectural landscape by examining my informants' everyday practices of discretion, which allowed them to conceal Masonic spaces and Masonic experiences in plain sight amid the profane world. Chapter 2, "Initiations," explores the multiple ritual and social paths that would lead particular people to become Freemasons. The subjectivity at the center of my interlocutors' self-cultivation projects was fundamental to their sense of self, and it could be more accurately described as *inter*subjectivity—the desire to become a brother. Gender relations within the lodges, however, marked and mediated the initiation of women to such an extent that women were often accused of "imitating" men's lodges, and their very conditions of possibility as women Freemasons were called into question. In chapter 3, "Brotherly Love," I therefore analyze the humanist notion of "fraternity" that Freemasons pursued. Reviewing the history of women's lodges in Italy, which emerged from within right-wing upper-class sensibilities and in opposition to feminism, I ask why and how women Freemasons remade themselves into abstract and unmarked *brothers*, and what their gender politics illustrate about the ideological workings of liberalism. Chapter 4, "Speculative Labor," aims to demystify what Freemasons actually do by examining the content and practice of Masonic work, which is the intellectual pursuit of both arcane, esoteric knowledge and of the Eurocentric body of art, literature, music, and classics ideologically defined as "high" culture. Focusing on the latter, this chapter reads the marginalization of women in relation to discreet practices of accumulation and performance of cultural capital that, while ostensibly available to anyone, is nonetheless rooted in a highly elitist, racialized, nationalist, and gendered knowledge formation. Finally, in chapter 5, "Transparent Conspiracies," I turn to Italy's violent history of political terrorism to understand how *Freemasonry* has become such a loaded term, and to contextualize my interlocutors' efforts to remake themselves into transparent subjects who have nothing to hide, albeit with discretion. There I analyze women's conspicuous absence from conspiracy theories and state-sponsored investigations of Italian Freemasons as diagnostics of the ideological deployment of security and transparency discourses in a democratic country.

Readers will notice that at key points of transition between chapters I have inserted brief vignettes that I have called *passwords*. Passwords are what Freemasons receive when they are ready to advance from one degree of initiation to the next. By speaking the right word, they will be granted access to the temple when rituals inside are being performed at a correspondingly higher degree of initiation. These ethnographically driven scenes that I have inserted between chapters are also meant to function as passwords: each provides an interpretive key to decipher the chapter that immediately follows it. They also, however, crystallize some of the knowledge generated in the chapter preceding each of them, since, in accordance with Masonic teachings, knowledge is only really learned in hindsight. These passwords can be read on their own, or they can be read in the order in which they appear to transition between chapters. They are meant to convey some of those episodes of extraordinary insight that occasionally break the monotony of fieldwork research by clarifying certain findings or by directing the ethnographer's attention to what is "really going on." I chose to include these passwords to recreate for readers some of my own learning process, as I came to know the path of Freemasonry through the everyday practices of women and men Freemasons who shared their lives with me.

This book is neither an apology for nor a condemnation of Freemasonry. It is rather a work of feminist anthropology that relies on gender as an analytical entry point to the study of how particular values that have come to define "Western civilization" and its political subjects are practiced, embodied, and reproduced on the ground by a powerful community of practice that more than any other has laid claims to the Occident as a universalizing utopia. In the anthropological tradition of making the exotic familiar, my hope is to demystify Freemasonry for profane readers, but also to profane Freemasonry's stronghold on the reproduction of privilege and of European imaginaries of subjectivity. And to be absolutely clear, I write it as a profane.

When I started this project, I did not know what studying Freemasonry would look like. Indeed, I went tumbling down the rabbit hole and found myself doing fieldwork in places and situations far beyond my imagination. Temples, rituals, initiation paths, esoteric symbols that all exist right below the surface of everyday encounters in everyday urban centers have been shown to me in broad daylight, along with gala dinners, coffee houses, theaters and someone's private home. As my informants liked to say, "Masons have nothing to hide," and indeed nothing is hidden, but one must know how to look. Over the course of this research, I had to train myself to see differently, speak differently, and move differently, as my informants did, to navigate with discretion spaces of knowledge hidden in plain sight. Remaining conscious of my shifting abilities, my reinculcated *habitus* was not just another exercise in reflexivity. It was, for me, a necessary step along the path.

Spaces of Discretion

It is as though the practices organizing a bustling city were characterized by
their blindness. The networks of these moving, intersecting writings compose a
manifold story that has neither author nor spectator, shaped out of fragments of
trajectories and alterations of spaces: in relation to representations, it remains daily
and indefinitely other. ‹MICHEL DE CERTEAU, *The Practice of Everyday Life*›

"Di qua d'Arno," on this side of the Arno River, the center of Florence was
more often than not picture perfect. The brightly lit windows of fashion designer stores illuminated day and night a pedestrian path along very narrow
sidewalks, where people walked in single bidirectional lines, slaloming to avoid
dog excrement, and squeezing to fit on the tiny stretch of raised pavement
according to more or less explicit Darwinian hierarchies. Those who did not
make it overflowed onto the street below, if traffic allowed it, or just lingered
at the edge of a piece of sidewalk barely wide enough for their feet, as they
waited for their turn to walk. When a bus drove by, pedestrians on most sidewalks had to come to a halt, turn our backs against the fashion windows, hold
in our breaths and stomachs, and then just wait for there to be room to push
and move and spill again.

When I returned to Italy for a year of fieldwork research in the summer
of 2005, I decided to make a home in Florence. There were various reasons
for that decision. First, Florence is strategically located in the middle of the
country. After visiting lodges and individual Freemasons in different parts of
Italy I realized that, if I wanted to follow the widespread networks of Masonic
lodges, traveling would be an essential component of my fieldwork. Second,

the region of Tuscany broadly and its capital city of Florence specifically have a uniquely rich Masonic history in Italy, which makes Florence an especially important site for my project. Finally, the national headquarters of the women-only Grand Women's Masonic Lodge of Italy (GLMFI) were in Florence. During one of my early meetings with Paola Foggi, then Grand Maestra of the GLMFI, in her Florentine home, she had told me that their group was relatively small and did not have as many local lodges in other cities, unlike the much larger men-only Grand Orient of Italy (GOI), its subsidiary Order of the Eastern Star (ES) for female relatives of the GOI, or the mixed-gender Grand Lodge of Italy–Piazza del Gesù (GLDI).[1] While the national headquarters of those three other Masonic organizations were in Rome, they all had well established local lodges in Florence. Therefore, living in Florence would allow me to stay in close contacts with members of those lodges while also being attentive to the specificities of the women-only GLMFI, most of whose activities were based exclusively in Florence.

Growing up in Italy, I had been to Florence several times, mostly to visit its famous museums and quaint street markets. Living in Florence, however, was a rather different experience, one that entailed a sense of dislocation I had not anticipated. Scholars of Italy often comment on the lack of a cohesive national imaginary, which, for historical reasons, and particularly for older generations, tends to be replaced by *campanilismo*, an urban or regional imaginary of community, metaphorically centered on the *campanile*, the bell tower, of the local church. While I would argue that much of this localism has given way to a na-tionalist sense of belonging since at least the early 1990s, as the marked visibility of foreign immigration has provided a counterpoint for nationalist imaginaries and downplayed internal differences, experientially Florence still felt in many ways like a foreign site to me. The menus of local restaurants offered dishes I could not decipher, while grocery stores and household stores displayed names derived from the Florentine dialect. A *mesticheria*, for instance, was a small home-supplies store like the one at the corner of my street, where I could buy anything from nails and batteries to kitchen tools to stock my new home. In my hometown, a *mesticheria* was instead a specialized art supplies store, where in my schooldays I had bought canvases, paint brushes, and oil colors.

Even the experience of walking in Florence was different from what I was used to. Growing up just an hour north in the medieval city of Bologna, I had been spoiled by wide, tiled sidewalks, embraced by the protective arms of ever-present porticos, defiant of cars, motorcycles, and even rain. The pleasure of walking had been an integral part of city life. Walking in Florence, however, was not easy.

Unforgiving electronic eyes guarded all entrances to the city center, and their panoptic power kept most nonresident cars outside, circling around what is left of the old medieval walls, caught in an endless traffic jam. Those blessed with a resident permit, as well as taxis, buses, scooters, and all those willing to tempt fate, used to speed through so-called pedestrian streets, which, as I soon learned, in the center of Florence meant nothing more than streets in which people and authorized vehicles danced together to the loud rhythms of honks and sharp breaks. On days in which carbon monoxide levels in the air rose high enough to cause a pollution alert, not even permits could guarantee admission through the old walls.

Walking was thus often an unpleasant necessity, and typically a great source of stress among city dwellers. Insults, however, were relatively rare, even in high season, when crowds of tourists might linger a little too long in front of shiny windows or Renaissance monuments. Nose up in the air, they might stop the entire motion system of the single line of walkers behind them, who had nowhere to go and therefore just stood right there on the narrow sidewalk and waited, wishing out loud for a portable pedestrian honk or, alternatively, for a machine gun.

Walking or, rather, the impossibility of walking, was a common topic of conversation among residents. How was your day? It took me fifteen minutes to get between the Duomo and Piazza della Repubblica (a two-minute "walking" distance); it was impossible to get through, to *pass* through (*non si riusciva a passare*). Walker's stress in Florence often seemed to replace, or at least to accompany, driver's stress. More often than not, tourists were the target of blame and violent wishes.

With tourists, however, also came the promise of sunshine. Longer, warmer, brighter days illuminated the romantically polluted green waters of the Arno River, in which many Florentines would swear their grandparents could wash laundry but which now release a distinctive odor on humid days. At the beginning of the third millennium, the river's presence in the heart of the city is perhaps less functional and more aesthetic. It still divides the center in two halves. Whereas the northern half, known as *this* side of the Arno ("di qua d'Arno"), is home to most of the city's tourist attractions and to the train station, the bottom half, known as Oltrarno (literally "beyond the Arno"), is a popular neighborhood of artisans and students.

When I chose to live in Oltrarno, a few steps from Piazza Santo Spirito, many of my informants smiled with nostalgia. They claimed that it is hard nowadays to find true Florentines on this side of the Arno—"i fiorentini d.o.c.," they would call them, as if they were precious bottles of wine—but insisted that neighborhoods *beyond* the Arno maintained some "authenticity" in the artisanal shops scattered throughout the area. Several of my informants were born in Santo Spirito and felt a special affection for the neighborhood, although they believed it had since changed for the worse, becoming a prime site of drug dealing. Virtually all the Freemasons I met had long moved out.

Indeed, Piazza Santo Spirito at night resembled in many ways any leftist social center in Italy. Students and young drug addicts sat on the church steps and on the tiled floor of the piazza with dogs, guitars, cigarettes, joints, beer bottles, drums, and drugs in a cheerful party atmosphere. With its population of both Italians and foreign citizens, including students, workers, and documented and undocumented immigrants, as well as a visibly lively queer community, Santo Spirito offered an illusion of diversity so hard to find not only in the rest of Florence but also elsewhere in Italy. Black bodies, Asian bodies, queer bodies, drugged bodies, and other socially marked bodies walked through its streets with relative ease.

Soon after I moved there, a group of Eritrean asylum seekers occupied part of a building one block away from my apartment to protest the harsh conditions and long waiting times imposed by Italian immigration law in the many detention centers for immigrants. My landlady, who was a thirty-something white leftist activist, got involved with some of the left-wing organizations and Catholic charities that were trying to engage in various forms of solidarity with the Eritreans. Knowing about my background, she asked me if I could help out with some translations. Unfortunately, I had to inform her that I do not speak more than a few words of Tigrigna or Tigré, or really any other Eritrean language, since I was born in Italy and my multilingual Eritrean parents spoke to me only in Italian. Nonetheless, the occupation, which resolved positively within two weeks, was an indication of the kinds of tensions for which the neighborhood of Santo Spirito had become a stage, and of the conflicting agendas of neighborhood and business associations, left-wing social organizations, Catholic groups, and right-wing political parties that in many neighborhoods throughout Italy are increasingly clashing over the novel presence of racial others (see Carter 1997; Merrill 2006).

The Freemasons I knew in Florence always warned me to be very careful in Santo Spirito, especially at night. The large age gap between my informants and me meant that they often treated me with parental concern, and certainly insisted on driving me home after gala dinners or work sessions at the Masonic temple. I used to accept politely, although driving was often a nightmare, whereas walking around Santo Spirito was invariably a pleasure for me. Many of its twirling side streets were off the beaten tourist path, and I could walk uninterrupted past bakeries and Asian markets, wineries and calling centers, fruit vendors and bars. The biggest relief for me was to walk in Oltrarno without eliciting the constant gaze of others.

Watching others was a prime activity in the main half of the center, on this side of the Arno River, where the fashion business and the tourist industry are at their peak. It seemed impossible to walk "di qua d'Arno" without feeling the inquisitive gaze of strangers perforate my skin at all times. Over there, beautiful people sat on the outdoor patios of elegant cafés, people-watching and city-watching, speaking English, German, French, or Japanese. It was a rich kind of tourism, mostly white but also East Asian, primarily North American and Northern European. It was a tourism that engendered an entire underground economy whereby recognizing tourists was a crucial source of income for many. Walking through the streets of the center of Florence, tourists were targeted not just by pickpockets but also by street vendors with fake designer bags and artists offering to paint your portrait, write your name in Chinese, or guide you through the city's wonders in your own language. Even a well-dressed tourist would be given away by her way of walking, her shoes, or her overly polite hesitation in ignoring the harassing comments of men. *Passing* for a local was quite difficult, and yet passing would bring some distinctive advantages, such as better service and better prices at many establishments.

In the guessing game of who's who in the streets of Florence, I often felt like the wild card. Tourist? Italian? Immigrant worker? Exotic dancer? Within a sea of mostly fashionable, white bodies pushing to make their way through tiny sidewalks, I was, more often than not, among those who ended up on the street. Passing was never my strong point in Italy, but facing the uncomfortable gaze of others, I could certainly raise doubts.

"*Signorina!*"

A very old woman in a black dress with white hair pulled up in a bun startled me as I waited for the bus near my house in Oltrarno.

"Miss, be careful with your purse!" She tapped my right arm to demonstrate that my purse should remain securely clutched underneath my elbow, where it already was. Growing up in Italy, I learned to walk with my purse always protected under my arm, holding on to its strap, and carrying it on the side of my body away from the street. It is now an automatic gesture for me, and therefore, for a moment, I could not understand what the elderly woman wanted me to do that I was not already doing.

Then she pointed her finger at two young women waiting for the bus just a few steps away from us, and I understood. They had colorful sheer dresses layered on and long, straight dark hair flowing all the way down to their lower backs, their skin only a shade lighter than my own. They pretended not to listen, although the old lady was making no effort to conceal her contempt.

"Those are gypsies [*zingare*]," she informed me, using the derogatory term for the Roma people. "Be careful!" Then she returned to waiting for the bus a few feet away.

We all boarded the same bus when it came a few minutes later. The Romani girls and I smiled to each other briefly, and I wondered what had made me seem like a potential victim of theft in this elderly Italian woman's eyes, rather than a perpetrator, as I had been imagined to be many other times before while shopping at high-end stores or simply boarding a bus. I concluded that my business casual outfit (I was going to meet an informant during her lunch break) did not hurt, but that ultimately the fluidity of racial attributions and the presence of two Romani teenagers—an Other more marginalized, persecuted, and dehumanized than any other racial minority group in Italy and, arguably, in much of Europe—had ensured that, on that particular day, I passed.

Passwords

The notion of "passing" has been central to the elaboration of critical studies of race in Anglophone scholarship and, more recently, to feminist and queer studies as well (Butler 1993; Delaney 2002; Ginsberg 1996; McDowell 1986; Pile 2011). Judith Butler (1993), for instance, has famously read Nella Larsen's text, *Passing*, as a site of convergence in the articulation of both racial and sexual injunctions constituted through each other. Here, however, I am interested in a different version of passing, one etymologically cognate to the kind of passing that has preoccupied race and queer studies scholars, but also different in connotation. The practices of "passing" that I observed in my fieldwork, both my own and my informants', were attempts at *passare*, which is more accurately translatable as "passing through" or "advancing," as in learning the password ("la parola di passo") to a higher step of Masonic initiation, or passing through the city without harassment. For Freemasons in Italy, the point was not simply to pass *for* a more privileged identity category—as in Larsen's black characters, who pass for white—but rather to get *through* what they called "the profane world," the world of non-Masons, unmarked and undetected.[2]

Freemasonry's reputation in Italy as an elite secret and criminal organization underscored every aspect of my informants' relationship to the rest of society and to their own feeling of being persecuted, despite the privileged class positions of most members. For historical reasons and unlike members of Masonic lodges elsewhere, Italian Freemasons at the time of my fieldwork continued to be highly secretive and highly suspect. The vast majority of my interlocutors, for instance, concealed their identity as Freemasons even from their profane loved ones, and the location of their temples was known only to the initiated.

When I began my field research, I paid close attention to the reactions that a disclosure of my project would elicit among non-Masons in Italy. Although anthropologists are quite accustomed to researching topics that offend the sensibilities of dominant political parties or local people (Vidich and Bensman 2000), the specific reactions that mention of my project elicited among non-Masons in Italy are crucial to understanding both the status of Freemasonry there and also the discursive power of Freemason as an identity category. Oftentimes, people simply fell silent upon hearing the word *Freemasonry*. With a concerned look on their faces, they might ask me if I studied Freemasonry historically, through archival research. When I proceeded to explain that I studied Freemasonry ethnographically by interviewing Freemasons and observing their practices and daily lives, most would incredulously ask me how I got access. In some cases, people close to me even expressed concerns for my safety. A friend once told me to make sure not to ever let Masons blindfold me or take me into a car without a safety plan. While that reaction was quite extreme, I almost always received a polite exhortation to "be careful."[3]

In conversations with non-Masons, I found that their initial shock and fear at discovering what my project was about were usually followed by curiosity. What are Freemasons *really* like? Where are their temples hidden? Are Freemasons just a political and financial business network, or do they actually do rituals? Are there really women Freemasons, too? Such prurient curiosity entwined with widespread repugnance about Freemasonry was a sign of the organization's powerful status in Italy. The intensity of public sentiment about Freemasonry—manifested in proposed legislation, animated political debates, or hushed kitchen table discussions about this or that coworker whose promotion inspired jealousy and suspicion—also reified at every juncture the inescapable truism of Freemasonry as the most powerful secret society in the country.

Walking through Florence one day, on this side of the Arno River, I stumbled upon a powerful reminder of why studying Freemasonry could seem so daunting for Italian audiences, even to a degree that might be hard to fathom in other countries. I went the wrong way behind the famous Uffizi Museum, and found myself standing in Via dei Georgofili. It was a quiet alley, away from the hustle and bustle of the museum and its adjacent street economy. There was nobody there. It was easy to understand why someone had chosen precisely that alley to place a bomb in 1993 that had taken innocent lives, destroyed part of the Uffizi, and woken up a country that had just begun to sleep comfortably again. Between the late 1960s and the early 1980s, Italy had been devastated by terrorist acts, but by 1993 the period of terror was supposed to be over. I stopped under the memorial plaque that commemorates those who died in that bombing. It reminded me of all the times growing up that I had stood under a similar plaque: the one commemorating the victims of the Bologna train station bombing of 1980, the deadliest terrorist attack on Italian soil to date. In both cases, and regardless of what police investigations eventually uncovered, the usual suspects were Freemasons.

The question of Freemasons' secrecy needs to be approached from a few different angles. Here I focus in particular on Freemasons' often invisible presence in central sites of the Italian social and political landscape in order to begin to unravel a central paradox of my interlocutors' life experiences. Despite how steeped in secrecy their daily practices were, the Freemasons I met always maintained that they were not members of a secret society and that they had nothing to hide. Their relationship to each other in public spaces, to the profane world, and to significant architectural sites of Italian cities was therefore a relationship mediated by various forms of concealment and revelation. To analyze this paradox, I have borrowed a term my informants used frequently: *discretion* (see Mahmud 2012b). As I have seen it enacted by Freemasons, discretion can be defined as a set of embodied practices that simultaneously conceal and reveal valued knowledge. Being discreet was essential to my informants' way of being in the world, and it was an attempt to reconcile the different pulls between secrecy and having "nothing to hide."

For example, Freemasons enacted discretion in how they presented themselves in profane contexts. Although being a Freemason, unlike being a member of a racial group, is not generally considered to be a visible identity, my interlocutors moved through the profane social world in ways that intentionally marked and unmarked their own embodied status as Freemasons. A Freemason walking through the streets of Florence might blend in with other upper-middle-class, middle-aged Florentines, especially men, to an extent that might seem naturally indistinguishable to the normative gaze of profane viewers, trained to recognize only certain differences (of gender, of race, of class, for instance) as significant. As much as that was true, however, many of the Freemasons I met also took pride in their uncanny ability to recognize a fellow brother or sister in a stranger, and in making themselves recognizable to other Masons even in the midst of profane, public sites.

Like the controversial notion of "gaydar" in queer communities, these claims effectively assumed that Masonic experiences and identities were embodied in the form of a *habitus*, bodily dispositions that were neither conscious nor intentional, but which were nonetheless perceptible. To be sure, Freemasons have many explicit gestures and signs to aid their recognition of one another. For instance, men of the GOI had a secret handshake, while women kissed each other on the cheeks three times (that is, one more than in the common form of salutation in Italy). When greeting a woman, men would gesture as if to kiss her hand, but would instead stop in mid-air before the hand could reach their lips. Some Freemasons also wore rings or pins depicting Masonic symbols (usually drawn from the higher degrees of initiation and thus less popularly recognizable). Most of the Freemasons I met, however, did not display any identifiable markers of Freemasonry. Their belief that they could recognize other Masons—a possibility in which I too began to believe after some time—was not predicated on the presence of visible markers but on an ill-defined aura, "something Masonic" exuding from someone. Just like with the gaydar, the point is not that the process of Masonic recognition was infallible but, rather, that its possibility—confirmed by those particular instances in which it seemed to work in uncanny ways and without apparent explanation—served to propel a sociality of mutual recognition operating right under the surface of everyday interactions. Although such recognition could be said to be based on implicit class, race, or gender expectations, it is also more than those things in the eyes of its proponents. By virtue of being discreet, Freemasons could make themselves visible and recognizable to other Masons, while simultaneously preserving the secret of their identity from unwelcome observers who simply lacked the passwords to decode the habitus of a Freemason.

The practice of discretion was constitutive of Freemasons' relationships to each other as well as to the built environment: that is, better known and lesser known architectural sites of cultural significance, in which my informants could read traces of invisible or repressed Masonic histories. One sunny afternoon, for instance, I made an appointment to meet with Lucia, a sixty-year-old Maestra in the mixed gender GLDI. She asked me to meet her in Piazzale Michelangelo, the famous hilltop overlooking the city of Florence, where a bronze replica of the David stands above the panorama immortalized in so many postcards. From the busy bus stop where she met me we made our way through crowds of tourists taking pictures and soaking in the sun. Lucia pointed to the architecture of the vista, the piazzale, and the large mansion behind it, designed by architect Giuseppe Poggi in the mid-nineteenth century. It was one more instance, Lucia informed me, of the invisibility of Freemasons' contributions to the architecture of profane society. How many of those tourists really knew what they were taking pictures of? As was often the case with Freemasons, Lucia's comment ended there, confirming my eerie feeling that so much of the history, vision, and creativity of Freemasonry was inscribed in the very topography of the urban landscapes I traversed daily throughout my fieldwork, leaving traces as indelible as they were overlooked.

In the outdoor café where we sat to talk and have ice cream, I was confronted, as I often was, with the radical disjuncture that occurred whenever profane and Masonic spaces met in ways that challenged their discursive separation. Surrounded by tourists in colorful t-shirts, children spilling ice cream, and waiters running around to keep everyone happy in the busy high season, Lucia and I could disappear. Our conversation, which turned out to be about some of the darkest times of recent Italian history, about the conspiracy theories involving Freemasonry and the suffering of victims through two decades of terrorism, seemed quite out of place in the sunshine of Piazzale Michelangelo. The anonymity of a public space afforded us, ironically, the safest of spaces for sharing secrets. Unlike our phones or a temple or our homes, it could not be bugged. We did not risk being overheard by people who knew what to listen for. The profane world could contain us, rendering us invisible in the process, in a perfect enactment of transparency in its etymological sense of seeing right through us. Just like architectural sites scattered throughout Florence, Rome, and many other cities all over the world, we could stand misrecognized and unrecognized, in what I would call a Masonic "space of discretion"—a liminal site of intimacy hidden in plain sight amid the profane.

Sitting at a café in Piazzale Michelangelo, Lucia pointed down toward the city, at its towers, its medieval walls, its domes. "Can you see it? Can you see the works [opere] of Freemasons? We are not secret. We are everywhere!" As Lucia reminded me, Freemasonry was to be found in public spaces, in restaurants, convention centers, art galleries, coffee shops, office buildings, museums, and cities' main squares, as much as it existed in privately owned residences, temples, or lodges. Masonic symbols and signs could be read in the architecture of Italian cities as much as in the body of a stranger, who could be recognized as a brother or, less often, as a sister. With the use of discretion, Freemasons could learn to see a second version of reality superimposed over the existing one, neither concealed nor explicit. By the logic of discretion, objects had the power to radiate beyond their material limits to suggest a thickness of interpretation for those in the know. Discretion required an understanding that objects are at the same time in plain sight and hidden from view. Symbols are everywhere and events are public, but only the correctly conjured public has the knowledge necessary, be it esoteric or social, to decipher, to participate, to see. That is why Lucia and I could sit together outside a café overlooking the city of Florence in its architectural splendor and she could say we were overlooking "the [architectural] works of Freemasons."

The "Native" Ethnographer

One of the students said, "I thought homophobia meant
fear of going home after a residency."
And I thought, how apt. Fear of going home. And of not being taken in.
‹ GLORIA ANZALDÚA, *Borderlands/La Frontera*›

On this side of the Arno River, in Piazza della Repubblica, there is a café called Giubbe Rosse known as the birthplace of futurism. It is often overcrowded with tourists paying triple price for a single shot of espresso and hardened bread sandwiches. Its famous red awnings expand onto the wide tiled piazza as a reminder of the café's historical references: the red jackets, the *giubbe rosse*, of Garibaldi's soldiers conquering the Italian nation into being, in Gramsci's words, "as hegemony of the North over the South" (Cited in Verdicchio 1997: 26) It might be a coincidence that the Giubbe Rosse café towers over the piazza dedicated to the Republic. The piazza itself, like the nation, was erected over the debris of previous destruction in what had been for centuries the Jewish ghetto of Florence. The narrow roads of the ghetto, gliding along the walls of densely populated medieval homes, were torn down as Florence prepared to become the capital of the new nation-state in 1865, while Rome was still under Vatican control. In their place, wide avenues were traced on the ground, converging on the newly shaped Piazza della Repubblica. In the center of the piazza stands the Column of Abundance, reconstructed and relocated there in the 1950s to resemble two of its prior incarnations in nationalist mythological history: the Renaissance "original," and the Roman column that supposedly stood there in ancient times. Locals often referred irreverently to this glorious reinvention of the nation's past as *il cazzone* ("the big dick").

While the red outdoor seating area of the Giubbe Rosse café was one of Piazza della Repubblica's most recognizable tourist spots, the inside of the café had long served a different crowd. Indoors, the café offered a tasty and inexpensive lunch buffet that attracted white-collar workers and city employees from the neighborhood. I often met informants there for a meal during their lunch breaks. The busy comings and goings of the café had offered a shield of privacy to our conversations, which put many of my interlocutors at ease despite the sensitive nature of our discussions. The indoor space of the Giubbe Rosse, however, had yet another function to fulfill in Florentine city life. It was mostly in the evenings that the back room of the café turned into an intellectual salon for poetry and musical discussions. It was in that very room, local histories recall, that in the early 1910s a group of intellectuals used to meet, and even got into a brawl, as the poetics and aesthetics of futurism were born (Rainey 2009: 16).

At the time of my research, the back room of the Giubbe Rosse continued to host weekly evenings of intellectual discussions; it was not much of a surprise to discover that many of those evenings were organized by Freemasons. Of course, none of the events I attended at the Giubbe Rosse mentioned Freemasonry explicitly. It would have been entirely possible for customers to hear a presentation on literary or artistic figures of European modern history without necessarily realizing that the emphasis on esoteric symbolism, which characterized most of the symposia I attended there, was one of those clues Apprentice Freemasons learned to recognize when they first tried to look for their brothers or sisters in seemingly unmarked public spaces. It might also have been entirely possible for the uninitiated to stumble into the back of the café and not recognize the familiar faces of local lodge members sitting at their usual spots in the audience. Like many other public appearances of Freemasonry in Italian cities, the Giubbe Rosse was a wide-open secret.

One night, a couple of months after I had moved to Florence, I made arrangements to meet Angelo, a young Apprentice from the men-only GOI. He had called me, not the other way around. The Worshipful Maestro of his lodge, who was a close friend of my aunt's husband, had told Angelo about me, my research, and my relationship to his lodge brother (my uncle). With the authority of his position, the Worshipful Maestro had charged Angelo, an Apprentice, with the task of meeting me, showing me around Florence, and "assisting" me as needed. The Apprentice, of course, obliged his master's orders, and that is how I came to receive a phone call, out of the blue, from Angelo offering his services to me. I wondered if his task was simply to assist me or also to keep an eye on me, but I gladly accepted his invitation anyway.

Angelo turned out to be a thirty-five-year-old man, which is quite young for a Freemason. On average, Italian Freemasons are over the age of fifty. I crossed Ponte Vecchio, the bridge from Oltrarno, to go meet him on this side of the Arno, where he lived. He was well educated and well traveled, with a large amount of disposable income, and although I never found out for sure what his vague corporate job was, after a few months I started to suspect that he might be an international arms dealer. Angelo always laughed along when I teased him with my suspicions about his job, but he never confirmed or denied them.

At his suggestion, we agreed to meet in Piazza della Repubblica under the "big dick," which serves as an easy meeting spot for Florentines. From there we could walk into the Giubbe Rosse together for one of their special events. When we arrived at the café, the place was packed and all seats were taken. In the back room, a man with long gray hair was giving a lecture on some of the key figures in classical music to an audience of maybe fifty women and men. We were late. Holding our jackets in our arms, Angelo and I stood at the edge of the room listening for a few minutes to catch the end of the lecture. I could see him making eye contact with some of the people in the audience, exchanging nods and winks, and the occasional wave. Angelo leaned over and whispered in my ear, "Do you see that man over there?" With a slight movement of his chin, he pointed to a slender fifty-something man sitting in second row, wearing a beige cashmere sweater. I nodded.

"That's Valentino Marchi."

"The one from the GLDI?" I asked quietly. I had heard from someone else, a woman in the GLMFI, that a man by the name of Valentino who was in the mixed-gender GLDI sometimes organized public events to teach Masonic values, even though those events might not necessarily be advertised as Masonic per se. My informant had told me that she was not sure how she felt about Valentino's activities and the associated risks of "exposure" they carried. When I realized that the Giubbe Rosse served as an intellectual coffeehouse for Freemasons, I put two and two together.

Angelo gave me a long look, and then confirmed my suspicions. "Yes, the one and inimitable Valentino. But how do you know about him?"

"I pay attention," I told him, in part not to reveal my sources.

"Hmm, I'll have to remember that," Angelo said with a smile, "but for now just act as if you didn't know [*fai finta di niente*]."

Right then the lecture came to an end, so we joined in the applause. As the crowd started to come toward the door, Angelo excused himself to go say hello to some people, and asked me to wait for him outside. Even if Angelo had not warned me, I knew better than to approach Valentino directly without a proper introduction. Preliminary fieldwork had taught me how important it was to be discreet when interacting with Freemasons, especially in public locations. I assumed that Valentino had probably already heard all about the researcher from the United States who was in town studying Freemasonry, since news had a way of traveling at light speed within Masonic networks. I trusted that at some point we would set up a meeting, which we did months later. However, approaching Valentino in public and without warning might have spooked him, and it might have hindered my future research possibilities. I also realized that because Angelo was only an Apprentice, and, moreover, he was in a different Masonic Order from Valentino, it would have been highly inappropriate for

him to take the initiative to introduce us. I knew I had to wait for a more senior figure, ideally someone in Valentino's own GLDI, to do so. For now, I just
waited patiently in the piazza among a small crowd of lecture attendees who
had clearly been dying to light up their cigarettes again now that new laws had
banned smoking inside public buildings and businesses in Italy.

A few minutes later Angelo joined me outside. He was laughing.

"Do you know what my friend in there just asked me?"

"Who, Valentino?"

"No, no, a friend of mine . . . someone I know from around here."

"What did he ask you?"

"He asked me who the beautiful girl with me was. He said he thought you
were an exotic dancer I hired as an escort!"

"And what did you tell him?" I asked, looking down at my jeans, sweater,
and light jacket.

"I told him that actually you are a PhD candidate from Harvard University
writing a book on Freemasonry, and so he went, 'Oh wow, then she must have
balls!' And I said to him, oh yeah," Angelo continued in an overly accented and
emphatic tone, "she *definitely* has balls!"

In the spirit of ethnographic prowess, I kept my composure and laughed off
the sexist-cum-racist remark, figuring it was neither the first nor the last.[4] Indeed, my identity became early on a source of polite and yet insistent questions
in my fieldwork. This was all too familiar to me. For as long as I can remember,
my identity has been a source of confusion, questions, and disbelief for new
acquaintances in Italy.

I was born in Bologna, in a country that, unlike the United States , does not value
nativity. Italian citizenship—whether in the legal or affective sense—has little
to do with the accident of birthplace. The question "Where were you born?"
is therefore utterly irrelevant in most discussions of national identity in Italy,
and I only heard it rarely. Rather, parentage and "blood" carry the weight of
tying subjects to the nation-state. "Where are your parents from?" was a much
more common question that people asked me. My parents migrated to Italy
from war-torn Eritrea, following the path of many other postcolonial diasporas.
Ironically, many people in Italy do not realize that Eritrea used to be an Italian
colony, and that there is therefore a fairly simple explanation for the following,
interrelated questions: "Why Italy?" and "Why do you speak Italian so well?"
(i.e., as a *native*).

When I began my research, I thus returned as a "*native* ethnographer"
(Narayan 1993; Weston 1998) to a country where this epistemological cat-

egory makes little or no sense. One afternoon, for instance, a Maestra in the mixed-gender GLDI introduced me to some of her Mason brothers and sisters at her home, explaining to them that I had come from the United States to do my research. Then she turned to me looking confused and asked: "She is American . . . you are American, right? . . . Or, Italian American, right?"

I shook my head, and then I politely answered all her questions, again, for the benefit of a puzzled audience. I was born in Bologna. Yes, I studied there through the *maturità* (license exam at the end of a *liceo*). I went to a university in the States. No, I travel on an Italian passport. Usually, people would still look at me puzzled at that point.

Sometimes I felt generous and volunteered the solution without them having to ask: both my parents are from Eritrea (small-country-next-to-Ethiopia-in-East-Africa). Other times I would let them wonder some more: "Do your parents live in Italy?" (My mother does), "Are you Italian?" (Do you mean my passport?), and even "Were you born in Italy?" (Yes). By this point, the most persistent inquirers would find the winning phrasing: "Where are your parents *originally* from?" Others would be blunter, pushing their demanding curiosity in the language of xenophilia: "Look how pretty you are; your skin is black; I can see you are not Italian. Tell me, *really*, where are you from?"

The visceral confusion so marked in many people's reactions to me in Italy was fairly easy for me to understand. It was not my race alone—after all, colonial propaganda and Italians' migrant experiences in other countries had made most Italians aware of the existence of black bodies well before foreign immigration from the global South became a newsworthy phenomenon in the early 1990s. Thus, I knew it was not simply the shock of racial difference (as in the old anthropological trope of the only white man among "natives") that made many people, including some of my informants, stare at me in a quiet stupor upon first contact with me. My appearance certainly made me noticed, but it did not make anyone pause in utter disbelief. For that, I had to open my mouth and speak, too.

Frantz Fanon wrote that as a postcolonial Francophone subject there is nothing more exasperating than to be told, "How long have you lived in France? You speak such good French!" (Fanon 2008: 18). I speak Italian as someone who was born in Italy and who spoke it at home as a mother tongue, who attended Italian schools from kindergarten through high school, and whose entire social world during formative years was experienced in Italian, in Italy. More specifically, I speak Italian with the accent and intonation that would be expected, through a normative judgment, of someone of my generation, who grew up in an educated household in northern Italy. I am what is popularly referred to as an educated "*native* speaker," and I speak Italian with an accent of privilege that appears antithetical to my body.

For many American readers, this discussion may seem odd, and not only because Italian racial taxonomies are different from their American counterparts. Scholars of race know well, at least in theory, that racial classifications are socially constructed in different places and times, and that the same body will therefore be read differently in different contexts. In the United States, for instance, I have experienced multiple and contradictory readings of my racial positioning, shifting both over time and from east coast to west coast between "black" and "brown" (the latter has no immediate correspondent in Italian racial discourses), or between Mediterranean and South Asian (wrong sea and wrong continent, respectively). In Italy, on the contrary, I have typically been identified by others as consistently and unequivocally black. Moreover, the particular historical configuration of racial ideologies and nationalism that has come to prevail in the United States has engendered the possibility of being, simultaneously, a citizen and a member of an oppressed minority. As such, a subject can speak (and be recognized) from the standpoint of an American national identity—albeit a qualified, hyphenated, marginalized, and marked American identity.[5]

Upon first learning of my academic training in the United States, many of my informants were quick to put their doubts to rest, assuming I must therefore be African American—a category with which they were familiar thanks to movies and travels—but with some unclear Italian connections and an excellent mastery of *their* language. In their mind, the category of "American" did not preclude the possibility of multiculturalism and racial diversity, and it was thus easily applicable to me. The Italian context, however, continues to be rather different. While the history of Italian nation-state formations, and the ideology of national identity that ensued, are beyond the scope of this research, their effects on the ground are epistemologically and methodologically tied to my fieldwork encounters. My informants' reactions to me are not separable, in other words, from larger structures of belonging that have shaped subjects' relations to the Italian nation-state.

If the nation-state ideology has succeeded in equating parentage with birth, heritage with language, and subjectivity with citizenship, all the while imagining a racially homogenous community of whiteness, then the entanglement of these categories on an everyday basis produces the experience of "dislocated identities" (Shohat 1992) for the native speakers who do not *look* like native speakers. When a black body walks through the streets of Italy, in some places it might still elicit a gaze (Carter 1997; Pinkus 1997). It is not, however, until that body speaks in ways that undermine the prevailing common sense of nationalist fictions that it is stared at in disbelief. That disbelief, in turn, sets in motion a quest to find alternative, rational explanations, as hopeless as the attending questions were ill formulated.

My racial otherness within Italian society took on additional symbolic value in relation to Freemasonry. For the members of this Enlightenment-born society, liberal humanism was an explicit ideological commitment. Most of my interlocutors therefore wasted no time in assuring me, upon first meeting me, that they believed in the equality of all races, and that they were against any form of intolerance. Freemasonry, as they recited in a familiar refrain, and despite mounds of evidence to the contrary, "accepts anybody." Sara Ahmed has argued that "diversity-proud organizations are often the ones that defend hardest against hearing about racism. It is as if speaking about racism is to introduce bad feelings into organizations; it is as if you hurt or bruise the ego ideal of the organization as being diverse" (Ahmed 2010: 591). While I do not question the sincerity of my interlocutors' assurances, I remained conscious throughout my fieldwork of the fact that discussions of race seemed to pierce the virtually all white space of Italian Freemasonry only when I did, and only as a litmus test of Masonic values.

I have often reflected on the combination of reasons that made it possible for me to do the fieldwork research that I did. As I have discussed elsewhere, the importance of the rising discourse of transparency in the early 2000s cannot be underestimated in Freemasons' decision to open up to me, especially when considering that my personal contacts with some high-ranking Freemasons provided me with much needed references to approach their secretive organization (Mahmud 2012a).

Throughout this research, several of my informants continued to ask me whether I would like to be initiated. In most cases, they were simply surprised that a profane would have such an interest in Freemasonry, and assumed I would want to be one of them. Some even insisted that it would be best for my research if I joined a lodge, so that I could have access to the esoteric rituals that the profane cannot witness. After all, the same credentials that had allowed me to pursue this project in the first place—my aunt and her husband's legitimating status in the Eastern Star and in the GOI, my own pedigree from a prestigious university, an upper-middle-class background, and the knowledge that I would be producing scholarly work on Italian Masonic experiences—made me an acceptable candidate for lodges open to women. Being a marked, racial other, I could also inspire the humanistic call for liberty, fraternity, and equality, on which all Masonic lodges in Italy—even the men-only GOI—based their claim that they accept "anybody." I could potentially embody the exception of diversity that would confirm the rule of Masonic liberal humanism.

The Masonic and the Profane

Race, however, was not the only element of my subject position to mark a significant difference between my informants and myself. My left-wing feminist politics were often at odds with my informants' largely conservative political identities. I tried not to make an issue of it, although sometimes they teased me about it. One time, for instance, I joined a group of older GLMFI women for a ritual celebration of the solstice in the backyard of the country home of one of the sisters. As they carefully picked particular plants from the garden to burn ceremonially in a bonfire to perform the ritual of St. John, one of the sisters turned to me and said, "I bet it's bothering you that we are killing all these plants for the ritual!" She winked at me, and then turned to the others: "I bet she is for the Green Party!" We all laughed together. Given my informants' profoundly anti-Communist sentiments, and their only occasional tolerance even for socialism, which in Italy has often had right-wing Fascist leanings anyway, it was no wonder that the Green Party was as far as they could see in the wide expanse of the Italian Left. I laughed along, and decided not to disabuse them of that notion.

Perhaps the single most important difference, however, between my interlocutors and myself was my status as a "profane" (f: *profana*, m: *profano*)—someone who has not received a ritual initiation and, therefore, has not been accepted into the Masonic brotherhood. *Profane* is an emic cosmological term by which Masons in Italy designated both non-Mason people and the social world outside of Masonic ritual spirituality. *Profane* was thus the opposite of *Masonic*, in that it often served to contrast behaviors or affiliations and to mark differences of identity. For instance, someone's Masonic work (in a temple) could be distinguished from their profane work (at a law firm), just as easily as the struggles of the Masonic world (e.g., ritual initiation, the pursuit of a difficult path) could be expressed in contrast to the social issues of the profane world (e.g., immigration, education). In my informants' usage, *profane* did not necessarily carry the negative connotations of vulgarity and degeneration that the term has acquired colloquially in English. Proficient in Latin and schooled in the esoteric cosmological traditions that provide the basis for Masonic spirituality, they used the word *profane* quite consciously in its etymological sense. *Pro fanum*, in front of and outside the temple, indicated a subjectivity in contrast to that of the *initiate*, from *in itere*, or going *inside* (the temple).

Several religious traditions refer to the profane or secular in opposition to the sacred, and in many contexts the Freemasons I worked with partook of that usage, which implies a spiritual hierarchy between the two. There is no doubt that Freemasons experienced their spiritual path as a betterment of themselves and of profane society more generally. However, unlike some religious groups, they did not separate themselves completely from the decadence of a profane world. On the contrary, the two spaces were highly integrated in their day-to-day lives, as Masons did not aspire to leave the profane world for an ascetic existence but strived instead to better the former through a spiritual improvement of themselves. Through this spatial metaphor, the profane and the initiated marked a dialectical relationship of belonging and separation, as outsider and insider respectively, in which the two positions were mutually constitutive rather than mutually exclusive.

Although I began my research knowing that, as a profane, I would encounter limitations to my ability to observe or take part in the rituals of a society of initiates, after some time my informants began to make exceptions to the purportedly strict rules of separation between ritual spaces and profane spaces. As an "honorary sister," I was often allowed to cross the boundaries between esotericism and exotericism, secrecy and transparency, the Masonic and the profane, discovering in the process that those boundaries were hardly ever firm (Mahmud 2013). Of all the "exceptions" that occurred in the course of eighteen months, the most significant ones where those in which I, a profane, was allowed inside Masonic temples.

The day I saw a Masonic temple for the first time I thought I was simply meeting an informant at her place of work. The woman who showed it to me, Daniela, was a Maestra in the mixed-gender GLDI. She lived in a city in northern Italy, and I had gotten her number from one of her brothers from a Florentine lodge of the GLDI. He had recommended I talk to her mostly out of convenience because I was about to spend a week in the city in which she lived. By then I had realized that each person's network spanned different chapters (lodges) of the same organization, such as the GLDI, as well as different organizations, such as the mixed-gender GLDI and the women-only GLMFI. In this case, the brother I had interviewed lived in Florence and worked in a Florentine lodge of the GLDI, but he could easily put me in touch with Daniela, who worked in a GLDI lodge in a different city.

When we had spoken over the phone, Daniela had sounded friendly, although she had also been careful not to mention explicitly anything related to Freemasonry. I had grown accustomed to this practice of discretion during phone conversations—which could have been tapped or overheard—as well as in public places. As in a game of Taboo, I had learned to phrase my interest in general terms, such as "women's participation in certain forms of association," without ever uttering potentially troubling buzz words, like Freemasonry, esotericism, lodge, brothers, or temple, so as to respect my informants' privacy. It was usually enough to start by naming the person who had given me their number for the context of the conversation to be unmistakable. When I called Daniela, it was clear that she had been advised to expect my phone call, and already knew my name. She offered to meet me that afternoon in her office, gave me the address, and told me the name on the doorbell: "Cultural Institute for Social Studies."[6]

The office was located in the historical center, among some of the oldest and most expensive real estate in the city, in a noble building. When the large, double wooden door buzzed open, a series of staircases, hallways, and private gardens came into view. I walked up to the second floor, passing what seemed to be mostly law firms and private medical practices, until I came to a small, unpretentious door left ajar with a brown doormat that had seen better days. I was about to knock when a woman in her late thirties with long brown hair and a white linen dress opened the door. "I'm glad you found it," she smiled, but suddenly paused to stare at me.

I was familiar with that pause. I recognized it because it happened all the time, with Masons as with non-Masons alike, in Italy. We had only talked over the phone. Daniela had heard my voice but did not know what I looked like. As her eyes scrutinized my appearance, she did not lose her smile or her manners for more than a few seconds, then quickly opened the door and invited me to take a seat.

Daniela was very affable. In the privacy of the office, which was empty on a Sunday afternoon, we discussed my project and her membership in the mixed-gender GLDI without the need to use euphemisms. From a room in the back she brought me copies of a magazine, *Officinae*, which the GLDI published monthly and sent out to its members. When I asked her how I could get some copies, she said she was not sure, but that if I needed any she would be happy to get them for me.

Almost two hours went by, as we sat on the elegant leather couches of the beautiful waiting room. I thought it was odd that something called "Cultural Institute for Social Studies" could afford to be located in such prime real estate. I asked Daniela if the institute was affiliated with the university, and what the nature of her job there was. She giggled and confessed that actually the institute did not exist, and that she did not have a job there. This was the site of a GLDI lodge. Daniela laughed again as she told me that occasionally they received phone calls from people who had found the institute listed in the phone book and wanted to learn about their activities. When I asked her why they needed to use a fake organization as a façade, Daniela's tone became more serious. "We are in Italy," she reminded me. Freemasonry has such a negative reputation in Italy that she felt it would not be safe or wise for them to make their location publicly known.

"Can you imagine?" She asked sarcastically. "'Masonic lodge' listed under *M* in the yellow pages!" It was not the first time I had heard that joke—one very common among Freemasons in Italy—that surely they should list *Massoneria* in the phone book, under the letter *M*, right after the Mafia. She said she feared possible attacks, and a façade organization protected them from unwanted scrutiny.

"So, have you ever seen a temple?" she asked me in a cheerful tone. When I had attended the annual convention of the GOI in 2004, I had been inside their ad hoc temple, temporarily located inside the auditorium of the convention center that the GOI had rented for three days. However, I had never seen a "real" temple, I told her. Daniela got up from her armchair, and offered to take me to one. First, though, she wanted to ask me a question. "Do you think you will be initiated?"

It was a difficult question to answer. I was certain I did not intend to join Freemasonry, but it was hard to explain why. The simple answer, which usually satisfied the inquirer, was that I did not think I could write an "objective" book about various Masonic lodges if I were bound by the rules and obligations of one in particular. Given the discursive power of objectivity outside of anthropology and other critical social studies, this was usually convincing enough.[7]

Daniela, however, did not seem interested in my attempts at an explanation. As soon as I told her that I was not planning to join, she stopped me. "The reason I asked you," she said, "is that if you think you will join I do not want to take away from you the experience of seeing a temple for the first time."

She was smiling, and her face seemed to glow as she shared with me her memories of her own initiation. The first time they take you into the temple for the initiation, she explained, is a priceless experience. She did not want to take that away from me. I reassured her that I was not planning to be initiated, and so she invited me to follow her.

I had assumed we would be leaving the office, but Daniela did not take either her purse or her jacket, so I left mine behind as well. I followed her down the hall, where in a small closet left ajar I thought I caught a glimpse of black robes hanging. She led me into a small study with functional office furniture.

A messy desk, some filing cabinets, and a couple of bookshelves were a far cry from the elegant waiting room in which she had received me.

"This way," she pointed. Next to the bookshelf, I noticed that the white wall appeared to have some hinges painted over. Daniela walked past the desk and gave the bookshelf a gentle push. I realized then that the bookshelf was on casters. As it rolled a little more to the side, it revealed behind it a small door craftily painted of the same white as the wall. Daniela opened the door for me, and with a smile she invited me to step forward into the concealed room.

I stood for several seconds on the threshold of the open door contemplating the sight before me. Inside the room, I could see an original eighteenth-century vaulted ceiling rising high above a black and white checkered floor. A throne on the far end of the room and rows of antique wooden chairs on either side, each with a sword resting next to it, were arranged to form a U-shape. Two tall Greek columns framed the entryway, and zodiac signs, stars, and planets had been carved all over the walls to symbolize the night sky. It was breathtaking. All those stories I had always heard about Freemasonry's secrecy were just overdone mythologies. And yet, there was a Masonic temple in all its splendor, literally hidden behind a bookcase.

Daniela stood next to me beaming with satisfaction. I noticed over time that my interlocutors seemed to enjoy the spectacle of Masonic ritual spaces and of the surprised reactions they could elicit. "This is the *small* temple," she announced proudly. "The big one is on the other side."

That afternoon had been the first of many exceptions. As a profane not initiated into the Masonic fraternity, I knew I was not supposed to see the temples. Over the course of my fieldwork, however, I was taken to several other temples, in various cities, even in different countries. Most were in undisclosed locations, something that made sense in the social world I was studying. More precisely, temples were usually hidden behind the façade of a nonprofit cultural association (*circolo culturale*) that was legally registered and listed in the phone book. For many of my informants, it was not only a matter of privacy but, more importantly, a security issue. I often heard them voice concerns about what might happen if word got out about the location of their temple, and their fears ranged from receiving hate mail to "what if a madman puts a bomb outside?"[8]

When Daniela and I said good-bye that afternoon, she walked me to the door, and as we were standing there I suddenly noticed a small compass and a square—unmistakable Masonic symbols—stitched on a corner of the brown doormat. Surprised, I told Daniela I had not noticed them before. How could I have missed them on my way in? Daniela smiled knowingly, and told me that it is always easier to see things in hindsight (*col senno di poi*).

Conclusion: Spaces of Discretion

> And I began to question everything around me: the houses, the shop
> signs, the clouds in the sky, and the engravings in the library, asking them
> to tell me not their superficial story but another, deeper story, which
> they surely were hiding—but finally would reveal thanks to the principle
> of mystic resemblances. ‹UMBERTO ECO, *Foucault's Pendulum*›

When I first began this research, I shared the common assumption and misunderstanding of Masonic lodges in Italy as "secret societies." I remember sitting
in the outdoor patios of Florentine cafes, among tourists, business people, and
groups of friends. After turning on my tape recorder to interview an informant,
an hour or two would go by talking over coffee about life in the lodge, the
struggle to "come out" as a Mason to one's family, the fear of repercussions at
work, the exhilaration of growing into a better person along the path. I remember looking around, each time, at the waiters busy clearing tables and at the
other customers sipping their drinks, and I could not help thinking what an odd
scene it was. There we were, in plain sight, discussing someone's life experiences
in what is romanticized to be one of the most powerful secret societies in the
world. What if someone had overheard us? What would they think? What could
they do? Was the crowded anonymity of a café (or a park, or a street, or a train
station) enough to guarantee my informants' confidentiality? The banality of
the location did not seem worthy of Freemasonry's legendary mystique. How
could something so secret exist in a space so public and mundane?

To come to understand Italian Freemasonry not as a secret society but as
a "society of discretion" is to recognize that Freemasonry, although secretive
in many ways, is an organization that operates nonetheless in direct relationship to the rest of society. The values, beliefs, and relations of Masonic lodges
extend into the profane world creating fraternal networks that span regions
and sensibilities. With the expressed goal of bettering society by bettering
individuals, Freemasons may change from robes into evening attire; they may
discuss the work of Botticelli instead of the alchemist Papus; they may use
legal pads instead of a compass and a ruler. But they do not stop their lives, as
Freemasons, outside the temple. Unlike sects that separate themselves from
the profane world, the Freemasons I knew embraced it and lived within it with
various degrees of "being out."

What I have called "spaces of discretion" are liminal sites reconfigured as Masonic, private, or even secretive by the craft of those occupying them. They are
ostensibly public spaces, such as coffee houses or rented-out convention halls,

or perhaps even lodges temporarily open to profane guests, but in which only a correctly conjured public would be able to know and to recognize Masonic activities. They are therefore simultaneously in plain sight and yet invisible to most, and they are rendered meaningful by the practices of discretion of those who pass through them.

Discretion was not just a means for Freemasons to skirt the question of legality (secret societies are illegal in Italy) under the threat of criminal prosecution. The practice of discretion was also generative for my informants, who could effectively conjure an enchanted world of symbols and of fellow Masons by learning to make meaning out of material traces or embodied dispositions found in plain sight amid the profane, and who were often able to carry out their Masonic craft in those profane spaces thanks to the obliviousness of others.

Over the course of my fieldwork research, I began to see and recognize the social topography of discretion, whereby the way in which a friend might comment on a particular work of art or might reference an interesting book he or she had been reading lately on ancient Egypt could open up a hidden world of symbols and connections that most non-Masons would fail to see. Discretion became for me a kind of coded visibility in which certain symbols and signs, intelligible only to those who have been trained to recognize them, were in plain sight, hidden not by an act of concealment but by the beholder's own illiteracy. Learning to recognize code words, visual signs, winks, gestures, whispers, and innuendos became as important to my fieldwork as conducting interviews, but not because a Masonic lodge is a "secret society" in the legal sense that the Italian constitution prohibits. Rather, it is because a Masonic lodge, like other social groupings, has its own shared, implicit common sense and language, although among Freemasons such arrangements are made explicit.

In Florence and other Italian cities, a process of dematerialization and de-signification of the material markers of Freemasonry allowed my interlocutors to "pass" through public spaces without fear of being indicted as Freemasons by others. In the process, they also reinforced their sense of belonging to an esoteric society that had taught them to see beyond the surface of reality and to recognize the world as a "forest of symbols." To be sure, the objects and sites that my interlocutors could identify, through the use of discretion, as Masonic were very often imbued with the markers of privilege. Feeling hailed, for instance, by architectural features of nationalist significance or by the artistic works that have come to define what counts as "high" culture, my interlocutors formed an exclusive community of belonging characterized by elitism and prestige, as much as by its discretion.

As I discovered during preliminary fieldwork on train rides to the North, the South, and the East of Italy and across boundaries that divided sensibilities, attachments, and social positions more than geographies, Masonic "fraternity" is not a neatly enclosed whole but a world of esoteric connections stretching out amid the profane and always existing within multiple spaces—spaces that one is trained to see and recognize. I therefore had to undergo a "process of enskillment" (Elyachar 2011) to train myself, with the help of my informants, in the art of discretion. The intimacy that I could develop with my informants, the trust that I could earn, and, therefore, the access that I could be granted to the ritual spaces of Masonic lodges depended very much on my own ability to be discreet. *Passing* was for me an epistemological necessity to open a window into the path of personal and societal transformation that Masons undertook.

PASSWORD I

———— * ————

One early morning my cell phone rang and woke me up. Still half asleep, I saw my hand reaching past the remote control, over a quivering glass of water, feeling for the familiar shape of rounded cold metal antenna. My eyes glanced at the caller ID flashing a yellow light with her familiar name. I got up right away and cleared my throat for my best possible morning voice. I was surprised to receive a call from her. Over the previous months I had come to think of her as an aunt, a guide, a mentor. She had helped me more than I could ever repay. She had opened her home to me and had welcomed me into a world that so few among the profane can ever expect to be privy to. For that alone, I was usually the one doing the calling. Rarely did the Grand Maestra call me. "What are you doing tonight?" It was her usual cheery voice.

That night I held my purse tight to my side, as I walked through deserted streets and alleyways, wondering if I had the right address. She had told me to come at 10:00 p.m. sharp. She had given me the address and the name written on the intercom outside the gate. She had instructed me to ring the doorbell three times, and someone would come for me. Except for a few cars driving by, the residential neighborhood at the outskirts of Florence city center was already asleep. I had taken two buses to get there, and the only sound reverberating in the night was that of my heels. Had I dressed appropriately? I feared my elegant coat, black pants, and high heels might make me an easy target in a city night. As I walked ten, fifteen minutes, the architecture around me started to morph from small apartment buildings into wide villas, clean white façades, and tall black gates surrounding their front yards.

I counted street numbers until I stood outside the right place. On the door there were three names and as many doorbells. I rang the one I was told, which in hindsight I could have guessed because of its ingenious reference to Roman mythology. I rang it three times. About a minute passed without anything happening, then the gate suddenly unlocked, and I stepped carefully into the dark garden among tall trees and unkempt grass. The Grand Maestra had told me to go underground, and indeed there were stairs leading to the basement of the villa. As I approached them, I realized a man was standing at the bottom of the stairs under fluorescent lights.

He could not have seen me from where he was. I held my breath for a few seconds, observing his outfit, making decisions. He was an ordinary Italian middle-aged man, a short gray beard, a dark blue suit with a pin on his chest. He looked like many others I had seen before, and I knew who he must be. I took a deep breath and walked toward the light. He saw me. He stared at me for a second or two, evidently making his own decisions about me, then he whispered something I didn't catch, and motioned for me to come down.

When I reached the bottom of the stairs, I followed the man through a narrow hallway with short ceilings. It was a basement, but the overhead lights gave a bright yellow tint to all the framed certificates, insignias, and emblems hanging along the walls. The man led me to a small room at the end of the hallway, then held the door open and whispered for me to walk in. At first sight, it looked like an ordinary office, with unremarkable furniture that made it functional if not comfortable. Beyond the stacks of books and piles of papers lying around, however, wall decorations revealed the room for what it really was, at least part of the time: an antechamber. I had read about it in esoteric books, but I had not seen one.

A woman rushed in. She was wearing a long black robe, and around her waist she had a white apron with colorful symbols etched on. She, too, was whispering.

"Do you need to change?" She asked me. I gave her a quizzical look. "Here, if you need to change, you can go to the other room." She pointed toward somewhere behind her shoulders.

I began to tell her that I was not sure whether I should change, but she was in a hurry and ran out before I could finish my sentence. The man offered me a seat, still staring at me, but I was glad to give my feet a rest. Within a few minutes, the woman ran back in, apologizing for the mix-up. She said the Grand Maestra told her to ask me to wait here. They would call me as soon as they were ready. Then she rushed back out, leaving me in the company of a stranger to ponder my luck.

I was inside a Masonic temple.

It had taken me several months of fieldwork to receive this invitation to see an active Masonic temple for the very first time. I had seen one other temple very early on, when I had met Daniela in what I believed was a research institute but turned out instead to be the site of a temple of the mixed-gender Grand Lodge of Italy (GLDI). That temple, however, had been empty when

Daniela showed it to me, mostly to pique my curiosity. I had never seen a lodge in session. Until that very morning, I feared the invitation might never come. After all, my interlocutors had made it clear that as a profane I would never be allowed inside a temple during rituals—a categorical restriction to which I had agreed because my interest was primarily in Freemasonry as a social organization, rather than in esotericism per se. When the Grand Maestra of the Grand Women's Masonic Lodge of Italy (GLMFI) had called me that morning to invite me to the temple for part of a ritual, it was the first of many exceptions to follow. As a profane ethnographer who slowly became an "honorary" sister—the same way that many anthropologists become honorary members of the social groups they study—I was eventually allowed to cross the fine line between profane and Masonic spaces more and more.

That night a woman was being initiated. The profane, myself included, were not allowed to witness the full ritual ceremony. Apparently, the man was not either. He sat at the desk in the office/antechamber where we waited, and smiled at me.

"I am a brother too, in case you are wondering. I am in the GOI."

I thought to myself that actually there was no mistaking that. Somewhere between the aging gray hair of his beard and the pin on his expensive suit, something about his eyes and his polite mannerisms, he had the habitus of the Grand Orient of Italy (GOI) down to an art form. I smiled back. Within the first few months of fieldwork I had become a believer in what I would call the Masonic "radar"—the ability many brothers and sisters claimed allowed them to recognize one another among strangers. That night, however, he was, in a sense, almost as much of a profane as I was. A man from a men-only lodge that continues to exclude women was sitting in the antechamber of a temple belonging to a women-only lodge. That night, karma meant he was not a brother; he was just a guest.

We waited in the antechamber for almost two hours. The man seemed happy to have company. He was in a talkative mood, and after I introduced myself as a researcher he took care of the rest of the conversation. The woman being initiated that night was someone dear to him. He had come for her. After a few minutes of listening to interesting stories of Masonic life, I pulled out a pen and notebook from my purse, sat it on the desk, and asked the man if he wouldn't mind me taking some notes. He wouldn't, he said, and so I began to write all that he was saying.

Every so often, someone new would come in to check on us, each time wearing a ritual gown. I had met all these women before at gala dinners and receptions, but that night they were all wearing black robes with badges of different colors on their white aprons. They would whisper hello, apologize again for the delay, and assure us that someone would come get us when it was time for us to enter. Then they each disappeared again into the bright hallway, but not before urging the man to take good care of me. Even the Grand Maestra herself came once. In her regalia she looked both matronly and majestic. She pulled me into her arms to give me one of her typical big hugs, and then disappeared again within a few seconds.

It was almost midnight when it was time for us. The woman who had asked me whether I needed to change when I first walked in came back. "Please, you can follow me now." It became clear to me what her role was, based on my readings about Masonic rituals. She was a Tyler, guarding the temple, monitoring access, running errands. I hesitated for a second, then decided to leave my coat and purse in the office, and headed out of the room, unencumbered, after the woman and the man. We walked in the bright hallway again but took a left turn into a more spacious room on the side. It looked like a formal dining room, with a dark wood oval table in the middle. I guessed that must be where ritual feasts—known as agape dinners—took place. On one wall, a French door with opaque glass panes was being opened from the inside of yet another room, just as we approached.

"This way, please."

I slowed down my pace upon reaching the threshold of the door, hoping the man would enter first, but the gentleman was predictably smiling with his arm extended to invite me to precede him. The Tyler had stopped by my side too, and was nodding encouragingly for me to keep going. So I entered first.

The sight was overwhelming. All the symbols of Masonic temples had been reproduced in this basement room. Columns made of cardboard, zodiac signs along the walls, a draping cloth covering the ceiling to reproduce a dark blue sky, candles and a wooden podium, rows of chairs on three sides of the room, forming the classic Masonic U-shaped seating arrangement. As I entered, I could see rows of women in black robes and embroidered white aprons sitting on my left and on my right, staring at me in silence. I knew most of them, but I had not seen them in their ritual garments before. Straight in front of me on a high wooden stage, presiding over the temple from a richly ornate throne, was a forty-something red-haired woman whom I remembered meeting once before. She was looking at me. On her left side, I recognized the Grand Maestra, sitting off-center. For a moment, I stood puzzled at this seeming hierarchical misplacement. It was naïve of me, but I had assumed the Grand Maestra of the

GLMFI would be in charge in that particular lodge too. Each lodge, however, functions as a chapter of the larger organization and has its own hierarchy, including its own Worshipful Maestra sitting in the place of honor.

I stood awkwardly a few steps from the door for what felt like a very long time, unsure of where to sit and unwilling to break the silence of the temple to ask. The Worshipful Maestra seemed to notice my confusion, and smiled at me from her high throne. Then she extended an inviting arm toward two empty chairs on her right side. "Please," she finally spoke, "come sit at the Orient."

I knew enough about the esoteric topography of Masonic temples to understand just how important her words were. The Orient, from which all light irradiates to enlighten the lodge and its members, is the designated esoteric site of the Worshipful Maestra presiding over a lodge and, occasionally, of her most important guests. When she invited us to join her at the Orient, specifically sitting on her right side, I knew she was bestowing upon us the status of guests of honor.

I walked to the seat she had indicated, the brother following close behind me, and I sat at the Orient, contemplating the view before my eyes. The Worshipful Maestra began to speak. She welcomed us into the temple as her guests, but she informed us that all "works" were now closed. The lodge was not operative at that moment. Instinctively, I glanced at the Bible lying on the wooden pedestal that I had just walked by in the middle of the room. Every temple has a holy book to offer spiritual guidance during ritual works. Lying on top of it, a compass and a square—symbols derived from the material origins of operative stonemasonry—are kept in either an open or closed position to signal the equivalent status of the lodge. Sure enough, the compass and the square on top of that Bible had been closed, indicating that rituals were no longer being performed. As profane outsiders, neither the GOI man nor myself could have been allowed to enter a Masonic temple otherwise. Letting us in at all was already an extraordinary overture.

The Worshipful Maestra proceeded to explain that although works were closed, they would now read aloud a *tavola* ("tablet") prepared by one of the sisters on the topic of that day's holiday: March 8, International Women's Day. In Masonic terminology a tavola is more or less a research paper written to develop a specific, usually assigned, topic and then delivered during a lodge meeting. It is the Masonic equivalent of homework. The Worshipful Maestra emphasized that the tavola would only be read, but not commented upon or discussed in any way, because, once again, works were closed. Right on cue, one of my interlocutors, who was a member of this lodge, stood up from her seat and walked to a wooden podium located near the door. Her tavola began with a brief history of International Women's Day, and continued to discuss the symbolism of the mimosa flower, which is the typical gift offered to women in Italy on March 8. Her analysis traveled through time back to the Temple of Isis in ancient Egypt, back to Solomon's Temple, and back to our days, tracing the acacia plant family as a life-giving symbol among goddesses and heroes.

When the sister finished her reading, the Maestra reminded everyone not to discuss the tavola because works were closed, and instead turned toward the man and me and offered us an opportunity to speak. Caught by surprise, I felt rather unprepared for public speaking inside the temple. Fortunately, the man stood up first this time, and seized the opportunity to offer unsolicited criticism of the tavola we just heard. Some of the sisters were discreetly making eye contact with me, smiling, winking, and shaking their heads in disapproval. When he sat back down, it was my turn to get up and speak. Right as I was about to say something, the Grand Maestra, who until that moment had sat quietly on the left of the Worshipful Maestra, interjected loudly: "Come on, Lilith, show him now!"

An eruption of laughter in the room broke the solemnity of the moment. I thanked everyone for their hospitality and for allowing me inside the temple, and I reminded them of my ongoing research, briefly introducing myself to the few sisters there whom I had not met before. "Her name is Lilith," repeated the Worshipful Maestra to a nodding audience, as soon as I finished. Then, much to my embarrassment, she added: "And that name alone is enough." The cabbalistic etymology of my first name, revitalized in feminist exegesis, had clearly not escaped the members of a women-only esoteric lodge.

I chose to describe my first visit to the Florentine temple of the GLMFI to illustrate some of the practices of discretion that I observed while working with Freemasons. As is typically the case, the temple was in an undisclosed location, something that was common and expected in the social world I was studying. More precisely, the temple was located within a legally registered nonprofit cultural association. Knowing that several of my informants were active in the association, I had suspected that it could be the site of the temple, but I could not be sure until I was finally invited in, several months into my fieldwork. The practice of hiding a temple behind the façade of a nonprofit association was quite widespread in Italy, as I had discovered early on when I was taken to see Masonic temples in other cities, and it was the result of a political history of violence that has seen Freemasonry and Italian institutions pitted against one another.

Whenever my interlocutors invited me (and other guests) to the temples or to other Masonic ritual sites, the boundaries separating the spatial metaphors of the initiated and the profane were revealed to be more porous than they were rhetorically made out to be. In the scene I described, the Worshipful Maestra presiding over the rituals insisted that all "works"—that is, Masonic ritual works—had been closed. Nonetheless, a tavola was read in my presence and all sisters wore their ritual robes. Moreover, I was invited to sit in what the Worshipful Maestra explicitly called "the Orient," which is to say a ritual space, rather than "the podium" or "the stage," as that same space would have been called had the lodge not been operative. There was an obvious tension between the Worshipful Maestra's firm claim that works were closed and the acts of disclosure through which she and her sisters shared some elements of Masonic esotericism. That tension, I would suggest, is a product of the untenable discursive separation between the esoteric and the profane—a separation made even more unlikely in the case of Freemasonry with its commitments to effecting social change by means of a ritual self-cultivation path. The profane and the Masonic are mutually constituted (Mahmud 2013).

My first invitation to a GLMFI temple came on a night in which a woman was being initiated. The ritual had taken almost five hours to complete, and I had spent a good part of it in the antechamber waiting to be called in. The ritual was so long because of the prescribed formulaic exchanges and choreographic moves required for the conferment of the degree of Entered Apprentice, the first one in the Masonic pyramid. Members of the lodge played specific, assigned roles in the ritual, and very little was left to improvisation. Indeed, the accuracy of the performance, measured against century-old texts of Masonic rituals, was crucial to ensure the legitimacy of the lodge. Rituals, in other words, had to be performed correctly. This was all the more important for the GLMFI, a group whose claims to Freemasonry were often called into question by the larger and more established mixed-gender GLDI and by the men-only GOI. Unlike those wealthier organizations, the GLMFI could not afford to rent more than a basement for their temple, and certainly could not afford to own historical buildings in the center of a major Italian city, where a vaulted ceiling would likely be an existing architectural feature of the space and not an optical illusion created with a cloth or with three-dimensional painting techniques. The sisters were often self-consciously ironic about their poverty, but also took it as a source of pride, for they did not need the spectacular temples of the GOI to be Freemasons. "Our temple is underground," one sister told me, "not because we have anything to hide but because it's cheaper to go underground."

Even though the Greek columns might have been made of cardboard and the starry sky was painted, rather than carved, on the flat ceiling of a basement, the symbols of a Masonic temple were reproduced impeccably. Indeed, the position of each item in the esoteric topography of the space was as important as the correct and timely recitation of ritual formulas by Masons playing particular roles. It was especially important if there were guests in the audience. Whether the latter were representatives of foreign Masonic lodges with which the GLMFI had a treaty of friendship, or whether they were brothers from the men-only GOI, who were technically considered profane because the two groups did not recognize each other, the sisters of the GLMFI knew that they would be judged in part on their ability to perform esoteric rituals correctly in a site built to reflect accurately the codes of Masonic ritual architecture. Indeed, upon walking inside the temple, and despite the fact that it was in a basement, the spectacle was breathtaking. In hindsight, I understood exactly what Daniela meant. She had let me peek at my first temple a long time before this one, but the one she had shown me had not been in use that day. Nonetheless, before leading me through the bookcase that concealed the temple's door, Daniela had asked me if I was sure that I would never be initiated. If I were to be initiated, she had told me, she would not wish to rob me of the experience of walking inside an operative temple for the very first time.

Initiations

I, of my own free will and accord, in the presence of Almighty God, and this Worshipful Lodge, erected to Him, and dedicated to the holy Sts. John, do hereby and hereon most solemnly and sincerely promise and swear, that I will always hail, ever conceal, and never reveal, any of the arts, parts, or points of the hidden mysteries of Ancient Free Masonry, which may have been, or hereafter shall be, at this time, or any future period, communicated to me, as such, to any person or persons whomsoever, except it be to a true and lawful brother Mason, or in a regularly constituted Lodge of Masons; nor unto him or them until, by strict trial, due examination, or lawful information, I shall have found him, or them, as lawfully entitled to the same as I am myself. I furthermore promise and swear that I will not print, paint, stamp, stain, cut, carve, mark, or engrave them, or cause the same to be done, on any thing movable or immovable, capable of receiving the least impression of a word, syllable, letter, or character, whereby the same may become legible or intelligible to any person under the canopy of heaven, and the secrets of Masonry thereby unlawfully obtained through my unworthiness.

All this I most solemnly, sincerely promise and swear, with a firm and steadfast resolution to perform the same, without any mental reservation or secret evasion of mind whatever, binding myself under no less penalty than that of having my throat cut across, my tongue torn out by its roots, and my body buried in the rough sands of the sea, at low-water mark, where the tide ebbs and flows twice in twenty-four hours, should I ever knowingly violate this, my Entered Apprentice obligation. So help me God, and keep me steadfast in the due performance of the same. ‹ *Oath of an Entered Apprentice Freemason* ›

The initiation of a Freemason begins with a death ritual. Before a profane is allowed to enter a temple to be initiated to the degree of Apprentice Freemason, he or she is made to wait alone in an adjacent room, known as the Chamber of Reflections. This dark, windowless room has funerary symbols as its sole decoration. Austere philosophical maxims engraved on black walls and a sickle and a skull placed prominently on a candlelit desk next to a piece of paper and a pen that the neophyte must use to write his or her "will" conjure a space of symbolic death. The *memento mori* scattered in the dark shadows of the Chamber of Reflections are meant less to instill fear in the neophyte and more to guide him or her into a state of solemn contemplation, serving as potent reminders of his or her imminent ontological transformation from a profane into a Freemason.

Many of my informants told me that their time of introspection in the Chamber of Reflections was one of the most significant moments along their initiation path. Writing their wills in the darkness and solitude of the chamber, listing all the material longings and preoccupations that they were about to leave behind, they had to abandon symbolically all remnants of their profane lives to prepare to embark on the esoteric quest of Freemasonry. Some described that experience to me as "a leap in the dark" (*un salto nel buio*), for they did not yet know what they would find on the path ahead after they were reborn, symbolically, as Apprentice Freemasons.

In the Chamber of Reflections there is a sign that reads "VITRIOL" that functions as a forewarning of the path ahead. VITRIOL is a Latin acronym: *Visita interiora terrae rectificandoque invenies occultum lapidem*. For those who know how to decode it, it contains a fundamental reminder of Masonic philosophy. In the Chamber of Reflections—the spatial prequel to the beginning of the path—most neophytes, however, do not yet know how to interpret it. It is only in hindsight, after having advanced to higher degrees of Masonic initiation, that my informants said they finally understood teachings that were previously unintelligible to them. This Latin acronym could be translated literally as "Visit the inside of the earth, and by rectifying it you will find the hidden stone." Most Freemasons interpret this maxim as a metaphorical exhortation to look deep within themselves and correct the vices and faults of their souls. Traveling to the inside of the earth is for them a symbol of the spiritual, inner journey they undertake to discover themselves and remake themselves into better people. Within this symbolic framework, the "hidden stone" (*occultum lapidem*) is generally understood to be a reference to the philosopher's stone, a century-old object of alchemic desire and imagination, cast as the mythical prize awaiting Masons at the end of a journey of self-discovery.

The philosopher's stone represents the potential for transformation and improvement—the legendary ability to turn metals into precious gold. As compensation for a path of self-cultivation, the philosopher's stone is therefore a symbol of the Masonic utopia: the very *possibility* of transforming society by transforming individuals. One person at a time, one consciousness at a time, my informants believed that society as a whole could be perfected. Through a Masonic path of self-cultivation, described esoterically as the ultimate quest for the philosopher's stone, profane individuals are thus remade into new members of society—reborn, so to speak, into new subjectivities, as better people, as *brothers.*

The initiation of an Entered Apprentice is the first of many ritual initiations that mark a Freemason's advancement through the Masonic esoteric path. Next come the second and the third degree, Fellow and Master (f. *Maestra*, m. *Maestro*), which complete the initiation levels of what is technically known as a Masonic "Order." A Masonic Order is what most profane see of Freemasonry, if they see anything at all. Beyond the third degree, however, many Master Masons choose to enter a much more secretive Masonic "Rite" and pursue further degrees of ritual initiations—up to thirty-three degrees in the Ancient and Accepted Scottish Rite prevalent among my informants[1]—to advance their knowledge of esotericism and of mysticism.

To each new initiation corresponds an increase in annual membership dues, additional fees to complete the ritual ceremony, and new regalia to purchase. The Masonic path can thus be a life-long endeavor, requiring a huge investment of time and money. The first initiation ritual does not simply transform a profane into a Freemason but, more precisely, it transforms a profane into an Apprentice Mason, establishing the condition of possibility for a long process of self-cultivation, of which it only marks the first step.

In this chapter I explore the subjectivity to which Masons aspire: who they are and who they want to be. Anthropological studies of subjectivity have understood the "subject" to be not an individual, psychological, unified self, as in the common Western view of a "true inner self," but rather a corporeal experience of personhood produced by historical contingencies and social structures.[2] Etymologically, *subjectivity* ties a notion of the self to political subordination. To study subjectivity ethnographically therefore means studying both power relations and the conscious-affective experiences of being particular people in particular contexts.[3] Practices of self-cultivation like those in which Freemasons engage are especially revealing of the craft of personhood insofar as those outer practices, such as rituals, labor activities, or creative endeavors, have been shown not merely to express practitioners' inner dispositions and values but also to shape and produce the very subjects who practice them (Abu-Lughod 1986; Herzfeld 1985; Kondo 1990; Mahmood 2005). In other words, it is by acting like a Freemason that a Freemason comes to be. An analysis of the power relations underlying Freemasons' practices of subjectivity makes it possible to decipher the social dramas of gender, class, or nation within which the lives of Italian Freemasons unfold.

Being Freemasons in Italy in the early years of the twenty-first century was for my interlocutors not simply a membership into a group but an identity category essential to whom they saw themselves to be. Yet, living amid the abhorrence of much of profane Italian society, often including their own profane family members, my informants inhabited a subjectivity riddled with contradictions, often feeling persecuted for who they were, despite the privilege and elitism of the lodges, and despite their own conviction in the righteousness of their self-cultivation path. The stated goals of Freemasonry to better society by bettering individuals under the Enlightenment principles of liberty, fraternity, and equality for all were a far cry from the dominant depictions of Freemasonry in Italy as a network of powerful men masterminding all sorts of corruption schemes and antidemocratic strategies for financial and political gain.

In exploring the meaning of Masonic subjectivity, I posit that it must first be taken seriously. The popular argument that portrays Masonic lodges as political lobbies where special interests can be advanced outside the purview of democratic checks falls short of explaining the degree of personal investment required to be a Freemason. Spending decades attending weekly rituals and meetings, studying esotericism and learning the arcane histories of secret societies across the globe, paying hefty membership dues, following a strict hierarchy of mutual responsibilities, all the while confronting the ostracism of mainstream society, is not the most efficient way of simply concluding a business deal or earning a promotion. Even if material benefits might have been accrued in some cases, the personal desires that lured people into this particular path of self-cultivation beg for a deeper analysis. As I tackle the question of who Freemasons were and who they aspired to be in this chapter, I therefore also explore the conditions of possibility that made the Masonic path an intelligible and desirable option for particularly situated individuals, and especially for women who have long been excluded and marginalized from most forms of Freemasonry worldwide.

The multiple paths that lead to a Masonic initiation are both contingent to the idiosyncrasies of personal lives and representative of broader patterns of social belonging. For most of my informants, the possibility of imagining joining Freemasonry—in a generic, unmarked sense—had first been conjured by people in their lives, such as family members, lovers, and close friends. The timing, modality, and context for that imaginative possibility, however, could vary significantly. Some had been born into Masonic families, learning about temples and lodges from a very young age and joining a lodge upon reaching the age of maturity. Others, had become familiar with Masonic teachings only as adults, through an encounter with a significant other or a friend, and had needed to rethink what they thought they knew about Freemasonry. Through an ethnographic reading of various personal stories of initiation that my inter-locutors shared with me, I trace "what is at stake" (Kleinman 1999) for them in imagining "Freemason" to be such a meaningful subjectivity, and what the conditions of possibility were for such imaginings.

Producing Subjectivity

On the day of her initiation to the degree of Apprentice Freemason, Claudia did not know what to expect. She told me that at the time she did not really understand what Freemasons did because she had never had a Mason in her own family. In her case, she had decided to join a lodge in the mixed-gender Grand Lodge of Italy (GLDI) because of a man with whom she had been involved. She was curious, but rather cautious.

> When I received my initiation I got there and I didn't know anything of what was about to happen to me. . . . In the moment when they took off my blindfold, and I saw all of them there with their hooded gowns, I said to myself, "I can't believe this! On the verge of the twenty-first century, they still dress like that!" I didn't know anything. I knew generally about [Masons'] ideals, but that ritual-ism [ritualità], what would happen to me during the initiation, I didn't know anything about that!

I first met Claudia at a dinner party at the house of one of her sisters in Rome, where someone pointed out to me that she was one of the youngest Mae-stre in the mixed-gender GLDI. In her late thirties, Claudia was indeed much younger than the other dinner guests, who were well over the age of fifty, as are most Freemasons in Italy. When I met her, Claudia had been a Freemason for almost ten years, and a Maestra for most of that time in one of the Roman lodges of the GLDI. "I went through the first three degrees very quickly," she explained, pointing out that the speed at which one advances in Freemasonry is very personal. "Some people can take a while."

The discussion I had with Claudia about her first initiation happened a few months after that dinner party in Rome, and only after Claudia had had a chance to get to know me better, running into me at Masonic events and at the houses of other brothers and sisters. She called me to let me know she would be in Florence for work, and so we decided to go out for an *aperitivo*. Similar to "happy hour," *l'aperitivo* is an increasingly popular in-between meal usually served between 6:00 and 8:00 p.m., before dinner. For the price of a drink, cafes and bars throughout Italy compete in offering their customers free food, ranging from bite-size snacks to abundant and delicious meals. Claudia and I walked together through the center of Florence, passing by Piazza della Repubblica, and Claudia smiled at the sight of the Giubbe Rosse café, where she had enjoyed a cup of coffee with many Freemasons throughout the years. For old time's sake, she decided we should get our *aperitivo* there.

As we sat in the back room of the café that is both a landmark of Freemasonry and, as the founding site of Futurism, a landmark of twentieth-century Italian intellectual history, Claudia described her memories of her initiation into the GLDI. Her brothers and sisters, people who had since become "family" to her, had looked "ridiculous," she told me, in those black hooded gowns. She insisted that back in the mid-1990s, when her boyfriend had introduced her to the social world of the lodges, she knew very little about Freemasonry. "I only knew the stuff we learn in school, you know? Garibaldi's *carboneria*, and mostly what the newspapers say, terrorism and all . . . but I trusted him and I trusted the people I got to know. They were excellent people [*ottime persone*]."

What Claudia had not realized, she told me, was how central the practice of rituals was to Masonic lodges. She had not expected the blindfolds and ritual garments that reminded her of silly movies about secret societies, or the old-fashioned formulas recited with rhythmic precision during the ritual. Claudia's avowal of ignorance about Freemasonry was the starting point in a narrative account that progressed to describe how she eventually came to acquire knowledge. Recalling her initial astonishment at what she perceived to be an anachronistic ritualism ("on the verge of the twenty-first century, they still dress like that!"), Claudia was speaking from a more knowledgeable standpoint—one from which her earlier impressions could now seem naïve.

Her account followed a pattern similar to that of many other Masons I interviewed. Recognizing her initial ignorance, she had learned that knowledge only comes in hindsight, and she could now see what she did not see earlier. She told me that it was only after she had initiated someone else that she really understood her own initiation experience, the importance of the symbolic death of her profane life, and the experience of being reborn among a group of brothers and sisters ready to guide her along a path they had walked before. Similarly, she said it was only after having been made a Fellow—the second degree of the Masonic hierarchical path—that she had understood her training in the first degree of Apprenticeship. Now, as a Maestra, she said she was finally able to see what she had been taught during her years of Fellowship. "It's like when in the tenth grade you really understand what you learned in the ninth grade," she explained, "or like when you understand the reasons for the end of your relationship a year later."

In hindsight, all my informants understood perfectly well the significance of Masonic rituals. The esoteric practices that might at first seem ridiculous, anachronistic, and off-putting, are in fact precisely what makes Freemasonry the unique spiritual social organization that it is. A Maestra in the women-only Grand Women's Masonic Lodge of Italy (GLMFI) who had come to Freemasonry later in life once told me that Freemasonry was not a social organization like any other. "If all I wanted was a club, another club," she said to me, "I would be content with the Rotary. But Freemasonry is not a club; it's a spiritual path and it is that esoteric aspect that gives me a reason to be here."

The "life and death" initiation rituals of Freemasonry follow the patterns amply described in the anthropological literature on rituals and secret societies (Luhrmann 1989; Simmel 1906; Turner 1969). An initiation ritual, purportedly transforming the neophyte's subjectivity from that of a profane to that of a Mason, marked the entry point not only into an organization but into a new status. Once initiated, a Freemason is a Freemason for life. Even if she were to stop attending the lodges, thus lapsing into a so-called state of sleep (*in sonno*), or even in the rare and more serious cases in which a Mason might be expelled from her lodge with what is symbolically referred to as a "death sentence," an initiation may never be undone. Once a Mason, always a Mason, and the self-cultivation path of a Freemason is always ongoing.

One of the first and most important lessons I learned doing fieldwork among women and men Freemasons in Italy is that for all of them being a Freemason was not simply a matter of membership into a group or a hobby. Being a Freemason was for my informants an ontological category, fundamental to who they saw themselves to be in the world. It was a subjectivity produced through the signifying power of an initiation ritual and maintained through the practices and further rituals of a self-cultivation path that, for many people, continued for decades. Some of my interlocutors told me that they were Freemasons before they were women, or Italians, or anything else, thus placing what could be misunderstood as a temporary membership or a professional affiliation in the same category as gender or nationality or heritage.

In the emic terms of my informants, then, being a Freemason was less similar to being in the Rotary or in another social organization, and more akin to being, for instance, "a Christian" among religious fundamentalists or "an American" in the nationalist logic of citizenship. It is a fundamental identity category attained through the rules and rituals of a religious or bureaucratic social system, whose loss could be brought about by nothing short of a profound rupture with or betrayal of its attending social system.

For contemporary scholars of gender or nationalism, it is of course easy to point out the illusory essentialism of any such claims to a foundational identity. After all, those categories of identity that are ideologically constructed to be natural—"all those things one cannot help" (Anderson 1991 [1983]: 143)—are only reified through processes of social construction. Gender, for instance, or even the notion of "sex" with its apparently unassailable biological fixity, have been amply deconstructed in feminist scholarship and revealed to be cultural constructs (Butler 1999; Fausto-Sterling 1993).

What is interesting about my interlocutors' insistence that being a Freemason was fundamental to their sense of self is that they relied on a commonsensical essentialism—the culturally based idea that some identity categories, such as sex or nationality, are natural, foundational, and constitutive—in order to naturalize as an identity category a structure of affiliation that would not be generally considered to be an identity category at all by dominant (profane) cultural conventions.

"This is what my parents don't understand," Claudia told me sitting in the back room of the Giubbe Rosse café, as she described to me her sometimes difficult interactions with her profane parents, who had never approved of her decision to become a Freemason. "They don't understand that this is who I am. I can't stop being a Freemason."

Being a Mason "Within"

While a ritual initiation worked to consecrate the production of "Freemason" as an identity category and the neophyte's first steps into a life-long path of self-cultivation, my informants often went further in their own identity claims, suggesting that to be a Freemason is actually to be a "Freemason within" (*Massone dentro*). The first time I heard this expression, I was at a ritual gala dinner with several of my informants. One of them took me over to another table to introduce me to an old friend, a profane woman whose husband was in the mixed-gender GLDI. After we met, I asked the woman if she belonged to the same lodge as her husband, but she promptly clarified that she was not a Mason. "She is a Mason within, though," said our mutual acquaintance, "and being a Mason within is what matters."

Since that first occurrence there were several other times in which I heard my informants refer to others as "Masons within." This descriptor was always used for people whom the speaker held in high esteem. Strikingly, the attribute could be applied to Mason brothers and sisters, who were formally members of a lodge, as well as to profane individuals who had never received a ritual initiation. Being a Freemason within seemed to be about a personal set of qualities one had independently of the teachings of the Masonic path or the active process of self-cultivation that it engendered. It was about an inner state of being rather than a transformation learned and practiced. As such, the idea of being a Mason within might appear to be in contrast to the very principles of Freemasonry, according to which anybody could walk the Masonic path after a required initiation ritual. The notion of being a Mason within added an inscrutable element of inner talent to what is otherwise a pedagogical training of the self that ostensibly anybody could undertake. Moreover, the attribution of the status of Mason within to a profane also served to reinforce and validate the Masonic qualities of the speaker, for it takes one to know one. Only a true Freemason could recognize a brother or sister by the very traits that all Freemasons aspired to cultivate along the initiation path, such as moderation of judgment, magnanimity, and discretion.

The traits that made one a Mason within seemed as ephemeral as the motives that had led a brother or sister to seek a formal initiation in the first place. Freemasons often described their desire to be initiated as a "calling" (*vocazione*). From the early days of my field research, I noticed they would smile, soften their tone, and talk about it as if they were trying to translate into words an unspeakable mystical experience. As a young Apprentice told me early on about her decision to be initiated in the women-only GLMFI, "Freemasonry is like a harbor where those who are searching for something may dock."

Profane family members of Freemasons were often very skeptical of the mystical tones that made the desire to be a Mason resemble a spiritual calling. The profane sister of a Freemason man, for instance, told me that her brother and other Masons "must not know what a calling is, if they think they felt one." In many cases, these profane relatives were under the impression that the material conditions underlying Masonic membership were much more relevant than any presumed connection with the spiritual. "They are just little power games [*giochini di potere*]," insisted the woman whose brother had for many years tried to persuade her to join a lodge. She said she believed becoming a Freemason could help her career, just as she believed it had helped her brother's, but she was not interested in those kinds of "games."

The Freemasons I met in Italy, both men and women, articulated to me time and time again the incomprehension they encountered daily when they confronted, as Freemasons, profane and thus mostly unfriendly social spaces. Those who came from profane families had in many cases found little support among their relatives, and often settled for peaceful living (*per amor di pace*) by avoiding the subject of Freemasonry altogether, rather than facing open hostility at home. Those who came from Masonic families needed nonetheless to negotiate their self-presentations among profane colleagues, friends, and neighbors.

In a few instances I heard my informants refer to the process of revealing their identity as Freemasons to profane people in their lives as an "outing," using an Anglicized term borrowed from the Italian gay rights movement to mean "coming out." Most Freemasons did not use this Italian neologism, but nonetheless described to me their experiences relating to profane loved ones in ways strikingly similar to the coming out stories so prevalent in queer studies literature (Decena 2008; Sedgwick 1990).[4] Not only was being a Freemason a core identity, brought about by a ritual transformation aimed to uncover and perfect a Freemason's true self, but it was also arguably a disparaged category, one that my informants believed to have been unfairly persecuted by Catholic and Communist forces in Italian politics.

During a social gathering I attended at the rural country house of one of the GLMFI sisters some forty kilometers outside Florence, as guests chatted and ate an enormous potluck meal on folding chairs in the backyard, the conversation turned to the experiences many had had dealing with profane loved ones who were unsympathetic to Freemasonry. Marina, one of the Maestre in the GLMFI, known in Masonic circles for her good sense of humor and her legendary culinary abilities—in addition to being a highly sought-out attorney with a private firm in the center of Florence—suddenly jumped into the conversation. She began to tell us about the difficulties she had faced discussing Freemasonry with her "blood sister" (*sorella di sangue*), a term Freemasons used to distinguish their profane siblings in their families of origin from their Masonic brothers and sisters. Marina told us that she had gone to her blood sister's house a few years earlier for Saint Stephen's—the day after Christmas, and an important Italian religious holiday—to exchange gifts and eat lunch. She and her sister had then found some time alone, and Marina had tried to explain to her sister that Freemasonry is nothing like what it looks like in the newspapers or on TV. She and her sister used to be close, and so Marina told us that she tried to convey to her sister that being a Freemason was her "calling," and that it was a part of her. No, she had told her sister, she could not quit.

Her blood sister had remained quiet for a little while, Marina told us, and then she had leaned forward to whisper to Marina in a concerned tone, which Marina mimicked for our amusement at the potluck: "Is it that you can't leave Freemasonry because *they* will not let you? Will they do something to you if you try to exit?"

The group of Freemasons to whom Marina narrated her story burst into laughter, of course, as they usually did, at the persistence of stereotypes about them in Italian profane society, and also, as one of Marina's GLMFI sisters was quick to point out, at the idea that any one of them could get Marina to do something she did not want to do. Next to Marina, Gianfranco, the husband of one of the other GLMFI Maestre and himself a Maestro in the men-only Grand Orient of Italy (GOI), rushed to the joke, adding that Freemasons are also known to eat children. "Do you know what you are eating at this party?" He asked us. Others jumped in too, to be clever, suggesting that perhaps all this Masonic talk of "death sentences" or the initiation oath, which threatens Freemasons who break the vow of secrecy with a very painful death, might have given others the wrong impression.

Hilarity and sarcasm mediated the expression of what I knew had been painful moments of familial ruptures in the lives of my informants. I knew that Gianfranco, for instance, had lost his childhood best friend, a magistrate, in the wake of the scandal that ensued when police investigations dragged the names of many Freemasons into the open after the P2 lodge was accused of plotting a coup. There is a saying in Italian, *si ride per non piangere*, we laugh so that we won't cry. Everyone at the potluck that day was laughing.

Franca, who until that point had been standing by the side listening quietly to the conversation, grabbed a chair and moved it into the circle so that she could join us. She was one of the most senior Maestre in the GLMFI, and I noticed that whenever she approached a group of Freemasons, others started to pay attention to her. Although she was known for the occasional snappy remark, Franca was usually jovial and well spoken. It was a sign of the respect she had earned that she could so easily convene an audience.

"This is why we have to be discreet," Franca stated matter-of-factly to a nodding audience. Being discreet was paramount to my informants' ability to live amid the profane in a society that largely viewed the lodges negatively by, for instance, negotiating their public presentations or even their self-disclosures among profane family members. Franca, however, was underscoring a particular aspect of discretion that related my interlocutors' everyday performances of self to their explicit pedagogies. In the Masonic learning path, discretion was also a didactic tool.

"One must learn things when one is ready," Franca continued. "If one learns things too early, one cannot understand them." Gianfranco concurred with the Maestra's assessment. Behind her cryptic words was an epistemology familiar to all those present. Knowledge comes in hindsight in the Masonic path, as new symbols and esoteric teachings help Freemasons make sense of earlier ones. Knowledge must be imparted with discretion, or else it risks overwhelming its recipients with the paradoxical effect of obstructing the learning process. Holding something back, discreetly, may therefore be not an act of concealment but a necessary step in the transmission of knowledge.

"There are things about Freemasonry, allegories, symbols," Franca continued, "that the profane are not ready to understand. Revealing too much would only lead to misunderstandings." The practice of discretion, which made it possible for Freemasons to exist as a secretive but not secret organization within Italian society, also mediated the transmission of knowledge among Freemasons in a way that made both disclosures and concealments crucial to the learning process.

"For example, the *death sentence*," Marina added, referring to the Masonic term for the expulsion of a brother or sister when he or she is found to be in violation of the rules of the lodge. Since an initiation can never be undone, a symbolic death is the only way to leave Freemasonry. "In reality," Marina continued, "we don't kill anyone by ripping their tongue out and throwing it into the sea." According to my interlocutors, revealing too much to the profane would not only cause a betrayal but it would also cause profound "misunderstandings" of Masonic values and esoteric beliefs, especially in a country where Freemasons have been associated with murderous conspiracies.

"Well, not anymore!" Gianfranco added, in reference to the death sentence, as the others, amused, rolled their eyes. "It's really unfortunate. Really, just my opinion." Then we all mused about the people whose tongues we thought should be ripped out.

Initiation Paths

Although profane readings of Freemasonry as a network for material gain fall short of explaining the degree of personal investment that life in the lodges required, my interlocutors' own explanations typically failed to account for the material conditions underlying lodge membership. Freemasons' elusive references to a "calling" emphasized the individual's relationship to an existential quest at the expense of any acknowledgment of the social context within which such a calling could unfold, including pre-existing family ties to Freemasonry. In their haste to assure me that anybody could be a Freemason, my interlocutors often left out the social conditions of possibility necessary for an initiation to take place.

The rules of admission to Masonic lodges, first spelled out in the eighteenth century in Anderson's *Constitutions*, were an expression of Enlightenment notions of political subjectivity, whereby only freeborn men of good character were eligible for an initiation to *Free*-masonry, the speculative masonry of the literate classes. All others—women, slaves, the disabled, the poor—were not admitted into the lodges not because of any inherent deficiency on their part, but rather because their historical conditions of dependency (women's on their male relatives, slaves' on their masters) meant that their ability to pursue reason and morality was irremediably compromised by the material circumstances of their existence. If Freemason men did not allow women into the lodges, it was, according to them, because women are not free.

Although membership requirements have changed somewhat over time and in different contexts, the claim that anybody could be a Freemason is still hyperbolic and does not account for ongoing socioeconomic and gender restrictions on initiation. The screening process that prospective initiates had to undertake to enter Italian Masonic lodges, for instance, required them to provide references from current Freemasons. In a country where most Freemasons do not openly reveal their identity and where Masonic temples are hidden from view in undisclosed locations, that task would be hard to accomplish for someone who did not already have a personal connection to a Mason. At a more fundamental level, the notion of becoming a Freemason could not be desirable, or even conceivable, to a profane in Italy who lacked the social capital necessary to imagine that possibility. Virtually all the Freemasons I met in a year and a half of fieldwork had come to know Freemasonry through a loved one.

In the next few pages I tell the stories of Margherita and Valeria, both members of the women-only GLMFI but with profoundly different personal histories of initiation. Margherita, born in a Masonic family, was one of the founding members of the GLMFI, whereas Valeria, a much younger Maestra, had only discovered Freemasonry as an adult. Their experiences are illustrative not only of the multiple paths that can lead one to seek a Masonic initiation but also of the institutional mechanisms that structure lodges and their members' relationships to each other. Together, these two stories can offer some insights into the sociopolitical context in which women Freemasons in particular came to receive an initiation, and on the conditions of possibility for their desires.

Margherita's Story

Margherita was in her late sixties when we first met, at the very beginning of my fieldwork research. She was introduced to me by a few other Masons, who insisted she was someone I needed to speak to about my project because she would be able to help me. A retired lawyer who had been at the forefront of the struggle to establish a Masonic lodge for women back in the 1970s, Margherita turned out to be indeed quite an extraordinary person to encounter. Both her father and her grandfather had been high-ranking officers of the men-only GOI, the largest and oldest Masonic organization in the country. Margherita liked to say that she had "grown up in the shadow of power," referring to her upbringing within a prominent Masonic family.

One afternoon soon after we first met, she invited me to her home. As we were sipping tea, she showed me some old family pictures and began to share with me memories of her childhood. She remembered going to play inside the temple with her little brother. Their father used to take them there on the weekend, when nobody was using it for ritual ceremonies, and she and her brother used to run around for hours on the checkered floors of the temple, hiding behind neoclassical columns, fantasizing about all the stars and zodiac signs carved on the ceiling. Margherita thought it was a magical place straight out of a fairy tale. When her brother came of age at twenty-one, he was allowed to be initiated into the GOI, and he returned to that same temple where they pretended to perform rituals when they were children. Margherita told me how left out she had felt. In adulthood there was no space for her inside the temple. As a woman, she felt there was no space for her in Freemasonry.

To be accurate, Margherita had options. The second-largest Masonic organization in Italy, the GLDI, had started accepting women in the 1950s, so she could very well have been initiated into one of their lodges. Her family, however, had such a strong legacy in the men-only GOI, and the two groups had such a history of friendly rivalry, that Margherita felt that joining the mixed-gender GLDI would have been tantamount to betraying her father and her grandfather's memory.

There was also another option for Margherita. Because of her kinship ties to members of the GOI, she was eligible to join the Order of the Eastern Star (ES), an auxiliary para-Masonic group designed precisely to accommodate GOI Masons' wives, daughters, and other female relatives. Although the Eastern Stars do not receive a full Masonic initiation, they discuss esoteric topics, perform rituals, and dedicate themselves to philanthropy.

Margherita told me that was exactly what she did at first: she joined the

ES. After a few years, however, she became increasingly unhappy. As a child she had sneaked into her father's study to read some of his books and papers about Freemasonry. Crouched down outside the door of his study, she had eavesdropped on his esoteric discussions with lodge brothers. She therefore felt she had more knowledge about Freemasonry than a new initiate, and she knew enough to know that what they were doing at the ES was simply "not the same thing." The Stars (*le stelline*), she told me, were wonderful people. She claimed that she still thought of them as her sisters. For Margherita, however, what they were doing was simply not Freemasonry, and since childhood she had wanted to be a Freemason.

After a few years, Margherita's dissatisfaction had become a contentious enough issue within her ES lodge that she was put "on trial" by her sisters and was ultimately expelled through a "death sentence." I had known about it from some of my other informants in the ES, but I waited for Margherita to broach the subject. She did, and with surprisingly little resentment she assured me that she still had many friends among the Stars. "There is a reason for everything," Margherita told me, and leaving the ES was what prompted her to decide it was time to try something else. She told me that she had heard of a French Masonic lodge for women that happened to have a few sisters working in Rome inside a temple attended mostly by diplomats and other foreigners. Indeed, generally speaking, Francophone Masonic lodges have been more open to women than Anglophone ones. Margherita and other former ES sisters decided to work with the French group, trying to start a lodge of their own. In her words, she felt the need for a "true" Masonry.

The story of how Margherita and a few others eventually built an Italian women's lodge came in bits and pieces. It began over tea in her apartment that afternoon and it continued through dinners and meetings over the following months. Sometimes others would join the conversation or would share their memories with me in private interviews, thus contributing additional perspectives. Their narratives, just like Margherita's, were not always linear and did not necessarily present the events in chronological order.[5]

It was some time in the 1970s. Margherita told me they used to get together in temples—basements, she was careful to specify—with columns made of cardboard, stars hand-painted on the ceiling, and none of the splendor of the GOI temples she had seen in her youth. She explained that they "had to make do" (*dovevamo arrangiarci*), splitting the cost of rent and of government-imposed fees to register as a nonprofit association. She insisted they had always done things by the book, making sure their association had a legal status in accordance with state and municipal policies. The sisters often needed to adjust the ritual schedule to allow for breaks to nurse babies or cook dinner at home so that their husbands would have nothing to complain about, and then finally rush to the temple in the evening to perform rituals to the glory of the Great Architect of the Universe, the nondenominational deity Freemasons worship. This was a recurring story among the older women I interviewed, many of whom emphasized "tutti i sacrifici," all the sacrifices, they had to make to pioneer a women-only Masonic organization in Italy, which was finally chartered in 1990 after over a decade of working under the auspices of a French Grand Lodge.

Although the sisters' narratives contained implicit references to class and gender differences, marking the limited resources available to them in building a Masonic organization, their rhetoric was typically one of resilience, sacrifice, and personal and collective commitment. Rarely were structures of difference interrogated in their accounts.[6] Margherita thought that some of her sisters were "lucky" because their husbands sympathized with their endeavors, while others had to fight harder at home to be good wives, good mothers, and successful in their careers as well as in advancing through the Masonic path. For all of them, the pulls of family commitments, employment, and activism in Freemasonry followed the well-documented pattern of the "double shift" (triple, in this case), or the disproportionate amount of work women often have to do to fulfill a variety of social and familial responsibilities in Italy and elsewhere (see Goddard 1996; Plesset 2006).

The GOI and the GLDI had beautiful temples, fancy gala dinners, libraries, offices, and resources that could not compare. To be sure, Margherita told me, some of the sisters gave up in the end. Some left Freemasonry altogether when it caused too much familial strife. Others joined the mixed-gender GLDI. I met and interviewed some of those women who at some point had left the women's lodge for the GLDI, and they told me that they had wanted to experience the wide scope of fraternity that Freemasonry engenders. With only a few hundred members, the women-only lodge could not offer them the sizable national and international networks of fraternity that they had come to find through the much more established GLDI. Margherita said she really could not blame them, and confessed that she herself had often been tempted to leave. In the end, though, she had stayed and worked with others to build what eventually became the Grand Women's Masonic Lodge of Italy (GLMFI). She was understandably very proud of their accomplishments.

After hearing Margherita's story, I asked her and several other women what made them decide to stay and fight to create a new lodge for women. Why not simply join an already established mixed-gender group? Was it only because some of them, like Margherita, had a family legacy in the rival men-only GOI?

Or perhaps did they believe so strongly that Freemasonry should be single-sex? Margherita's answer was the same as that of almost every other sister I interviewed in the GLMFI. She told me that her decision to help found a women-only Masonic lodge had nothing to do, at least not in principle, with believing in a single-sex rite. On the contrary, she admitted that from a strictly esoteric point of view she was inclined to agree with the perspective of the GLDI, where women and men work together to effect ritual transformations by bringing together "the solar and the lunar" principles represented, respectively, by the masculine and the feminine. Margherita told me, however, that women needed to find their own space first, in order "to become conscious of themselves" (*per prendere coscienza di se stesse*).

I asked her what she meant by that, and Margherita invited me to consider for a moment the hierarchies of power apparent in the mixed-gender GLDI. There, she pointed out, women and men were nominally equal, but who held the position of Sovereign? Who sat on the Supreme Council, the highest governing body? Who presided over the High Chambers? Who was sent as an ambassador to meet lodges worldwide? For Margherita, the internal sexism of the GLDI was a microcosm of Italian society. While nominally championing gender equality, the GLDI maintained a glass ceiling that prevented most sisters from rising to the highest positions, which indeed, as I observed directly, were almost exclusively occupied by brothers.

"Maybe in a hundred years," she said in a somber tone. Maybe in a hundred years "society" will be ready to treat men and women equally. According to Margherita's assessment, the problem was historical, not essentialist, and it affected all of society, not only Freemasonry. Her rhetorical solution to wait a hundred years emerged clearly from a modernist and progressivist conceptualization of history, one central to the linear betterment of the Masonic self-cultivation path. For the time being, however, Margherita firmly believed that women needed a woman-centered space to learn to feel self-confident before they could be ready to "compete" against men in an uneven playing field. That is why they started the GLMFI, now a fairly well established women-only Masonic lodge with international recognition, but in the 1970s just a group of women who had learned about Freemasonry at home or from their friends.

Valeria's Story

Unlike Margherita, Valeria was not born to a Masonic family. Instead, she was one of the many women who came to Freemasonry as an adult. Valeria's story is in many ways representative of a fairly common pattern I encountered.

When we were first introduced by one of her sisters, she was forty years old, an accomplished freelance journalist who also held an administrative position in the city government of Florence. In her late twenties, Valeria had met Rosario, the man who would later become her life partner and for whom, despite the passing of time, she still had tenderness in her voice as she described him to me as an "extraordinary person." Although I had not met Rosario yet, I already knew of him, and I knew he was a member of the men-only GOI.

Valeria told me that when she had first met him she was struck by Rosario's way of being (*il suo modo di essere*). He seemed different from most people she knew, although she could not quite find the words to describe what exactly made him different in her eyes. His friends too had seemed different. It was not simply that they were kinder or more thoughtful or more *per bene* (polite, well behaved) than other people she knew. Struggling for words, she concluded that it was as if her partner and his friends had some sort of internal peace, some kind of serenity, that used to shine (*risplendeva*) on the outside. At first Valeria did not know what to make of it. Very early on in their relationship, however, Rosario disclosed to her that he was a Freemason. Valeria emphasized that he had seemed very open about it. It was an important aspect of his life, and he did not like to hide it, although she admitted to me that she had been shocked by his revelation.

When she first found out that her partner was a Mason, all Valeria could remember were some high school history lessons on the Risorgimento—Italy's period of nation-state formation in the nineteenth century—with some brief mentions of secret societies like the Mafia, the *carboneria*, and Freemasonry in the backdrop of accounts of Mazzini, Garibaldi, and other national heroes. With a smile, she told me that her mind had then quickly jumped to dominant media depictions of Freemasonry in Italy in the 1980s and early 1990s: conspiracies, terrorism, and the infamous P2 lodge.

As she recounted those moments to me, sitting in the living room of her apartment in Florence, Valeria laughed wholeheartedly at her initial naïveté, and she dismissed those first images of Freemasonry as utterly ridiculous in hindsight. She admitted that she had to overcome some ingrained prejudice about Freemasonry, which she attributed to the pervasive ignorance about it found in Italy thanks to the Vatican and to the Left. However, getting over those "stereotypes" was a rather quick process for her. From the moment Rosario told her that he and his friends were all Masons, Valeria decided that Freemasonry could not possibly be the eerie brotherhood that it was made out to be on TV. Her partner was such an extraordinary person, she explained, that if he could be a Freemason then it meant that Freemasonry itself must be extraordinary.

Valeria's narrative about her first exposure to the social world of Free-masons—initiated through a romantic relationship—revealed fairly common patterns of resignification and embrace of a Masonic identity. For many of my informants, especially those who came into contact with Freemasonry later in life, the choice to become Freemasons had required a profound ideological resignification of the dominant common sense that in Italy connotes anything Masonic as criminal, dangerous, and evil. In Valeria's personal narrative, the resignification process was relatively painless. By her own avowal, she did not know much about Freemasonry, except for some stereotyped media images, and she therefore did not hold as strong a negative opinion about it as many do in Italy. Even so, Valeria described a shift from belief in a Freemasonry that was nefarious and unimportant to belief in one that was positive and even central to her life. When confronted with the specificity of her partner's character, Valeria's beliefs about a generic category (Freemason) were called into question. Rather than leaving her partner, attributing to him any of the negative stereo-types about Freemasons, she was able to rethink instead her own assumptions about this identity category.

This is a rather familiar trope in antidiscrimination movements, as personal relationships with individual members of disparaged groups are often quite ef-fective in overcoming prejudice. Valeria's process of resignification, however, went a step further. She did not simply allow for the possibility that some Freemasons might be, like her partner, above their reputation, or that such reputations might even be unfounded. When she met an "extraordinary man," it was Freemasonry that she credited for his character, and for that sense of "internal peace" that made his way of being so extraordinary in her eyes. If he was such an extraordinary person, it was not *despite* being a Freemason nor *while also* being a Freemason. It was *because* he was a Freemason. He was not simply an exception to the rule of nefarious Freemasons. He was living proof that Freemasonry *must* be good.

Valeria's story echoed that of many others I met in that it ascribed to Free-masonry, as opposed to familial upbringing, personality, faith, profession, or any other identity-making site, a causal power to produce "good" people, "good" families," "good" values. It was not only Freemasons, however, who held Free-masonry capable of such life-transforming power. Most non-Masons I talked to in Italy spoke of Freemasonry as if assuming a seemingly limitless capability, on the part of the brotherhood, to shape the course of personal lives and politi-cal events. While profane portrayals of Freemasonry were typically negative, they nonetheless shared the sense that to be a Freemason was fundamental to a person's lifestyle, aspirations, sociopolitical alliances, career prospects, and commitments. "Freemason" was clearly an identity marker that carried a rare amount of discursive power in Italy.

Within just a few months, Rosario had invited Valeria to a white *agape*, as Freemasons' ritual dinners are called when they are open to profane guests. White agape dinners often provided the occasion of the first introduction between a prospective Mason and the members of a lodge. They usually looked like gala dinners in fancy restaurants or hotels rented out for the occasion, and they therefore offered an opportunity for the profane to become acquainted with Freemasonry amid a spectacle of opulence.[7] It was at that white agape, Valeria recalled, that Rosario introduced her to a friend of his—the woman who would later become Valeria's *madrina* (godmother, guide) in the women-only GLMFI.

When I began collecting life histories from my informants, I was surprised to discover that most of them had not made a conscious decision to join a specific Masonic lodge. With the exception of some of the older members of the GLMFI, like Margherita, who had intentionally cofounded a Masonic lodge for women, and those who at some point switched from one lodge to another, the vast majority of my interlocutors experienced initiations more like Valeria's. A loved one, a friend, or a family member had introduced them to a particular Masonic lodge or to the ES, and they had joined it. Indeed, and somewhat surprisingly, many Freemasons told me that at the time of their initiation they did not even know about the existence of other lodges.

My interlocutors' initial lack of awareness about Masonic groups other than their own seemed counterintuitive to me for various reasons. First of all, although the four organizations I studied were not always on the best of terms with one another officially, members of each had close personal ties of kinship or friendship with members of others. Any given social gathering, lecture, or white agape was likely to bring together members of the GOI, the GLMFI, the GLDI, and the ES. Second, given the commitment of time and money that membership in any Masonic organization requires, I would have expected a prospective applicant to research various organizations before making a final decision. Third, my informants often spoke of the gender and ritual differences among lodges as crucial to their experiences, usually claiming that they would not switch to another Masonic group precisely because of the particularities that they had come to value in their own. Nonetheless, the gender politics, ritual practices, or geographical presence of a particular lodge had been decision-making factors in a minority of the initiation stories I heard. When I asked my interlocutors how they had come to join their specific lodges, they usually answered that they had done so randomly (*è stato un caso*).[8]

Of course, the path that led neophytes to particular Masonic lodges was far from "random." The ways in which lodges courted prospective recruits, sometimes taunted their success in "stealing" members of others, and, at times, as was the case for Valeria, introduced prospective members to another lodge as a gesture of goodwill, were all part of complex politics of engagement in the landscape of Italian Freemasonry. These transactions and negotiations, which I found to be quite common, were indicative of the labor of production necessary for the making of Masonic fraternity.

Valeria's story is also significant precisely for what it tells us about the systems of exchange that make a neophyte's initiation possible and certainly not random. In her story, it is noteworthy that Rosario, a member of the men-only GOI, was the one to introduce Valeria to the women-only GLMFI, an organization that the GOI does not officially recognize. As her partner, he could have introduced her instead to the ES, the para-Masonic organization for female relatives of GOI men.

The modality of Valeria's introduction to her lodge was yet another example of the complex reality of Masonic relations in Italy, where a variety of Masonic lodges are officially bound by the existence, or lack thereof, of treaties of friendship and mutual recognition. Unofficially, however, brothers of the GOI often showed their support for the women-only GLMFI by assisting the sisters in locating suitable venues for their agape dinners, or by volunteering their services as guest lecturers during open receptions and talks sponsored by the women's lodge. Sometimes, brothers showed their support by introducing potential women initiates to the GLMFI, rather than to their own auxiliary ES. As I listened to Valeria's story, I could not help but remember the reassuring words of the Grand Maestra of the GLMFI when I had first discussed with her the challenges I feared I would face in working with four different Masonic organizations: at the end of the day, she had assured me, "everyone comes over for dinner."

The Traffic in Women

One night I was invited to the local temple of the GLMFI for the initiation ceremony of a new Apprentice by the name of Sara. Her story was very similar to Valeria's, insofar as Sara too had been brought to the GLMFI by a GOI brother with whom she was in a relationship. After the ceremony was over and all the sisters had changed out of their ritual gowns and into the elegant outfits of the profane world they inhabited, we mingled, laughed, and talked over food and refreshments at the agape dinner that followed in the small dining room outside the temple. This was a ritual agape, not a white agape, and therefore it was not open to the profane. The only exceptions that night were Sara's significant other (the GOI man), who was not technically a "brother" since his lodge and the GLMFI do not recognize each other, and I, the profane ethnographer turned "honorary" sister.

Everyone took turns in congratulating Sara, the newly minted Apprentice. She was a slim, short woman in her late thirties, much younger than most others, and looked fatigued by the four-hour initiation ordeal, much of which she had spent down on one knee. Right by her side, her male partner appeared quite moved by the moment. Perhaps it was the joy of the initiation, or perhaps it was the wine, but his eyes seemed red. I walked up to Sara to offer her my congratulations, and the Worshipful Maestra in charge of the lodge joined us. She thanked the man for first introducing Sara to them, just as Rosario had done for Valeria, and together they reminisced about how it had all come about several months earlier.

The Worshipful Maestra then turned to the brother and asked him somewhat loudly, in front of all of us, whether he had given Sara his "white gloves" yet. The room became suddenly quiet, as everyone waited for his answer. Upon reaching the third degree of initiation as a Maestro, a Freemason brother receives two sets of white gloves: one for himself, and another to offer to his "lady" as a chivalrous sign of commitment. This century-old custom continued to be practiced by the GOI, and the Worshipful Maestra's question that night was therefore an indiscreet inquiry into the relationship between Sara and her partner. Was Sara the woman to whom he would give his white gloves?

The man smiled, and for a moment I thought I saw his eyes watering.

"No," he answered thoughtfully after a long pause, as he reached for his partner's hand. "No, I did not give her my gloves." Then, looking directly at the Worshipful Maestra, he added: "Instead, I gave her to you."

Some of the sisters around us were visibly moved by that romantic heterosexual moment, nodding in approval at the sensitivity of this man, who could see what some of his brothers could not, who could see that giving his gloves to a woman was no sign of equality to that audience, no sign of freedom and fraternity, no sign of love, or agape, as they meant it. For a member of the men-only GOI to introduce his partner to a women-only Masonic lodge that the GOI considered irregular was in the eyes of those present a radical instantiation of agape, a love of humanity that Freemasons pursued above all other forms of love.

No, he would not give his white gloves to Sara to consecrate a status quo in which all she could be was a Freemason's significant other. Instead, he would give Sara to the Worshipful Maestra of a women-only Masonic lodge, so that Sara could be free to walk her own Masonic path, parallel to his and independent, sharing in that fraternity that was at the core of their sense of being.

I smiled along with my informants because I had come to understand and respect the significance of the Masonic path of self-cultivation for a particular class of women who sought their consciousness of gender outside the rubric of feminism and who fought for equality every day within structures of privilege. Yet, the feminist anthropologist in me cringed in a flashback to Claude Lévi-Strauss's classic theory of the "elementary structures of kinship," positing women as the units of exchange at the basis of kinship alliances made by men (Lévi-Strauss, Needham, and Bell 1969). As I was reminded in that very moment, Lévi-Strauss was not wrong about the widespread traffic in women's bodies and desires, but wrong in failing to recognize the heterosexist mechanisms underlying the process of exchange (Rubin 1975; Sedgwick 1985), in which it is also women who give and take each other. In a Masonic social world where members were precious commodities and leaders of each group often teased that they had "stolen" people from another, a brother's gifting of his female partner to the Worshipful Maestra of a women-only lodge put a powerful seal on an unpredictable alliance.

This gift exchange was a sign of the brother's commitment to the higher principles of equality and fraternity, and also of his support of women's initiation into Freemasonry, something that his men-only lodge would not condone. Remaking Sara herself into a gift, and turning the Worshipful Maestra into the gift recipient, the brother effectively changed every other term of this exchange but the one he occupied: that of the giver.

The fact that such a heterosexist transaction positing this man as the giver of his female partner could be understood by those present to be a romantic act, an act of love, is especially significant when interpreted in the context of long-standing social theories suggesting that the modern affect of "love" is ideologically deployed to mask the underlying political economy of families, kinship, class, and nationalist formations (see Engels 1978; Hardt and Negri 2009; Maira 2009; Ramaswamy 1997; Sommer 1991). In the history of Freemasonry, one of the recurring arguments against the possibility of initiating women has been that a Mason must be free, but that women are not truly free because of their subjugated status in relation to the men in their lives. This brother's symbolic gifting of his female partner to the Worshipful Maestra was therefore legible, in Masonic terms, as a profound act of love insofar as it liberated Sara to pursue her own Masonic path toward fraternity and equality. The kind of love the brother evoked was a love familiar to all those present; it was love as *agape*, a love of humanity far greater than the particular desires of *eros*. By literally giving his partner away to a women's lodge, the brother could be understood by himself and by his audience to have embraced fraternal love even at the cost of renouncing his own claims to Sara, and even at the risk of betraying his own lodge.

This romance of fraternity reveals the transactional engagements that render the lofty ideals of Masonic brotherhood materially possible as gendered practices. It raises the question, which I will explore more fully in chapter 3, of what fraternity with and among women could look like as they initiate and exchange each other, and what the conditions of possibility of such a brotherhood might be for the Freemason sisters committed to its pursuit.

One of the best-kept secrets of Freemasonry, my interlocutors told me over and over again, is that there are women Freemasons, too. The profane world is mostly ignorant of women's presence in the lodges, and the jaw-dropping realization—even the journalistic scoop (Meynell 2005)—of this social fact can elicit a chain reaction of incredulity, minimization, and awe that far exceeds the acknowledgment of women's presence in other men-dominated fields and institutions. Even when women were initiated and became, in fact, Freemasons, the patterns of inclusion and exclusion underlying their social struggle continued to persist in their claims to legitimacy and belonging. Are women as serious in their path? Are they as rigorous in following ritual procedures? Can they, ultimately, "really" be Freemasons? The more or less explicit term of comparison for such inquiries was always men's Freemasonry. Are women simply imitating men's Freemasonry, and does the latter hold a monopoly on Masonic legitimacy and authenticity?

Conclusion: Of Mimicry and Brothers

My intent in this chapter has been to explore the desires and conditions of possibility that made being a Freemason a meaningful and coveted core subjectivity for my interlocutors. Whether out of naïveté, curiosity, or greed, because of a mystical calling or family legacy, the Masons I met chose to enter an esoteric path ostensibly built to refashion who they were and how they inhabited their social world. In order to achieve their desired transformation, they subjected themselves to rigid ritual structures and significant financial and time commitments, in many cases lasting decades. My interlocutors exposed themselves to the risk of persecution, stigma, and ridicule in a society quite hostile to Freemasonry. Through ritual practice, they sealed the subject category of "Freemason" as a core identity, and then reified its ontology further by claiming that to be a Freemason is to be a Freemason within. Rather than dismissing my informants' labor of self-cultivation as self-serving "little power games," what could be learned about subjectivity by taking Freemasons seriously?

A plurality of Masonic experiences characterized my informants' lives in the lodges, and multiple paths led them to seek an initiation. Understanding the social conditions of Masonic initiations is crucial to understanding what it was that my interlocutors were after when they embarked on a long journey of esoteric self-cultivation. The most striking aspect of the Masonic path is that very little is known about it from the outside. Like Claudia, most of my informants told me that when they were first initiated they did not know what to expect, and that it was only through the knowledge quest that followed that they were able to understand, in hindsight, what they had learned at each step. Given the secrecy that surrounds Masonic practices in Italy, it is not surprising that most of my informants admitted that they had only learned what it meant to be a Freemason after becoming one. According to their accounts, it was somewhere along the initiation path that the subject category of "Freemason" was ascribed with meaning. How, then, I wondered, did it become an object of desire in the first place? What did neophytes want to be when they first chose to be initiated, before the category of Freemason was made intelligible to them?

The coveted subjectivity of Freemasonry is by definition relational. It is not only a desire to be something yet to be defined or yet to be discovered, but it is, more precisely, a desire to be *one of them*. For virtually every single Freemason I spoke to, the first impetus to join a lodge came from a family member or a friend, someone whom they trusted and admired. Joining Freemasonry was often an effort to feel closer to that person, or to follow in the footsteps of parents and grandparents, or "to have something to talk about with [one's] husband over dinner." In most cases, the desire was concretized after informally meeting several Masons at white agape dinners and galas and being introduced to their social world of esotericism and opulence. Even if a neophyte did not know exactly what Freemasonry was, or what to expect during an initiation ritual, he or she wanted to be *like them*. In other words, their desired subjectivity was, more accurately, intersubjectivity.[9] Before knowing what it means to be a Freemason, it was a desire to become a "brother."

I use the masculine noun *brother* here on purpose, despite the fact that most of my interlocutors were women, to call out the seamless discourse of fraternity underlying Masonic desires and principles. Insofar as masculine terms operate linguistically as placeholders for generic, unmarked categories, the *fratellanza* (fraternity, brotherhood) of Freemasonry is discursively masculine in its universal claims. The initiated enter a path of self-cultivation meant to refashion them into a particular kind of unmarked subject: a brother. The gendering of Masonic fraternity, however, had profound consequences for my women informants, whose pursuit of brotherly love required an explicit attempt on their part to become unmarked subjects.

Mostly invisible to profane accounts of Freemasonry, women Freemasons embodied an oxymoronic subjectivity. When their existence was recognized at all, they were accused of simply imitating men's Freemasonry and of not being "real" Freemasons. The problem of "mimicry" is not a new one, nor one that applies solely to women Freemasons. From those of us who are not deemed "real" Europeans because of our race to those whose gender expression marks them as not "real" women and men, many different kinds of subaltern subjects have long had to contend with the accusation that their subjectivity is not quite their own. This accusation delegitimizes subaltern life experiences and at the same time reifies the subject position of those they are accused of imitating as "natural" and "original." The question of mimicry has been explored in particular from the vantage point of postcolonial theory, which has attempted to recover an agentic, postcolonial subject from the influence of colonial hegemony (Bhabha 1994; Chatterjee 1993; Fanon 2008; Guha 1997; Mbembe 2001; Spivak 1988). Within that framework, Homi Bhabha (1994) has suggested that the civilizing aim of post-Enlightenment colonial discourse was to produce a colonized subject as "a reformed, recognizable Other, *as a subject of a difference that is almost the same, but not quite*" (86; original emphasis). Given colonialism's investment in both humanist claims (that all people are equal) and in the conquest of people deemed to be "others," the resulting "mimicry" of colonial subjects—their subjectivity as almost the same but not quite that of the colonizers—is for Bhabha a sign of the internal ambivalence of colonialism itself. It is in this internal ambivalence of colonial discourse that Bhabha also finds its weakness. Although much of the most thought-provoking scholarship on mimicry has emerged specifically from postcolonial contexts, the questions of authenticity, sameness, and equality that it has raised are worth asking of modern liberal discourses in all sites of their circulation.[10]

Masonic lodges have historically been coproduced with Enlightenment ideals of freedom and universal fraternity, and it might therefore seem odd to apply a postcolonial critique of liberal humanism to the very political subjects who not only "invented it," as one of my informants said jokingly, but who belong to the social groups that have structurally profited the most from the uneven, paradoxical applications of the logic of modernity: the white upper-classes of Europe. If I use the framework of "mimicry" to analyze the condition of Freemasons in early twenty-first-century Europe, it is not, then, to misrecognize the radical sociopolitical differences between my informants and colonial subjects, or to imagine a possibility of solidarity that simply was not there. To be sure, women Freemasons, despite their own struggles along gender lines, participated without question in the Orientalist and othering *bricolage* of Masonic esoteric knowledge that is crystallized even in the names of many Masonic lodges. My aim is to show instead that the subject-producing logic of the discourse of humanism is internally ambivalent regardless of where it is deployed, even in what might be considered one of its most "authentic" formative sites: European Freemasonry.[11]

Instead of conceding to certain Europeans primal authenticity as liberal subjects and relegating the predicaments of mimicry to those others who are "almost the same, but not quite," I contend that mimicry itself can be used to expose the instability of Freemasons' liberal subjectivity—that is, of Occidentalist liberal subjectivity—both women's and men's. My interlocutors had to labor to effect the self-cultivation that reified them as Freemasons. Being a Freemason was a subjectivity perpetuated through daily admonishments strengthened by ritual practices: to be fair, to be moderate and of "good character," to pursue knowledge with reason, to espouse the politics of secularism but under the spiritual guidance of a higher being, to defend the principles of freedom and equality for all, and to embrace universal fraternity. None of my informants were born that way.[12] Recognizing the mimetic efforts that even European subjects have to make to approximate the ideals of liberal humanism and to naturalize them can have a destabilizing effect on the claims of authenticity against which all other bodies are measured.

Rather than reduce women's initiation to Freemasonry to a simple mimicking of elite men's brotherhoods, I take the elaboration of a discourse of women's Freemasonry in its own terms, as a powerful and understudied expression of identity-based mobilizing for a certain class of women. Discussing gender, Judith Butler (1999) argued that a dissonant and denaturalized performance can reveal the performative status of that which is supposed to be "natural." If we take women's initiation into Freemasonry and their identities as Freemasons to be that dissonant performance, "derived, phantasmatic, and mimetic—a failed copy, as it were," then rather than despair its failures we can interpret it as a sign that the "ontological locales" of the authentically real and natural "are fundamentally uninhabitable" (Butler 1999: 186).[13] The controversy over the possibility of women's initiation can therefore be read diagnostically as a site of struggle where the authority of the Masonic discourse itself is disrupted and exposed in its partiality. A brotherhood of sisters, in other words, exposes the performative labor at the heart of the claim that Freemasonry accepts anybody. It is not that women are not "real" Freemasons, or that their initiation is "almost the same, but not quite" like that of a man. Rather, the initiation of women exposes the mechanisms that render the category of Freemason a meaningful subjectivity through a performative act predicated on powerful fictions of nation, Occidentalism, and manhood.

Brotherly Love

The persons admitted Members of a Lodge must be good and true
Men, free-born, and of mature and discreet Age, no Bondmen no
Women, no immoral or scandalous men, but of good Report.
‹JAMES ANDERSON, *The Constitutions of the Free-Masons*›

And the sister? Would she be in the same situation? Would she be a
case of fraternity? ‹JACQUES DERRIDA, *The Politics of Friendship*›

According to the official website of the mixed-gender Grand Lodge of Italy
(GLDI), liberty, fraternity, and equality are guiding principles of the life of a
Freemason. Among the three, however, the GLDI exalts fraternity as the highest
and most important because of its philosophical roots in an act of love: "This
elective tie [fraternity] can also be read as a Love tie: love in its meaning of
agape; a spontaneous love toward the other that does not expect to be requited;
an act of recognition of oneself in the other or, rather, in all others because
sharing the same nature" (GLDI 2012).

Fraternity is a peculiar form of love, one theorized and dissected with surgi-
cal precision over the centuries by philosophers assuming ancient Greek as the
starting logos for modern European imaginaries of community. *Eros*, *philia*, and
agape, the trinity of Greek love, are hard to translate in many contemporary
European languages that express *love* in a singular form, like the Italian *amore*.
Fraternity is not exactly any of the three or, rather, and depending on interpretation, it appears to lie somewhere in the interstices between friendship (*philia*)
and divine universal love (*agape*). As the GLDI's website informs us, Freemasons

understood fraternity to mean love as agape, an unconditional extension of love to all others "because sharing the same nature." As a product of Enlightenment humanism, the Masonic principle of fraternity my informants espoused was nominally universal, generalized to all people and specifically to all Freemasons. Even Freemasons who had never met each other face-to-face could partake in an affective imagination of community as a horizontal comradeship based on the claim of shared identity and on the deployment of "love" as the basis of political solidarity and affective subjectivity.

While this description suggests that Masonic fraternity is similar to the brotherhood of nationalism described by Benedict Anderson (1991 [1983]), the latter is, by its own definition, predicated on the contrast with an other, or multiple others—internal and external enemies, colonizing forces, misfits, traitors (Aretxaga 2003).[1] In contrast, Masonic fraternity is rhetorically constructed as translatable across borders of countries, races, genders, or ethnicities, and indeed able to make those social differences immaterial. The distinction between these two notions of fraternity, both emerging with the rise of modernity and shaping it in turn, is crucial not only for understanding the rhetorical power of fraternity but also for analyzing its enactments in twenty-first-century Masonic lodges.

Simply put, Masonic fraternity was humanist rather than nationalist. The very notion of love to which my interlocutors ascribed—that is, the *agape* of fraternal conviviality, the love of humanity—was therefore permeated by the immodest claims of Enlightenment liberalism and its unmarked subjects (Balibar 1994; Bhabha 1994; Fanon 2008; Gilroy 1993; Povinelli 2006). Despite its apparent commitment to inclusionary politics, Masonic brotherhood operated simultaneously on two explicit rhetorical tracks, one inclusionary and one quite exclusionary. On the one hand, adopting the universal claims of humanism, my interlocutors presented Freemasonry as a path that anybody could undertake. On the other hand, they explicitly espoused a commitment to exclusivity, for only those people of "good character" could be accepted on the path, after a careful screening process that included personal references and background checks. In this second sense, Masonic fraternity relied on a careful policing of membership boundaries to ensure exclusivity, internal cohesion, and external prestige—the markers of elitism (Shore and Nugent 2002).

The apparent contradiction between Freemasonry's universalizing Enlightenment claims and its literal codification of hierarchies of difference reflects the internal ambivalence of humanism itself, as a discourse simultaneously aggrandizing in its universal promises and particular in its privileging of a Eurocentric masculine rational subjectivity. Following Cornel West (1999), I take this apparent contradiction to be no contradiction at all but, rather, "the ignoble paradox of modernity"—modernity's reliance on the political economy of slavery as necessary fuel to propel its immodest claims to universal fraternity.

Indeed, because of Freemasonry's origins in the Enlightenment and the Enlightenment's origins inside Masonic lodges, there is a foundational correspondence between liberal modern discourses and Masonic principles. Many of the *philosophes des lumières* and their American political counterparts were Freemasons, such as Jean-Jacques Rousseau, Voltaire, George Washington, and Benjamin Franklin, and so were leading figures in women's rights and in national independence struggles throughout much of the world since the eighteenth century.[2] That historical overlap is deeply significant to contemporary Freemasons, many of whom told me they espoused a "secular morality" (*una morale laica*) founded on reason and on the "universal" principles of liberty, equality, and fraternity.

"Excuse me," a Maestro in the men-only Grand Orient of Italy (GOI) said during dinner once. "We are the ones who invented the Enlightenment!" His comment, spoken in a half jovial and half ironic tone, was met with laughter and nods by the small audience of Freemasons at the table. I do not intend to take it more seriously here than it was meant to be. Irony, sarcasm, wit, and jocularity are built seamlessly into the fabric of Italian conversations to a degree that may seem off-putting, confusing, or even rude to those not used to it. Spoken during a dinner conversation about the origins of Freemasonry, this Maestro's hyperbolic claim was nonetheless meant as a reminder of the deeply felt investments that all the Freemasons I met had in the values and ideals of liberal humanism.

In this chapter I propose an ethnographically driven analysis of the affective discourses and practices of fraternity—of brotherly love—at the core of liberalism. Situating this project within the geopolitical borders of Europe and amid white subjects, a consideration of the ignoble paradoxes of modernity can serve to expose the precariousness and internal contradictions of liberal humanist discourses even among what might be considered their political base. In addressing accounts of Masonic fraternity ethnographically, my aim is to explore fraternity's resilience despite its ignoble paradoxes not only as a perplexing abstraction but as a set of discourses grounded in the lived experiences of some contemporary European subjects.

Despite their historical exclusion from the institution of Freemasonry, women make claims to its promises of fraternity. The underlying question running through these pages is: what makes the inherently masculine notion of *fratellanza* (fraternity, brotherhood), founded as it is on the exclusion of most bodies from its expansive imaginings, such an appealing and compelling object of desire for women Freemasons? Why would they choose to commit their lives to its pursuit?

I approach this question through three lines of analysis: first, I explore my informants' lived experiences of fraternity—having brothers and sisters in the lodges for whom they developed feelings of love and care; second, I relate women Freemasons' fraternal practices to their distinctly right-wing politics and explicitly antifeminist rhetoric; third, I analyze my interlocutors' attempts to remake themselves into abstract liberal subjects, unbridled by corporeal and material differences that would otherwise preclude their possibility of engendering a brotherhood of sisters.

Tracing the material roots of fraternity and its embodiments in particular practices of politics and sociality—the process of "fraternization"—I seek to foreground fraternity's exclusive corporeality against its ideological representations as a universal, abstract, and thus disembodied set of affective attachments. To that end, I take fraternity to be an emic category for contemporary Freemasons and, more generally, for liberal subjects of the global North.

Fraternization

> On the field of battle, in the solitudes of the uncultivated forest, or in the busy haunts of the crowded city, [the tenets of Freemasonry] have made men of the most hostile feelings, the most distant regions, and diversified conditions, rush to the aid of each other, and feel a special joy and satisfaction that they have been able to afford relief to a Brother Mason. ‹BENJAMIN FRANKLIN›

A Masonic initiation turns a profane into a brother. The symbolic death a neophyte must undergo during the ritual serves as a prelude for him or her to be reborn into a new subjectivity that is, more precisely, intersubjectivity. Reborn among a community of brothers, the initiated will be endowed with a new ontological status as a Freemason and thus as a brother, and such a status may never be undone. *Once a brother, always a brother.*

Although brotherhood in esoteric terms is an intersubjective status produced through ritual work, many of the Freemasons I met told me that the affective bonds of fraternity took longer for them to experience than ritual time allows. At first, their lodge brothers and sisters were still strangers to them—strangers to whom they had made themselves vulnerable as they shared deeply intimate emotional experiences of the kind that an initiation ritual brings about, but strangers nonetheless. It was over time, my interlocutors told me, that they came to feel the interpersonal attachments, the strong fraternal bonds toward all of their lodge brothers and sisters, that in hindsight they said they could not live without.

Fraternity was therefore an ongoing project for them. Just as the initiation ritual that marks the ontological transformation of the profane into a Freemason is only the first step in a life-long esoteric path from Apprentice to Fellow to Master, and up to thirty-three further degrees, brotherhood too is a subject of cultivation. It was the process of fraternization, which produces and reifies fraternity as a lived experience, that I therefore set out to understand as I struggled to make sense of women Freemasons' embrace of a structurally androcentric organizing principle.

My interlocutors' stories of fraternity, both in the sense of what the principle of fraternity meant to them and in the sense of how they came to *feel* fraternity toward other Masons, were remarkably similar to each other. Their stories borrowed from a vast repertoire of allegories and tropes circulating inside the lodges. Some exalted, for instance, Freemasons' uncanny ability to recognize a fellow Mason in a stranger, perhaps while traveling through a foreign country. Some told of unexpected acts of kindness they had received from another Mason, even before they knew the other to be a Mason. Such modern-days stories, personal to the speaker, of mutual aid and recognition among Freemasons were often reiterations of the conventional narratives of Masonic parables, which were usually set in the ancient times of Masonic esoteric history: the temple of Solomon, the medieval guilds of stonemasons. They were inevitably scripted narratives of fraternity, although no less genuine as a result.

Is there no help for the widow's son? So goes the famous and formulaic cry for help that Freemasons in distress supposedly can speak to reach out to their brothers. The widow's son, depending on different esoteric interpretations I heard among my informants, could refer alternatively to Horus, the son of the Egyptian goddess Isis, or to Hiram, the architect of the temple of Solomon and foundational figure for Freemasons, who cried for help as he was being murdered for the secret keyword that would unlock the symbolic mysteries of his creation—the "lost word" that Freemasons' esoteric quest is after.

"Now, let's be serious, leaving jokes aside, have you ever tried to use it in a normal conversation?" Piero leaned back on his chair and unbuttoned the top of his shirt to allow his chest some room to breathe after the heavy meal. "Really, would you go up to a total stranger and say, 'Is there no help for the widow's son'?"

Everyone laughed at the idea.

"Ok, ok," said Giuliana pushing off the leftover roast in front of her. "Of course, it's clear that it's an allegory. Now there's no need to get undressed, please!"

"Well, he is right!" Massimiliano intervened from across the table on Piero's behalf, and began to unbutton the top of his own shirt. "We are all *fratelli* [brothers/siblings] anyway!"

The dinner guests who had come to Giuliana's house in Rome for the evening included a couple of her Eastern Star (ES) lodge sisters, their husbands (GOI), the Worthy Patron of her lodge (that is, a GOI brother supervising the work of an ES lodge), and Giuliana's own husband, Tommaso, who had been initiated into Freemasonry almost twenty years earlier, but who had been inactive for over a decade. Since an initiation may never be undone, Tommaso was technically a Freemason in a state of "sleep" (*in sonno*), although he joked that by now one could more accurately say he was in a coma.

The conversation at dinner had turned to fraternity, and I suspected that the topic had come up thanks to Giuliana's gentle nudging. I had arrived a few hours before dinner to talk with Giuliana alone, and she knew that I was hoping to understand better what some of my informants in Florence had already been describing to me about the meaning of Masonic fraternity in their lives.

The first time I met Giuliana was during preliminary fieldwork at the annual convention of the men-only GOI in 2004, one of the few controlled public appearances of Freemasonry in Italy, which brought together thousands of Freemasons, members of the press, and local authorities. There I had spent three days getting to know her and her sisters, helping them staff the ES info booth at the conference, while the GOI brothers performed rituals behind closed doors inside an ad hoc temple built within the convention center's main auditorium. That early encounter with internal Masonic divisions—whereby members of the auxiliary ES were banned from GOI's ritual works—had made me aware of the complex politics of fraternity among different lodges, which seemed to defy any simplistic dichotomies between Freemasons and the profane. Some Freemasons, I realized then, might only be recognized as Freemasons in certain contexts, and their recognition was mediated by bureaucratic processes, signed treaties among lodges, and diplomatic concerns, as much as by their gender or by the esoteric significance of the initiation ritual they received (see Mahmud 2013).

When I returned to Italy for fifteen continuous months of fieldwork, I lived in Florence but traveled frequently to Rome and other cities to visit Freemasons or to attend conferences, galas, and other special events. During one such trip, Giuliana invited me over to her house to talk and to have dinner with some of her friends. Giuliana was a middle-school teacher in her forties. Her father had been a thirty-third-degree Mason, and before he died he had made her promise to join "the Stars." When we first met at the convention, Giuliana had told me that her father wanted to make sure she would be taken care of, and that people would be there for her in times of need. That was why she had joined the ES, the auxiliary Order for female relatives of the GOI, soon after he passed away, when she was in her early twenties. When I went to see Giuliana at her place, in a 1950s apartment building in one of Rome's peripheral neighborhoods, I therefore wanted to make sense of the fraternal attachments that many of my interlocutors had described. I wanted to know if she had found what her father had wished for her.

Because of a series of life circumstances, Giuliana did not have the close-knit network of family and friends known for a lifetime that so many in Italy can count on. In a country where it is not unusual for adult family members to live together or at least in close proximity, or for childhood friends to remain close well into adulthood, and in which family-owned businesses and factories are a significant part of the national economy, Giuliana's life trajectory did not conform to the mold (Krause 2005; Plesset 2006; Yanagisako 2002). As a child, she had lived in other countries, primarily in Latin America, as the family relocated with her father's job, and her mother still lived abroad. She had moved to Italy to study at La Sapienza, the University of Rome, and had since built her life in the capital.

As we waited for the dinner guests to arrive, Giuliana told me that your Mason brothers and sisters are with you for life, a statement that echoed many similar claims I had heard from other informants. She explained that there might be people with whom you cannot get along because of a difference in personalities, but you will have to learn to work things out because the ties of Masonic fraternity will bind you forever. At your job, she told me, you might have colleagues whom you dislike, and you might be tempted to stay out of their way and ultimately keep them out of your life. In the lodge, on the contrary, you have to push yourself to embrace your brothers and sisters, even if it feels uncomfortable. In the process, she assured me, you learn new ways of relating to other people that can help you even in the profane world.

For Giuliana, as for many other Masons I spoke with, both women and men, the lodge was like a family. "Even if you do not talk to a [Freemason] brother or sister for fifty years," she told me, "in the end they are still your brothers." Giuliana was not simply regurgitating an ideology. She was very aware of the problems. She had experienced firsthand, for instance, the sexism of some of the brothers in the GOI, to which the ES is an auxiliary organization. She noticed their explicit jokes and sexual innuendos, or the ways they would hug a sister a little too long. She had also witnessed the veiled racism against some of the very few nonwhite sisters she had met. She liked to say that Freemasonry would have been perfect, had there not been human beings in it. Nonetheless, she firmly believed that the ideals of Masonic fraternity translated into deeply felt experiences of closeness, trust, and bonding. When it comes down to it, she explained, sisters and brothers are there for you, emotionally, financially, and otherwise, just as her father had taught her.

At the end of the evening, as we were saying good-bye, Giuliana leaned in to kiss me three times on the cheeks. "This is your house," she said. "The house of any sister will always be your house." Both her words and her gestures caught me off guard. It was not simply the politeness with which she extended her hospitality to me, but rather her invocation of fraternity—an inclusive gesture that seemed to embrace me into a network that I studied but to which I did not belong. Although two kisses on the cheeks are a common form of salutation all over Italy, three kisses were the gesture of recognition among Freemasons—the equivalent of the much mythologized "secret handshake" for men. The triple fraternal embrace, as it was known, was a very discreet gesture, one that could easily be dismissed by the profane recipient as a case of overeagerness. It was subtle but unmistakable.

With her words of hospitality and her triple fraternal embrace, Giuliana for a moment included me in her fraternity. I thanked her profusely, but then, out of ethnographic research ethics, I promptly reminded her that I was a profane. It is true that many of my informants had begun to treat me as an honorary sister, often allowing me to participate in spaces and activities that would normally be closed to the profane, sharing with me even some of their disappointments toward the lodges. I had also developed personal friendships with some of the younger Freemasons I met. Friendship and "cultural intimacy" (Herzfeld 1997), however, were quite different from the fraternity that comes from having shared the esoteric experiences of an initiation path walked side by side. That is what my informants usually pointed to as the basis for Masonic fraternity. Unlike the bond with one's family of origin or with one's best friends, the affective bond among Freemason brothers and sisters came from the knowledge of each other shared through an incommunicable spiritual journey.

Giuliana assured me that she had not forgotten that I was not a sister, but that it didn't matter to her. My aunt was a Star, Giuliana reminded me, and besides, over time she had come to think of me as a sister, too. "If you ever need anything, you can call on any sister."

For the women Freemasons I met, the "safety net" afforded by Freemasonry was a genuinely felt experiential reality of mutual caring, companionship, and support. Fraternity created strong affective ties among sisters who provided counsel and comfort as they negotiated their positions in Italian society as well as within their families. Sisters' relationships to one another went well beyond the walls of the temple, as they often sustained each other through mourning and through illness. As several of my informants extended to me the privileges of sisterhood, at least temporarily, during fieldwork, I benefited firsthand from warm welcomes and homemade meals.

For detractors of Freemasonry in Italy, this safety net of Masonic fraternity is nothing more than a corruption network used by socially privileged "brothers" to advance their social standing and careers. As central characters in Italian corruption dramas, Freemasons conjure the specter of nepotism for anticorruption profane critics who find the lodges' metaphorical and literal claims to kinship highly suspicious. The separation of kinship from politics is a hallmark of modern political thought. While familial metaphors supply the affective language of nation-states—motherlands and fatherlands, brotherhoods of citizens—kinship is not literally supposed to provide a medium of engagement in the democratic body politic.[3]

One of the earliest conversations I had with any of my informants about anti-Masonic narratives of corruption took place inside a lawyer's office. Marina, a Maestra in the Grand Women's Masonic Lodge of Italy (GLMFI), had invited me to meet with her in her office after a brief phone conversation we had when I first started fieldwork. Nobody at her prestigious law firm knew that Marina was a Freemason, and therefore she asked me to be "discreet." When calling her at work, or when writing to her at her work e-mail address, I was to avoid any reference to Freemasonry, the lodges, or esoteric matters. Discretion was standard practice in my interactions with Freemasons in profane settings, but given Marina's line of work I understood she might have had even greater concerns.

We set up an appointment at lunchtime, when her colleagues and secretary were sure to be gone for at least a couple of hours, as typical Italian work schedules allow for a lengthy lunch break. Marina herself came to open the door of her elegant law firm. I had wanted to meet with her because, as a lawyer, she could perhaps shed some light on the legal standing of Masonic lodges in Italy. Our conversation started out very technically indeed, as Marina explained that each Masonic organization is its own legal entity and that the sisters of her own GLMFI even had a taxpayer ID number for their legally registered cultural association. As we continued to talk about Freemasonry's reputation and some of its secretive practices, however, Marina started to get upset about what she saw as widespread prejudice against Masons.

"It always makes me angry," she said, "when people say that Freemasons do favors for each other [*si fanno i favori*]." She pointed out that the Freemasons she knew, her sisters, were like family to her. They were her closest friends, and everyone relies on their friends when they need something, not just Freemasons.

"Let's say you need a plumber, and your best friend happens to be a plumber. What would you do?" she asked me rhetorically. "Would you call a plumber you don't know from the yellow pages, or would you call your friend who is a plumber?"

According to Marina, the problem with dominant narratives of corruption was their selective applications to Freemasons. The same practices of sociality in which she believed everyone engaged (*lo fanno tutti*)—something as innocent as the act of calling a friend in times of need—were attributed nefarious motives only when discovered among Freemasons.

I found myself often mulling over Marina's rhetorical question in the months that followed, as I continued to observe my informants' fraternal bonds toward each other, as well as their unflattering depictions in Italian news media. Marina's skillful rhetorical construction was axiomatic to a line of argument that presented Freemasons as victims of an unfair smear campaign but also as holders of a very human art to engender private social relations and build face-to-face communities of friends and family.

Yet Marina and I both knew that there were no plumbers in the lodges. Her example, crafted with a lawyer's skill to put forward a convincing argument, relied on an erasure of the class status of most Freemasons and of the Italian state's investment in monitoring their activities. Nepotism, after all, is a form of corruption only relevant when the professional occupations of the social actors implicated in nepotistic practices raise public concerns. Family-owned small businesses, for instance, are not typically understood as cases of nepotism. Given the class composition of the lodges and, admittedly, my own political sensibilities, I couldn't help but wonder what if Marina's hypothetical friend was not a plumber but a judge? Or a university dean? Or a journalist? Or the chief of a hospital wing? Or a high-ranking bureaucrat in one of the government's ministries?

The fraternity of Freemasons posed a threat to the state because it would seem to materialize as a private fraternity, a secretive elite network, easy to map onto other secret groups that have long threatened Italy's democratic institutions. Freemasons' solemn promise to provide mutual aid to one another preoccupies the state because the effects of those private instances of fraternity could potentially be devastating for the public good. At the nation-state level, fraternity is supposed to be a metaphorical invocation of familial ties to ensure citizens' allegiance to an ideological abstraction. Freemasons' fraternity, however, carries the risk of too much literalism, and therefore evokes the specter of other subversive, family-based criminal organizations like the Mafia and the Camorra.

Either way, whether from the point of view of my informants or that of their profane critics, Masonic fraternity in Italy is commonly understood to be highly effective in producing social capital. In its enactments, Masonic fraternity literally and esoterically remakes strangers into brothers, and the latter might thus be more loyal to one another than to the national imagined community. Perhaps fraternity is such a powerful notion precisely because it *works*; it compels and obliges, as it reifies a peculiar form of kinship of choice that cuts across lines of blood and marriage, but reifies them as well in the process. And just as with kinship structures rooted in blood or marriage, fraternity's effectiveness as a form of social capital depends on its ability to negate its conditions of possibility: the rampant exclusionary practices that ensure that many others could never be brothers or sisters in the Masonic family.

The Impossibility of Sisterhood

Fraternity and *brotherhood* have different connotations in English, but in Italian they are both *fratellanza*, and although the term *sisters* (*sorelle*) has the same literal and political significance in both languages, *sisterhood* is not really a word in Italian, and certainly not one that my informants cared to coin. Women Freemasons constituted themselves into a *fratellanza*: a brotherhood. Using the masculine as the unmarked general concept of fraternity, my women informants did not wish to be just like men or to mimic the Freemasonry of men. Those common charges against them could not have been farther from the truth. What my informants aspired to do, in forming a brotherhood of sisters, was rather to ask more of the liberal notion of fraternity than men Freemasons have asked of it. They drew explicitly on a humanistic credo of liberty, equality, and fraternity for all in an attempt to forge a universal relationship above and beyond the constraints of specific, gendered bodies.

In *The Politics of Friendship*, which he explicitly equates to a politics of fraternity, Jacques Derrida addresses the grammatical elisions of the feminine and the discursive compulsion of the falsely neutral masculine in the liberal philosophy of fraternity. He pauses, as he often does throughout the text, to address the reader parenthetically—in passing:

> (You will not, perhaps, have failed to register the fact that we are writing and describing friends as masculine—neuter-masculine. Do not consider this a distraction or a slip. It is, rather, a laborious way of letting a question furrow deeper. We are perhaps borne from the very first step by and towards this question: *what is a friend in the feminine, and who, in the feminine, is her friend?* Why do "our" philosophers and "our" religions, our "culture," acknowledge so little irreducible right, so little proper and acute signification, in such grammar? [. . .] *How much of a chance would a feminine friend have on this stage? And a feminine friend of hers, among themselves?*) (Derrida 2005: 56–57, emphasis added).

The question that Derrida allows to furrow deeper is the question at the heart of my interlocutors' paradoxical life experiences. What is a Freemason brother in the feminine? And "how much of a chance" will sisters have at this liberal fraternity, with its falsely neutral promises of equality? Among all my informants the language of Masonic fraternity was pervasively masculine, especially given that *sisterhood* would be hard to translate into colloquial Italian. Members of mixed-gender lodges, however, went even further than members of women-only lodges, as they often chose to use the word *fratello* (brother), rather than the readily available *sorella* (sister), to refer to both men and women in an explicit attempt to deny material and corporeal differences within the lodges. *Brother* Lucia, for instance, a high-ranking member of the mixed-gender GLDI, introduced me to her *brother* Claudia, whom she had initiated into her lodge many years earlier. They did not want to stand out, to be marked as "different" from other (that is, male) Freemasons working alongside them in the temple. Therefore, most of the women I met in the GLDI had literally become *fratelli*.

Several of my informants pointed out that this linguistic choice is in line with similar erasures of feminine nouns in Italian professional contexts, whereby women might choose to use the masculine form of their professional title, such as lawyer, architect, or engineer, to avoid the lesser prestige, the ridicule, or the awkward sound (*suona male*) of the feminine equivalent, when one exists. Moreover, standard Italian grammar requires that all plurals referring to both masculine and feminine nouns be masculine, so that *brothers* would be the correct plural to indicate a group of both sisters and brothers. My interlocutors' choices, however, about when and how to push the limits of grammar, "Masonic tradition," or family expectations to refashion themselves as members of a brotherhood were political speech acts taking place in the discursive space of modernist notions of fraternity and Freemasonry. For some of them, linguistic creativity extended to appropriating the masculine "brother" as an attribute for themselves and their sisters, but *sorellanza* (sisterhood) was not a neologism I ever heard them utter.

The concept of sisterhood, however, has a long history in Anglophone feminist scholarship.[4] Approaching the topic of women Freemasons' quest for brotherhood from a feminist anthropological perspective, and especially in the context of American scholarship, could therefore lead to two potential misunderstandings of my interlocutors' experiences. First, in the hands of Freemason sisters, the Masonic project of unmarked, universal fraternity might be mistaken for an earlier version of global feminist sisterhood founded on an essentialist and Eurocentric notion of womanhood that elides the diversity of women's experiences across the globe under the guise of inclusionary politics (Mohanty 1988).[5] Unlike global feminist sisterhood movements, however, the sisterly bonds of Freemasons were explicitly exclusionary, limited to those women—mostly upper-class, mostly related to Mason men, mostly right-wing, virtually all white—who chose to embark on an esoteric initiation path and who recognized each other not through the indiscriminate embrace of shared womanhood but through a discriminatory rubric of secret signs, codes, and gestures.[6]

Second, from an anthropological perspective, any form of identity politics based on the notion of sisterhood or brotherhood may be dismissed as a mere strategic reliance on what used to be called fictive kinship to establish and maintain social alliances that do not fall under the rubric of either blood or marriage.[7] Various theoretical developments in anthropological studies of kinship have uncovered its Western bias in favor of biological ties (Carsten 1997), and have advocated for a shift toward models that can be more sensitive to local formulations of "relatedness" and of families of "choice" (Collier, Yanagisako, and Bloch 1987; Stone 1997; Weston 1991). Within such a framework, sisterhood is not merely a metaphorical and discursive strategy of social solidarity, but it is rather a category of relatedness in its own right to explain the everyday interactions of women Freemasons who experienced each other very much as sisters. Indeed, the convention among my interlocutors was to reserve the unmarked noun *sister* (*sorella*) or *brother* (*fratello*) for a fellow Mason, but to use the marked terms of *blood* sister and *blood* brother (*sorella di sangue*; *fratello di sangue*) to refer to their profane siblings in their families of origin.

The insistence on the familial language of brotherhood is quite telling of the assumptions embedded in Masonic social bonds. The communicative strategy used here—that which inscribes instances of friendship, collegiality, solidarity, or partisanship within a discourse of kinship—operates within a Masonic institution whose elaborations on family are historically very significant. Not only was Freemasonry a "brotherhood" at the time of Italian unification in the nineteenth century, when the nation-building process was very much phrased in the rhetoric of familiarity and familism, but Freemasonry was also a familial society insofar as its members, even across different lodges, have usually been related to one another. Wives, husbands, uncles, daughters, cousins, nieces, and grandparents are often all Masons, although they might be Masons in different lodges, some of which may not even recognize the others officially.[8]

Family ties played a particularly important role in my women informants' participation in Freemasonry. Unlike men, many of whom learned about Freemasonry through friends or colleagues, most of the women I met were first exposed to the path by men in their lives, typically their husbands or male partners. Their desire for sisterhood had therefore originated in many cases through kinship, although its actualization had taken different forms. For members of the ES like Giuliana or my aunt, kinship represented the central *raison d'être* of the group, and it was a formal requirement for admission. The sisterly bonds of the ES were therefore predicated on shared experiences of kinship—of knowing what it is like to be raised according to Masonic values, what it is like to have a husband who goes to the lodge two or three nights a week—rather than on shared personal qualities or interests.

Many of the women I spoke to in other lodges were very critical of the Stars precisely because of their membership requirements. The women of the mixed-gender GLDI and of the women-only GLMFI often referred to the Stars disparagingly as "the wives' club." In contrast, they often praised their own groups for vetting potential women initiates on the basis of their personal merit, rather than their kinship ties to brothers. Although most of the women I knew in either the GLDI or the GLMFI were in fact related to Mason men, kinship was not an official prerequisite for membership in those lodges. Members of the women-only GLMFI in particular had needed to travel well beyond the limits of familial kinship to establish fraternal bonds through transnational Masonic connections and start a lodge for women.

Margherita, for instance, who had been among the founders of the GLMFI, was one of the first to explain to me why she and her sisters had felt the need to start a Freemasonry for women only, instead of simply joining the mixed-gender GLDI or the auxiliary ES. Margherita's account of how she and her sisters had reached out to a French Masonic group that had a local lodge in Rome to begin their initiation path highlighted a typical characteristic of Masonic fraternity:

its deeply transnational quality.[9] Although kinship ties often created the conditions of possibility for women's encounters with Freemasonry, the pursuit of the universalist ideals of liberal fraternity had pulled my interlocutors far beyond the social networks of their families and communities of origin.

The F Word

When I first listened to Margherita's rationale for starting a women-only Masonic lodge, I thought her goals resembled closely those of women-only feminist co-ops of the 1970s. After all, it was the same historical period, and both groups had emerged out of a perceived need for consciousness-raising among women. I still remember—a zealous researcher with notepad in hand—the moment in which I asked Margherita the fatidic question: how did she think 1970s feminist movements related to the project of women's Freemasonry? Her dyed blond hair curling up around her face, Margherita took a long drag from her cigarette, leaned back on the couch, and shook her head knowingly.

"Oh, dear," Margherita told me, "dear, we are not feminists. We are absolutely not feminists."

The question of feminism and its potentially awkward relationship to Freemason women's activism became a central concern early on in my study. Margherita's response, as I learned soon thereafter, represented a position typical of women Freemasons. None of the women I interviewed, in any Masonic lodge, identified as feminists. On the contrary, most, including the younger Apprentices and Maestre I met, had very negative associations with the word *feminist*. I often wondered why these articulate, educated, professionally employed, socially active women who had been organizing around a struggle for gender equality were so adamant about *not* being feminists. What particular understandings of feminism made them reject the label so vehemently, and what investments did they have, in turn, in presenting their own activism to "raise women's consciousness" and "liberate women's minds" as explicitly not feminist?

Feminist scholarship has only sporadically tackled the topic of women's participation in movements that are explicitly antifeminist. Unlike movements that may not identify as feminist simply because geopolitical distance from that framework of reference makes it irrelevant or unhelpful, women's movements that are explicitly antifeminist often espouse a nationalist, conservative, or religious ideology that puts them at odds with the researcher's own commitments (Ginsburg 1998; Koonz 1987). Antifeminist groups have only started to be the objects of serious scholarly attention in recent years, despite the fact that, as Paola Bacchetta and Margaret Power put it, "feminist projects will benefit from understanding right-wing women precisely because in many cases they constitute major obstacles to feminism" (Bacchetta and Power 2002: 1).[10]

Similarly, Italian historiography has rarely taken seriously women's volun-tary contributions to right-wing projects. With only a few notable exceptions (Macciocchi 1976), women's complicity in Mussolini's Fascist regime, for instance, has largely been dismissed as either inconsequential or as a further indicator of the dictatorship's propagandistic successes. Only in the past two decades has Italian historiography begun to revise this portrayal, addressing the voluntary contributions of many Italian Fascist women to a dictatorship that often repressed women's rights with respect to work, education, family law, or reproduction (De Grazia 1992; Gallucci 2002).

The discomfort that many feminist intellectuals might feel about women's movements that do not organize around a feminist platform or that explicitly reject it may stem in part from a different understanding of what feminism means. Unlike American or French feminisms, Italian feminist movements have mostly developed outside of academic institutions, and gender studies programs at the turn of the twenty-first century were still relatively rare in Italian universities. In the 1960s and 1970s, feminist movements in Italy emerged primarily from within left-wing political parties—particularly the Italian Communist Party—rather than in relation to them. Feminist organizations often began as women's subgroups of the party, and as a cultural referent, feminism in Italy is therefore inextricably tied to the political framework of the Left.

One of the main concerns of Italian feminists of the 1960s and 1970s was the issue of "double militancy," both within a left-wing political party led by men and within women-centered spaces and consciousness-raising collectives dedicated to the cause of women's liberation (Birnbaum 1986).[11] While often embracing a Marxist-Leninist approach to women's struggles, many Italian feminists refused nonetheless to subsume the "gender question" to class struggle, thus causing tensions and sometimes splits within their own leftist political parties (Bono and Kemp 1991: 42).

What is perhaps the most striking difference between Italian feminist movements and much of U.S. feminist scholarship from the past few decades is the conceptualization of gender equality. Philosophically inspired more by French than by Anglo-American feminist scholarship (de Beauvoir 1949; Irigaray 1974), feminism in Italy has often carried an essentializing message of difference between manhood and womanhood that has downplayed internal differences among women.[12] In the Italian context, women's liberation was to be achieved not by arguing that women and men were equal, but rather by valorizing women's unique contributions and creating alliances of women across social classes.

The manifesto of a Roman-based collective known as Rivolta Femminile (feminine revolt) became a canonical text in this regard (Lonzi 1982 [1970]). Written by Carla Lonzi in 1970, the manifesto entitled "Let's Spit on Hegel" argues that the only difference that matters is the difference between women and men, and that the Hegelian slave-master dichotomy underlying Marxist class struggle fails to address the more crucial question of gender struggle:

> The difference between woman and man is the basic difference of human kind. A black man may be equal to a white man, a black woman to a white woman. Woman's difference is her millennial absence from history. Let us profit from this difference. . . . Equality is what is offered as legal rights to colonized people. And what is imposed on them as culture. It is the principle through which those with hegemonic power continue to control those without. (Translated in Bono and Kemp 1991)

This Italian feminist approach to gender difference, which explicitly rejects the false promises of equality as a hegemonic tool and posits an essential difference between woman and man, ironically lends itself aptly to conservative approaches to gender questions, such as those espoused by most of the Freemasons I knew. In Masonic esoteric cosmology and rituals, a primal difference between solar and lunar forces was understood to be representative of an essential difference between masculine and feminine principles, which, in turn, were understood to be embodied by men and women, respectively. My interlocutors often relied on cosmological arguments to support their views for or against women's initiation into Freemasonry. For instance, several members of the men-only GOI justified to me the exclusion of women by claiming that women are characterized by a lunar essence that would be incompatible with Freemasonry, which is a "solar cult." Members of the mixed-gender GLDI, on the other hand, explained to me that both complementary principles (lunar and solar, feminine and masculine) must conduct ritual work together in order to achieve perfection. Although they came to radically different conclusions regarding the initiation of women, the Freemasons I knew across different lodges shared as their premise a fundamental belief in the cosmological difference between women and men.

My informants' belief in an essential and binary gender difference was strikingly similar to the views articulated by prominent Italian feminists of the 1960s and 1970s. It is therefore all the more important for a feminist analysis of conservative organizing to understand the motivations behind women Free-masons' explicit rejection of feminist discourses that, at least at first sight, would not appear to contradict my informants' deeply held beliefs. Virtually all my informants from different Masonic lodges adamantly told me that they never identified as feminists, although most of them had lived through the 1960s and 1970s feminist movements that swept through Italy at the same historical moment in which the idea of a women's Freemasonry began to gain more vibrancy. After my initial gaffe with Margherita, I learned to be more discreet when approaching the subject of feminism with my informants. Nonetheless, whenever I touched on the similarities I perceived between Italian feminist projects of the 1970s and women's struggle for inclusion in Freemasonry, my interlocutors appeared confused, uncomfortable, or outright offended by the analogy.

For many of the women Freemasons I knew, feminism as they knew it was clearly irrelevant. Older Freemasons remembered watching "those feminists" (*quelle femministe*) at street protests, shouting and rallying, attempting to bring about women's liberation (*la liberazione della donna*) through what they saw as sexual promiscuity, and they found them to be misguided. Franca, for instance, a Freemason in her sixties and one of my key informants, told me explicitly that even as a young adult she had not felt that emancipation (*emancipazione*) would come from having sex with multiple casual partners—a position that she attributed to Italian feminists, and which alluded to the "free love" slogans of her youth. To her, liberation and respect of her body meant being free to have sex with the man she loved, rather than with just anyone. It was not chastity that she wanted either, a position attributable to the Catholic influence on morals in Italy, and which in Franca's eyes was just as "extreme" as that of "free love." Instead, she wanted to find self-determination and self-respect, both important Masonic objectives, through a reasonable middle ground.

Like many of the other Masons I interviewed, Franca, now a grandmother of two, remembered 1970s feminists as promoting an agenda that would give women beneficial treatment and, thus, "charity," rather than justice. Our conversation quickly turned to the present day, and to an issue that had taken central stage in Italian media at the time of our conversation in 2005. That year, the minister of equal opportunities appointed by the right-wing coalition government of then prime minister Silvio Berlusconi had presented a bill for review that would have set minimum quotas for women's representation in Parliament. Although the bill ultimately failed to gain enough votes to be approved, mostly because of a lack of support within right-wing parties themselves, the issue of "pink quotas" (*quote rosa*), as it became popularly known, engendered a lively debate about women's equality in Italy and about appropriate methods of redress.

Discussing it with several of my informants at the time, I had realized that they too had considered the issue and had strong opinions about it. Bringing up the topic of "pink quotas" during our conversation about feminism, Franca told me that she would be offended to be elected only through an act of affirmative action (*discriminazione positiva*). Echoing the words of several other sisters I had talked with, Franca told me explicitly that "1968 is long gone," and that nowadays women "have no excuses" for needing measures like quotas to achieve equality. Though she conceded that in the historical moment of the 1960s and 1970s there might have been a need for feminism, she argued that the need had been met. In a rhetorical turn characteristic of postfeminism, she asserted that it was now women's responsibility to prove ourselves equal. Why accept the "charity" of pink quotas? Why not run for and gain office just "like men do?"

Rhetorically, Franca's discussion of the proposed bill framed it within larger class and market ideologies. Conceiving of pink quotas as charity, she not only refused them but she also felt personally offended by them. Her comments are especially interesting in relation to the class subject positions reproduced through Freemasonry, which is a philanthropic organization in addition to being an esoteric society. According to classic social theoretical definitions of gift-giving, charity need not be a disinterested activity but, rather, one that obliges the receiver (Mauss 1925). Philanthropy has often been a driving force in mobilizing women from powerful segments of society (Gordon 1990; Koven and Michel 1993). For upper-class women like Franca, who are negotiating their social positions vis-à-vis the men in their lives, to be givers rather than recipients of charity is paramount to establishing their upper-class gendered subjectivities. It is within this class logic that pink quotas could appear unacceptable, as they position women as receivers of aid—the antithesis of women Freemasons' labored identity.

Franca went further in her discussion of pink quotas. Not only would quotas for women be offensive, at least to the sensibilities of her particular class position, but they would also be unnecessary. Claiming that the mission of feminism had long been accomplished, Franca insisted that women were no longer at a disadvantage and that it was therefore up to us to prove our worth. Such a neoliberal conceptualization of gender struggles, indebted both to market models of competition and to an individualistic ideology of meritocracy, echoed prevailing Masonic constructions of the (unmarked) subject: anybody could be a Freemason, even though most of us are not. So too, anyone—any woman—had already achieved equality.

After listening closely to her perspective, I asked Franca what she thought of the abysmally low numbers of women representatives in the Italian Parliament. Accepting the emic terms of the discourse, our conversation was strictly about gender, comparing the opportunities of a generic woman with those of a generic man, assuming these categories to be independent of other social identities that might affect access to opportunities, including class, race, or citizenship. It was a conversation, in other words, that followed my informants' conceptualization of gender rather than my own, partly because of their own social positioning, partly because of the gender binaries underlying their esoteric cosmology, and partly because the very discourse of feminist scholarship in Italy has been framed in binary terms.

Franca's response was once again similar to that of many other women Freemasons, although remarkably more succinct. After a longer elaboration of the lack of self-awareness among Italian women, which she thought contributed to the dearth of eligible women political candidates as well as to the misinformation of women voters, Franca summed up her point in one sentence: if Italian women are not elected to Parliament in larger numbers, it is because "le donne italiane sono coglione" ("Italian women are *testicles*").

The English translation of the Italian word *coglione* (here used adjectivally, in a feminized, plural form) as *testicles* fails to capture both the raunchiness and the connotation of the term. Unlike the expression "having balls" (*palle, coglioni*), which means being daring or having courage both in English and in Italian, "to be a coglione" in Italian implies a sheep-like idiocy, perhaps better expressed by the colloquial but offensive terms *dumbass* or *moron*. Underlying Franca's remark was a belief that women's consciousness (*presa di coscienza*) is failing, thereby producing a dissatisfaction with the proposed remedy of quotas, which might repair the Parliament's image but fall short of producing actual change. For Franca, Freemasonry offered a path to consciousness in which every individual would become the best person she could be. Through Masonic self-cultivation and collective work, she believed that women could learn to respect themselves and take charge of their own existence in a male-dominated society. Pink quotas were, in her mind, little more than a feminist shortcut that did not afford women the opportunity to prove themselves just as capable as men.

Many of my informants described to me their struggles to assert themselves in male-dominated professional work spaces, fighting to earn the respect of their male colleagues first and foremost by learning to respect themselves. They felt they had been effecting change day by day at home and at work, and they saw nothing respectful in the loud street protests or the free-love discourse that they had come to associate with feminist "extremists."

Such a concern for respectability and good taste is a hallmark of European bourgeois sensibility (see Mosse 1988) and of Italian notions of character and appearance, tying together morality and aesthetics in the popular expression *fare bella figura*. For Freemasons specifically, however, moderation was the key to healthy living, and it was a core principle they tried to live by. Characterizing feminism as extremist was an effective rhetorical strategy to dismiss its political or social message in a Masonic context where extremisms are, by definition, anathema and where, for instance, far-Left political parties are often described as extremist. Interestingly, the members of the women-only GLMFI were often the most vocal in their disavowal of "feminist extremists," perhaps because they themselves were sometimes accused of being radical lesbian feminist extremists by Freemasons who had chosen a different initiation path, whether by joining an auxiliary group (ES) that would not challenge the hierarchical preeminence of the men-only GOI or by joining a mixed-gender lodge (GLDI). Creating women-only spaces and promoting women's emancipation through consciousness-raising have long been staples of feminist organizing, and the constitution of a women-only Masonic lodge could easily be attacked in sexist and homophobic terms by other Masons unsympathetic to their cause.[13]

My informants' representations of 1970s Italian feminism and of contemporary (2005) feminist projects tended to portray them as a unified movement, characterized by moral failures (promiscuity, lack of respectability), illegitimate political demands ("charity" in the form of legislation favorable to women), and misguided sites of action (the street, rather than homes or work spaces). Echoing a famous feminist slogan, several sisters in different lodges told me, "I am mine" (*io sono mia*). They felt they had come to own and know themselves through a Masonic path of self-cultivation. It was not in the streets that they believed change could be brought about, but in their own homes, in the office, in the lodges, and ultimately deep inside their own souls.

Besides, as another older woman Freemason, a Maestra in the mixed-gender GLDI, once told me jokingly, "Those women [feminists] were burning bras. Should I have burned my La Perla bra? I don't think so!"—referring in this case to the foolishness of burning an expensive designer bra (La Perla used to be the premier high couture Italian lingerie maker) on the altar of feminism. My interlocutors' comments often illustrated the merging of bourgeois sensibilities and political affiliations in their dislike of feminism.

As I listened to the stories of so many older Freemasons, it became clear that their positions regarding feminism could not be separated from their own political affiliations with the Right. Most of them came from the upper and upper-middle classes, ascribed strongly to right-wing ideals, and opposed firmly the traditional Left, which in the 1970s was embodied primarily by the Italian Communist Party, then the third-largest Communist party in the world (Kertzer 1980).[14] Given the foundational history of Italian feminism within the Left, to espouse feminism means to espouse the class politics of the Left, too. For Italian women who could not identify with the proletarian premises of feminism, but who had been exposed to the Masonic path in their social circles, Freemasonry thus offered a valid alternative for social activism.

The intellectual challenge of accounting for the experiences of gender-based movements within frameworks explicitly hostile to feminism lies, in many cases, in such movements' opposition to the specific agendas that have come to define Euro-American feminist activism. In the case of Italian women Freemasons, however, the *content* of their political beliefs in many cases accorded with local feminist positions. Although there were instances, like the issue of pink quotas, where the Freemasons I knew aligned with right-wing parties, often the official positions that lodges (including male lodges) took on current social issues, from a woman's right to choose to supporting public education, access to health care, and even immigration reform, were strikingly similar to left-wing positions insofar as they were based on liberal discourses of human rights and individual freedoms that have been the foundations for many feminist and liberal legal victories. Committed to a secular morality that historically put them at odds with the Vatican, most Freemasons were also against Catholic pressures on Italian political life that have historically curtailed feminist political goals around issues such as family law and new reproductive technologies.

The difference between women Freemasons and Italian feminists may have more to do with the former's apparent contribution to the masculine hegemony of Masonic lodges—their deliberate support of a system that structurally excludes them—than with any sustained allegiance to the political opinions of right-wing parties. Feminist scholars have warned against the tendency "to see women as identified with male games, or as pawns in male games, or as otherwise having no autonomous point of view or intentionality" (Ortner 1996: 16). The question of Freemason women's antifeminism should therefore be framed as an issue of agency, rather than false consciousness. If we are to take seriously their modality of social activism within a male-dominated, elite society, then we could ask how women Freemasons in Italy cultivated an agentic subjective consciousness, *una presa di coscienza*, which was neither entirely complicit with their subordination nor defiantly resistant against the existing hierarchical structure.

A growing body of feminist scholarship in recent years has embraced precisely this latter line of inquiry to address women's participation in religious movements that seem to run against liberal feminist projects.[15] In her ethnography of women's piety movements in the mosques of Cairo, however, Saba Mahmood (2005) has eloquently challenged even the notion of agency underlying feminist anthropologists' accounts of subaltern subjects. Mahmood's argument is that even where feminist scholars have been able to appreciate agentic practices of resistance occurring outside the rubric of feminism, they have nonetheless recognized women's agency only when it appeared to subvert and resist structures of oppression. Mahmood writes that "agentival capacity is entailed not only in those acts that resist norms but also in the multiple ways in which one *inhabits* norms" (15). To recognize agency only where it enacts the goals of progressive feminist politics is to take as universal the political aims of liberalism, predicated on the autonomous self's desire for freedom. Instead, Mahmood severs the notion of agency from the subject-centered goals of progressive politics in an attempt "to parochialize those assumptions—about the constitutive relationship between action and embodiment, resistance and agency, self and authority—that inform our judgments about nonliberal movements" (38).

While Mahmood's valiant effort provides an excellent framework for the feminist study of nonfeminist gender-based movements, her own ethnographic material emerged from a sociohistorical context—piety movements in late twentieth-century Egypt—where the etic categories of the anthropologist may be at odds with the emic categories of her ethnographic subjects. The latter did not share the liberal political ideas of autonomous self-realization, progress, and desire for freedom that, while historically produced through European modernity, have become normative for much of Euro-American feminist scholarship (Mahmood 2005: 153–155).

Unlike participants in the "nonliberal" movements Mahmood studied, the women Freemasons with whom I worked did ascribe to the values of progressive politics, and they sought agentic self-actualization within a market-driven social economy as much as within the social ties of their family networks. The relevant question haunting a feminist analysis of antifeminist and yet *liberal* European movements like Freemasonry is not how to detach the notion of agency from that of progressive politics to do justice to our interlocutors' experiences. Nor can the question be framed simply within the dichotomy of false consciousness or resistance. After all, it is undeniable that women Freemasons genuinely derived a strong sense of personal realization through the Masonic path, even though in doing so they may not have posed a considerable challenge to either male dominance over Masonic institutions or to Italian gender relations more broadly.

The question—perhaps more uncomfortable from a feminist perspective—is rather about the unintended compromises and contradictions inherent in the agentic enactment of progressive subject-centered politics, especially when they are effective. As privileged women decided to participate in the structures of masculine Masonic fraternity to advance their goals for self-cultivation, what incarnations did their transformations take, and what other relationships of solidarity with differently positioned subjects did they have to forego in order to abstract themselves to the unmarked status of *brothers*?

Abstracting Liberal Subjects

Only among you, in America, are liberals left-wing. ‹ *Maestra in the GLMFI* ›

The abstraction of liberal subjects is one of the fundamental paradoxes of humanism. Particular positionalities, such as "men," are abstracted as placeholders for generic categories, such as "human beings." In their historical configuration as liberal movements, the most visible Euro-American feminisms and proto-feminisms since the eighteenth century have largely partaken of the liberal political strategy of abstraction, producing the generic "woman" as a subject in need of representation.

In recent decades, critiques of liberal abstractions seem to have become commonplace both in radical strands of feminism and in fields of inquiry like anthropology, feminist scholarship, and ethnic studies.[16] Scholars and activists, for instance, have revealed that the political signifier of the unmarked "woman" typically conceals a particular kind of white, middle-class, heterosexual, *cis*-woman whose concerns and needs are not representative of many other women (see Butler 1999; hooks 1984; Weston 2002). Even seemingly uncontroversial "human" rights discourses have been shown to have been hatched in a markedly Eurocentric and masculine context (Merry 2006). To say now that all ostensibly generic categories are in fact seeped in particularity, despite their apparent abstraction, would therefore be akin to "discovering hot water," as the Italian saying goes.

In these myriad critiques, the abstractness that allows some particular subject categories (e.g., white middle-class women) to become generic subject categories (*just* women) is usually understood to be a convenient mask to maintain the privilege associated with their particular positionality. Hagar Kotef (2009), however, has proposed an alternative framework to conceptualize liberal abstractness. Cautioning against the dangers of dismissing abstraction as nothing more than a pretense, Kotef has suggested instead that we take it seriously as a project of liberalism, "a regulative idea that is never actualized but still cannot be thought of simply as a façade" (496) To understand how the abstract woman can come into being, Kotef tracks "an attempt to *remove* the different elements in this intersection of categories in order to arrive at a desired void at its heart, to strip from the discursive object of what-would-be liberal feminism all the concrete counterparts (such as race or sex) that may impede its desired universalism" (496). Recognizing that the abstractness of unmarked subject positions is an intentional project of political liberalism foregrounds the question of how such an abstraction may be realized or, more accurately, given that liberal abstractness is never fully realized, of how it might be approximated through various practices of decorporealization.

It was common for my informants to insist that social differences of class or even gender simply did not matter inside the temple, where Masonic hierarchies and roles such as Tyler, Warden, or Worshipful Maestra superseded profane statuses. As we discussed fraternity at dinner at Giuliana's house, for instance, Massimiliano, who was in the men-only GOI and was married to one of Giuliana's ES sisters, said that "inside a temple, it might be a nurse who must guide a doctor, or it might be that a university professor has to listen to a student."

I often heard my interlocutors make similar claims about the radical equality they found in the temples, which they understood to mean a lack of social and embodied differences. Their claims, which were especially surprising to me when coming from women Freemasons, rested on two rhetorical moves. First, my interlocutors often overstated the social diversity of the lodges to begin with, by giving examples of a much wider range of occupations (plumbers and professors, nurses and doctors, or carpenters and architects) than those I saw represented among the Freemasons I met, who were mostly professionals with advanced degrees. Second, they then proceeded to assure me that inside the temples all differences absolutely disappeared, despite the fact that in other contexts many women Freemasons I spoke to, for instance, expressed deep disappointment about the ongoing glass ceilings they faced in mixed-gender lodges and about their marginality to Freemasonry as a whole. My interlocutors therefore had to both underplay and overplay material differences in order to claim that inside the temple they saw none.

The certainty with which both women and men Freemasons of all ranks and lodges throughout my fieldwork assured me of the immateriality of differences inside the temple begs the question of how social differences could seem to disappear completely, at least in their eyes, when they were also so clearly identified as differences in other contexts. For embodied differences not to matter inside the temple, they had to be intentionally dematerialized in order to pursue a utopian project of equality.

Among Freemasons, a wide range of esoteric and pedagogical practices were meant not only to instill docility, but also to make bodily differences less apparent. All lodges, for instance, required some kind of ritual garments, such as robes and decorated aprons, which functioned as uniforms to cover visible markers of difference among practitioners. Moreover, the process of corporeal dematerialization was made literal by Masonic ritual requirements, which prescribed that all metals be left outside the temple upon entering. Stripping the neophyte of metals before her initiation, and also expecting initiates to leave metals outside upon entering the temple to perform routine ritual work, is a rule meant to remind Freemasons of the vanity of material possessions. A Maestra in the mixed-gender GLDI once explained this rule to me by saying that inside the temple it would be distracting to have someone flaunting a Rolex watch or gold necklace because "inside the temple we are all equal."

More than a concealment of conspicuous markers of wealth, the ritual interdiction against metals is also supposed to teach initiates to let go of material objects and to embrace the value of charity, which is a central tenet of Freemasonry. Kotef (2009) points to philanthropy as a central technique for the abstraction of liberal subjects because it shows the giver to be free of material concerns, while imbricating the recipient in the gross materiality of physical needs. In the early twenty-first century, volunteerism in the fields of arts, education, or children's well-being still characterizes the activities of many privileged women both in the United States and in Europe, as was the case among Freemasons in Italy. Although most of my informants reluctantly admitted they did not devote much of their own time to volunteerism, they could proudly inform me that lodges often collected money for donations to various causes.

In Italy, where a welfare state provides free health care, education, and a host of other social services, and a strong Catholic presence provides charitable services for the most marginalized social groups, there has not been as much of a need for private philanthropic endeavors.[17] Rosa, for instance, the Worthy Matron of an ES lodge in Florence, compared the charitable practices of her group to those of their sister lodges in the United States, where the ES are headquartered. Rosa pointed out to me that in Italy, unlike in the United States, there is less need for private citizens to finance new hospital wings or schools.

She also added that many of the ES sisters she had met during her travels to the States had financial means but were not professionally employed. Her Italian sisters, she told me, confirming a pattern I had noticed too, were busy professionals, and most of them did not have the free time necessary to volunteer, although they certainly made financial donations, she assured me, as a lodge. Philanthropy, mostly in the form of monetary donations, contributed to defining the scope of my informants' organization, which, despite its secrecy, also strived to maintain a strong presence in civil society.

The moral implications of Masonic philanthropy, however, were far from straightforward in Italy, and Freemasons' donations did not always elicit the responses my informants hoped for. When I met with Marina, the lawyer who explained to me some of the legal and bureaucratic workings of the women-only GLMFI, she also told me that there had been cases in which their donations had been refused. "Pecunia non olet," Marina had admonished me, citing a Latin adage. "Money doesn't stink. Even the Romans already knew that." Then she had added with an exasperated tone that there were people in need in Italy who nonetheless would not take Freemasons' money. As a result of having their gifts returned to them, Marina told me that the GLMFI had learned to donate anonymously instead. By persisting in their commitment to philanthropy even at the cost of donating anonymously to those charities that would otherwise turn down financial gifts coming from Freemasons, the sisters proved their civic responsibility in the face of their critics. Marina's message was that it was not important to her and her sisters to have their donations acknowledged by their recipients. They practiced philanthropy simply because they believed in helping others. The act of donating anonymously even when their help was not wanted or appreciated suggests that philanthropy was a defining activity for my informants, who insisted on positioning themselves as givers, on knowing themselves to be givers, regardless of whether anybody else knew it too. Freemasons' philanthropic endeavors were therefore important to how my informants saw themselves, and they were one technique of their abstraction as liberal, upper-class subjects.

As an intentional project, abstraction had significant stakes for women Freemasons whose own gendered corporeality had long served as the basis for their exclusion from the practice of Freemasonry. Being a Freemason was a subjectivity at the core of their existence: it was who they really were inside, as my interlocutors often reminded me. And yet, the discursive impossibility of their subject category—a woman Freemason, always contrasted to an unmarked (and therefore masculine) Freemason—made their need and desire to be abstract all the more urgent. As all the women Freemasons I spoke to told me, they did not want to be "like the men." What they wanted was to be Freemasons in a generic, unmarked sense. In other words, they wanted to inhabit a truly abstract category, one that was not simply a mask for a particular brotherhood of men, but which could encompass the universality it promises: a *genderless brotherhood*.

One of the most revealing conversations I ever had on the subject of fraternity was with a Freemason by the name of Emma who was a long-standing member of the women-only GLMFI. When I asked Emma what her reasons had been for remaining active in the women's lodge, despite its lack of resources and despite the backlash against Freemasonry in Italy, she spoke of the ideals that Freemasonry stands for in the eyes of its members.

> I stayed because when I have a strong conviction I can be quite stubborn, and because I did believe in universality, in this way of opening up to others, not being constrained by borders, races, religions, and going farther, outside and beyond. You count as an individual for who you are, not for what might appear or for what it looks like outside. That's something that always appealed to me.

Fraternity, equality, and liberty were not only a distant echo of the French revolution, lost in contemporary political discourses for Emma. They were inscribed in a particular way of being in the world, one that could free itself from the corporeal constraints of races, borders, or physical appearance ("what it looks like outside"). Her belief in universality was a belief in the possibility of abstracting her sense of self ("who you are") from what she experienced as the weight of material and embodied differences. Although feminist scholars have shown the material body to be a semiotic and discursive construct, rather than a natural given (Butler 1993; Haraway 1991), Emma's comments reflected a dualism of self/body, spirituality/materiality that is a familiar ontology for many Europeans. Just as Freemasons leave metals outside before entering the temple, Emma wished to leave behind the burdens of social and material differences in order to ascend "farther, outside and beyond," to a place where everyone could count "as an individual" because material differences would presumably no longer matter.[18] Her rhetorical exaltation of individualism to counteract the perceived ills of social differences ("borders, races, religions") is characteristic of the political philosophy of liberalism that informed Freemasons' common sense. As in liberalism, here too individuality is invoked to achieve a homogenizing effect: not that everyone will be different from one another, but that differences will no longer matter at all. By being "who you are" and counting "as an individual," a woman Freemason like Emma could hope to abstract herself from the material constraints of her gendered body.

While Emma's wish to ascend to a place "farther, outside and beyond" was metaphorical, the act of traveling, the freedom of movement, of leaving the home, of entering the political sphere, is another one of liberalism's techniques for producing abstract subjects in contrast to the bodily oppressions and imprisonments that characterize abject others (Kotef 2009). From a phenomenological viewpoint, mobility is a process of dematerialization of the body (Merleau-Ponty 2002). Indeed, as we continued the conversation, Emma began to tell me about her travels in connection with her work for the GLMFI.

> The first time I traveled abroad [for the GLMFI], I remember seeing the "Royal Café" in London, near Piccadilly. There's a little wooden staircase, very beautifully engraved, leading to a temple underneath. It's a beautiful, old temple where we worked. That was a mixed-gender lodge with both women and men. Obviously it was not part of the regular English Lodge, unlike the GOI, but it was a beautiful lodge. It was a meeting of the CLIPSAS with lodges from countries all over the world. I'm talking about over ten years ago.

As one of the first members of the GLMFI—not quite a founder like Margherita and others, she told me, but there almost from the beginning—Emma had soon risen through its ranks, and she therefore started to travel as a representative of her lodge to Masonic meetings abroad. Although all Masonic lodges derive their legitimacy from the recognition they receive from lodges of other countries, establishing international diplomatic connections was especially important for a Masonic organization as young and as small as the GLMFI. The women-only lodge had received its initial charter, authorizing it to operate, from a French lodge, and transnational connections and treaties of mutual friendship continued to be central to its development plans even at the time of my fieldwork, when the GLMFI was already an independent Masonic organization with its own charter.

Emma's travels instantiate two hallmark principles of liberalism: its supranational aspirations, and the "freedom of movement" characteristic of cosmopolitan, liberal subjects. Her official trip to London is especially significant because of what it reveals about liberal fraternity. As the representative of a women's lodge, Emma was not in London to visit the United Grand Lodge of England (UGLE), whose historical dominion over Freemasonry continues to exclude women. Rather, Emma was there to meet with representatives of other worldwide lodges that either because of their membership policies or because of differences in esoteric practices did not fall under the purview of the UGLE. Emma's diplomatic travels were part of systematic efforts to build fraternity and forge political alliances among lodges that for various reasons were all at the margins of official Freemasonry: that is, Anglocentric and masculine.

Underneath a café in the city of London, in the heart of that Masonic hegemony that continues to deny the conditions of possibility for Emma's and her sisters' existence, her enduring efforts to be nonetheless fraternal reveal the extent of her attachment to fraternity's promises. "In the end we formed a chain. We held hands together, and everyone read the first paragraph of Anderson's *Constitutions* in their own language. That made you feel the fraternity and the universality. I never wanted to say, 'Whatever; why should I bother?'"

What Emma was describing without saying so explicitly was a "chain of union," a ritual that Freemasons sometimes performed to solidify fraternal bonds. I had participated in one myself once. According to Masonic esoteric teachings, sometimes group rituals like the chain of union can produce what is known as an *egregore*. The concept of the egregore has resonance in a variety of Western Mysteries and esoteric traditions beyond Freemasonry. It is a psychic entity thought to emerge from shared, intersubjective experiences during rituals as a sort of collective mind (Mainguy 2004). Sometimes even large crowds and mobs where emotions run high might unintentionally conjure an egregore. The appearance of an egregore was usually taken as a sign of how powerful a ritual had been. For instance, during dinner after several hours of ritual works in the temple, I heard a group of GLDI Freemasons remark that the egregore had been especially strong that day. Emma's description of the event echoed similar accounts my informants gave of their feelings of fraternity after rituals. Many described it as an out-of-body sensory experience that presented fraternity as a collective energy, an egregore, conjured through the ritual chain of union of the Freemasons present at the meeting.

As members of Masonic lodges from all over the world held hands together to form a ritual chain of union, Emma said that one could "feel the fraternity and the universality." Her words exemplified the ways in which Masonic rituals and practices produce the sensory and affective experiences of their political ideals. Fraternity as a rational, Enlightenment principle can translate into Masonic treaties of mutual alliance that bring people "from countries all over the world" to stand together in a chain of union. But it is the ritual practices of men and women forming a circle in an underground London temple that produce the exhilarating experience of fraternity that inspired them in the first place. Fraternity, in other words, was reified through the rituals that conjured it into being. Through a process of ritual abstraction, personal differences among individual ritual participants were literally dematerialized giving way to a shared, out-of-body, intersubjective experience of fraternity. In turn, that sensory experience during a ritual moment legitimated the belief that fraternity was there all along, as a principle to feel and to hope for, as a *real possibility* to strive for.

The rest of Emma's story, however, was an account of precisely the failures of fraternity:

> Outside events were not favorable to us. First it was the P2, then the bombs. At some point we received memos [from foreign lodges] saying that they could no longer write to us, or that we should not write to them abroad because there might be something dangerous about using the addresses . . . all very unpleasant things that were hard for us. Clearly, this made it hard for us to open up, to invite more women to join us. . . . The problem was not our secret; it was problems that were outside of us and that had nothing to do with us, but we had to pay the consequences too.

Emma had mentioned that during that trip to London she had been the guest of a mixed-gender lodge not recognized by the UGLE. It was a trip to consolidate alliances among groups that were already excluded from the official fraternity of hegemonic lodges. However, after the scandal of the deviated Masonic lodge P2 shook the highest levels of government, and after the 1993 bombing in Via dei Georgofili near the Uffizi museum in Florence, for which Freemasons had initially been prime suspects, even the sisters and brothers who had "felt" and shared the fraternity of a chain of union in London refused to be associated with Italian Freemasons. The Italian state campaign against Freemasons in the 1990s had tapped into pre-existing imagery to reinvigorate a conspiracy of corrupt, dangerous, satanic Masons. Not unlike the McCarthy era in the United States for those suspected of Communist sympathies, it was a time in which being a Freemason—or being suspected of being one—had potentially dramatic repercussions for one's social life and status in Italy and beyond. Among other effects, this prosecutorial strategy against Freemasons undermined their networks of solidarity, their fraternity, as it sought to push Masons to save their own skins rather than to follow the Masonic injunction to aid a brother in need.

Despite recognizing the fragility of fraternity as a source of political alliance, however, Emma persisted in her beliefs because she "can be quite stubborn" about deeply held convictions. What is especially interesting analytically is how fraternity could become such a deeply held conviction despite its ongoing failed enactments. Gaining discursive strength through rituals that presented it as prediscursive, fraternity could, in a sense, take on a life of its own. Its failures could be attributed to the human imperfections of people carrying it through, rather than to the internal limits of its own discourse, and any instance of its enactment could become a sign of fraternity's inherent value.

In a sense, evidence of fraternity's repeated failures could do little to deter its subscribers who, like Emma, knew that fraternity's appeal was in the promise of a yet-to-be-actualized future and of a love so selfless as to transcend the limits of worldly differences. The personal transformation she and the others wanted to achieve could only be actualized intersubjectively by becoming a brother, and "brotherly love" or agape was the explicit paradigm with which they explained to me their quest to engender a better world. *Amore eterno*, or eternal love, was the wish expressed at the end of a Grand Maestra's allocution to her lodge. *Amore* would also be the guide of a new apprentice through the hurdles of her initiation. When my informants used the Italian word *amore*, love appeared as an external force, almost as an egregore, descending upon the people to whom it was bestowed, to guide them, protect them, or make them better. The failures of brotherly love did not dissuade my interlocutors, who knew how much labor their self-cultivation path required to remake the profane into a liberal abstraction of brotherhood. If anything, present failures could fuel an even stronger longing for that world, as Emma put it, "farther, outside and beyond" the lived constraints of raced and sexed bodies, where you can be who you really are.

And wouldn't I agree with that? She asked me, looking straight into my eyes. Wouldn't I want to live in that world too?

Conclusion: Fraternity and Its Discontents

Fraternity is the highest principle of Freemasonry's humanist credo. Among my interlocutors, fraternity was an explicit goal, an affect to cultivate through practices of fraternization meant to solidify their bonds of love and care for each other. By learning to relate to one another fraternally, the Freemasons I met also learned how to relate to others: profane coworkers, neighbors, family members, acquaintances. The lodge provided a training ground for what would ultimately be a fundamental transformation in my interlocutors' subjectivity and in their sociality. Learning to be brothers in the lodge, Freemasons could therefore learn how to be fraternal in the profane world too. That is the ultimate goal of Freemasonry: to better society by bettering individuals.

The difference in scale between the brotherly love shared by a group of Freemasons in the lodges among themselves and the brotherly love of humanist fraternity—love in the sense of agape, capable of translating across all borders—

is the fundamental contradiction at the heart of the Masonic project and also at the heart of the liberal discourse of humanism, of which Freemasonry has historically been an accomplice. Anybody could supposedly be a brother; and yet, not only are most of us not brothers but our chances at fraternity are also substantially reduced by fraternity's roots in the political economy and in the gendered and racial discourses of the "unmarked subject" of European modernity.

Subaltern subjects worldwide have long known that the promises of universal fraternity were never really meant for them (although hope springs eternal). By focusing on the experiences of upper-class European subjects like women Freemasons, however, it is possible to expose the laborious efforts necessary to keep fraternity discursively vibrant, desirable, and effective even where it would seem to be the most "natural" or, at least, to come closest. Not only did women Freemasons believe in brotherly love, but they actively produced it among themselves and in relation to men Freemasons, despite their ongoing exclusion.

To recognize fraternity as a set of promises, rather than a fait accompli, allows one to better understand why and how the women Freemasons I knew endured in their allegiance to this liberal principle, despite repeated disappointments. My interlocutors' attachments to Masonic fraternity could be described as a "cruel optimism," in Lauren Berlant's (2006) sense of the term. What is cruel about it is not simply that fraternity will not be fully actualized, and has already been frustrating, but that in the process of maintaining an affective attachment to it, the women Freemasons I met had to remain attached to compromised conditions of possibility that defined their very sense of life and selfhood.[19] They had to remake themselves into abstract brothers—that is, genderless brothers—so that they too could experience fraternity. That lived impossibility, that contradiction in terms, was in a sense the "price" to pay for inclusion into Freemasonry, and even that was not quite enough, as evidenced by women's ongoing marginalization and invisibility within the brotherhood. In return, however, my interlocutors were able to engender a *feeling*, an affect, which was both material and discursive, and which was for them life-affirming: the feeling of walking through life alongside brothers and sisters. The feeling that through their labor of love they might be coming one step closer to living in that world, as Emma put it, "farther, outside and beyond."

"They'll think I am mad [*matta*]," Emma told me toward the end of our meeting. When she said "they," she wasn't referring to anyone in particular. Just people, in general. "They'll think I am mad, but I believe in it, I have always believed in [fraternity]."

If fraternity lends itself to madness it is because its vertiginous orientation to the future is always already conscious of its impossibility, betrayals, and hypocrisies; and yet it remains central to surviving in the present, to infusing present life with meaning. It is a revolutionary madness, and if some of my interlocutors' ideological premises in an abstracted individualism that was also in many ways disembodied made their approach inimical to leftist and feminist political projects centered on the recognition of material and embodied differences, the mode of fraternity they espoused has nonetheless been historically contagious. Whether in anticolonial struggles, in liberal and radical feminisms, or in Masonic lodges, the liberal discourse of fraternity has broken a lot of hearts, but it has also inspired and fueled revolutions and social movements. It is certainly madness, but of the utopian variety.

Performing rituals in the lodges two to three times a week, devoting their lives to a self-cultivation path meant to remake them into brothers, Freemasons produced fraternity as an intersubjective affect. The ongoing controversy over women's initiation into Freemasonry, however, exposes the limits of fraternity both in its material applications and also in its discursive consistency. By *marking* women's presence to forbid it, allow it, or simply to debate it, masculine Masonic discourse alienates its own post-Enlightenment language of universal fraternity, liberty, and equality, at the same time as it realizes fraternity into a community of practice that feels just as loving to its practitioners as my family of choice feels to me.

If the subject position of a "woman Freemason" continues to appear so oxymoronic, it is precisely because of the discursive play of the masculine notion of fraternity, which propels not only Masonic practices but also the modern strand of humanism at the heart of liberal political philosophies. As a learning path, Freemasonry teaches that all bodies are equal. Inside temples, ritual gowns, just like uniforms, hide individual differences to create a cohesive esprit de corps. Not all bodies, however, are equally likely to be granted access to the temple in the first place. Not all bodies speak its passwords with equal command. Some who cannot meet the elusive criteria of "good character" or who may not meet the gender and financial requirements of a particular lodge may remain standing outside the temple, *pro fanum*. Those who enter, in turn, will be refashioned into ostensibly unmarked persons, abstract liberal subjects, such that several Masons over the course of my research assured me that when they are inside the temples they do not see men or women, rich or poor, but only brother Masons, working together, as the saying goes, "to build a prison for vice and an altar to virtue."

PASSWORD II

———— * ————

The huge expanse of the Main Hall of the Grand Hotel had been converted into a restaurant to hold what the profane waiters and hosts kept referring to as a "gala" but which the rest of us knew to be a white agape. The hall was filled with round tables dressed in white linen cloths to accommodate the approximately one thousand guests who had flocked to town for the occasion. I sat next to Elisa, an Eastern Star, who was sitting next to her Worthy Patron, the GOI man in charge of supervising her ES lodge. Elisa had been born into Freemasonry on her father's side. Her mother was from Cape Verde, and Elisa had inherited a light brown complexion that made her the only person of color in the room other than me. At the age of thirty-nine, she was also younger than average.

Before long, Elisa's Worthy Patron, Piero, came back to our table from a short absence. Like many of his GOI brothers, he was a white man in his sixties with a well-groomed gray beard, small round glasses, and a belly that he liked to point to as proof of his human frailty in the face of the temptations of gluttony. Earlier, when he had introduced me to the other guests sitting at our table as a researcher working on Freemasonry, he had joked that my thesis should be called "On the Size and Quantity of Freemasons' Eating Practices," or, with an overdone dialect inflection, "Quanto magnano li Massoni" (how much those Freemasons eat). I kept running into him at agape dinners, with their multiple courses of food and their seven ritual toasts with champagne.

Looking excited, Piero apologized for interrupting the conversation at the table, but he wished to introduce everyone to the brother standing next to him, a very dignified-looking man about twenty years younger than Piero. "This is Abdulmannan. Did I say it correctly? Abdelmunnan . . . yes, Abdelmannan." The brother remained impassable. "He is a brother from Jordan," Piero explained cheerfully to all of us at the table. Then, directed at me, "You see, this shows that we do accept anybody in Freemasonry without any distinctions of religion or background, et cetera."

Abdelmannan kissed Elisa's and my hands, as GOI brothers do upon being introduced to a woman, then took an empty seat across from us next to the group of men who were already sitting at our table, and who had mostly been ignoring Elisa and me, despite our attempts to join their conversation. Feeling invisible had allowed Elisa and me to have our own conversation, but she needed to talk to Piero, so she excused herself momentarily and stepped away for several minutes. Guests were still coming into the hall, and with nothing better to do in Elisa's absence, I found myself listening to the live band entertaining us that evening. They were performing an obnoxious rendition of an aria from Mozart's *Don Juan*, made tolerable only by contrast with the previous song, the painfully touristic *O Sole Mio*.

As the song came to an end and I started to clap, the men at my table turned to look at me, as if they had suddenly been reminded of my presence. The man sitting closest to me, who had introduced himself as Vittorio when I first sat down, asked me why I was clapping, since I didn't seem to be enjoying the performance any more than the rest of them were. "For their efforts," I shrugged, and pointed out that the other tables were also clapping. Vittorio looked at the hundreds of Freemasons in the ballroom, and he said with some complacency that he thought many of them were probably enjoying it.

The men returned to their conversation, this time mocking the musicians and debating which of Italy's most famous orchestra directors and singers had been the best ones. Pavarotti, they concluded, was like the Roman general Pompey. Pompey could have been remembered as the greatest Roman general, but unfortunately for him there was a Caesar, and next to Caesar he would inevitably be second best. As the live band finished their next poorly played song, however, Vittorio decided to join me in a short applause this time. "It's for their efforts," he told me.

As our first course was served, the men had moved on to discussing zodiac signs. To be exact, they kept guessing (mostly correctly) each other's sign, insisting that it only takes a few minutes of meeting someone to read their essence. Their guesses were uncannily accurate, and although the act of guessing someone's sign might look rather like a parlor trick, I had heard some Freemasons talk about the importance of knowing how to read other people.

Vittorio turned to me during the next music break, and he guessed my sign correctly, Sagittarius. Then he added that he thought I had a good ear for music. He was being polite, but I told him that I didn't think so, and that I've never studied music. He explained that some things, like how to appreciate music, cannot really be taught.

Elisa kept coming back and forth to our table, eating with us but also getting up between courses to greet others. I joined her once, and another time I went to say hello to some sisters I knew who had arrived late. Through much of the dinner, however, I remained sitting at the table and, after a little while, Vittorio and I began to converse.

He was seventy-four years old. Our conversation was casual at first. We started out talking about the public lecture series that had run parallel to the ritual works for the duration of the convention we had both attended. Vittorio confessed that he found those lectures boring, and then proceeded to describe in simple terms what he believed would have been a pedagogically more successful format. It sounded as though he was referring to the Socratic method, and I asked him if that was what he meant. Indeed, he confirmed that he was. He had clearly given a lot of thought to pedagogy. As he continued to discuss the importance of studying for self-improvement, Vittorio mentioned casually that "we are not meant to live like beasts." Then he paused and stared at me as if he were waiting for me to respond.

I often had a paranoid feeling, when I was in the company of Freemasons, that my cultural capital was being tested. At first it was just a hunch, but over time I grew more sure of it. If I could demonstrate my knowledge with a few right answers, my interlocutors, and especially the men Freemasons I talked to, would begin to open up significantly. It was as if cultural capital worked as a password to let me into their discussions of esoteric and Masonic practices by proving that I was capable of understanding them. I could not be sure, of course, but I decided to treat Vittorio's pause as if it were a test of me, and I responded by completing his statement.

"We are not meant to live like beasts . . ." he had said and then paused.

"But to follow virtue and knowledge," I added.

He had paraphrased in modern Italian a verse from Dante's *Inferno*. When I responded with the next verse, I recited it in the fourteenth-century original to show that I had read it. To be sure, most people educated in Italy would have been able to recognize that very famous verse at least well enough to paraphrase it. If this was a test of my knowledge, which I thought it was, it was not a particularly challenging test. Nonetheless, it seemed to work. Vittorio looked pleased.

The next thing that came out of his mouth was that he was not only a Freemason, but also a Knight Templar.

The shock on my face must have given away my thoughts. As I confessed to Vittorio, I thought the Templars were extinguished in the fourteenth century. Vittorio acknowledged my confusion, and explained that the church had attempted to destroy the Templars in 1307. "Do you know the story of Jacques de Molay?"

I knew that the para-Masonic children's organization for the young sons of GOI brothers was called "de Molay." The girls' equivalent, a precursor to the Order of the Eastern Star, was the "Rainbow Girls." Vittorio proceeded to tell me the story of Jacques de Molay, the famed Knight Templar who was tortured and executed by the Catholic Inquisition. He told me it was Friday, October 13, when the Templars were attacked, and that is why that day is considered so unlucky.

Vittorio claimed that the Templars had never disappeared. They had gone into hiding, seeking refuge in Britain after the papacy had successfully dismantled their Order in Southern Europe, and they had kept their knowledge alive into the present. Vittorio was asserting historical continuity between his group and the Templars of yesteryear. He insisted that modern Templars are not simply trying to recreate a chivalrous and religious Order modeled after the ancient one but that they are actually the legitimate heirs of that Order. Although he conceded that modern Templars have adapted some of their practices to our time—they no longer practice celibacy and they are no longer active soldiers—he insisted that the spirit of their Order had resisted the corrosion of time.

It is not uncommon for members of contemporary esoteric groups to trace their genealogical roots to far distant sects, and even to claim, despite historical evidence to the contrary, to be the direct descendants of an uninterrupted lineage of practice. According to Vittorio, the Templars never stopped existing, although that's what the Catholic Church would like us to believe, he said. According to him, they simply went into hiding and, over the last few centuries, they hid within Masonic lodges.

A natural pause in the conversation gave me time to think. I thought of the long tensions between the Catholic Church and Freemasonry in Italy. Where did Knights Templar fit into the topography of Italian secret societies? For all the historical claims my interlocutors made about Templars hiding out in Masonic lodges, political conspiracies might tend to place the Knights Templar, if they still existed at all, in the realm of Opus Dei, the Vatican secret organization that along with Freemasonry and the Mafia completes the trinity of Italian conspiracy theories. Many Freemasons consider Opus Dei to be their nemesis; it is rumored to have far more tentacles reaching into civil society and governmental institutions than the lodges have ever had.

I hesitated for a moment to think about how best to phrase my next question. It nonetheless came out clumsily. "Vittorio, I hope this doesn't offend you, but I was wondering . . . I was wondering if being a Freemason and a Templar ever seemed . . . if it was hard for you to reconcile being a Freemason with being a Templar."

Vittorio gave me a nice smile, and he seemed to have read my mind. "It's true that a lot of Templars are in Opus Dei. But some of us, many of us, are here [in Freemasonry]. Let's not forget that the church, because of greed, excommunicated both Templars and Freemasons. We have a great deal in common." He continued to tell me that the reason he became a Templar was that for him being a Freemason was not enough. Sometimes, he said, he felt his heart was restless. "Cor nostrum inquietum. Do you understand Latin?" He asked me.

"Inquietum cor nostrum," I said for an answer, "donec requiescat in te." It was a passage from the writings of Saint Augustine: "Our heart is restless, until it rests in you." I was surprised I still remembered it from the days of studying Latin in a *liceo*. As for my Latin, I admitted, it was very rusty.

Vittorio paused to look directly into my eyes again, as he had done before. Next to him, the other men were absorbed in their conversation. Elisa was gone again. The shrills and trumpets of the performance carried loudly over the room. For a moment, in this public space surrounded by hundreds of people, we were alone. As I learned time and time again, when I met my interlocutors in cafes and restaurants, or for a walk through town, the safest places for an intimate conversation were the most public. The cacophony of city noises offered a cover to our conversations, and we could go unnoticed in a sea of busy people.

Suddenly, Vittorio's demeanor started to change. He was now speaking softly and solemnly. He began a long discussion about his pursuit of a higher truth, the love quest, the quest for love as agape that is Freemasonry. And he told me about the ability to read people by looking into their eyes. Like many other Freemasons, he seemed to believe firmly in the eyes' ability to see beyond the surface of things to read other people but also to read clues traced in the landscape. It was a skill that had to be practiced, he told me. It was a skill he learned through esoteric works, but that he had also tried to teach his daughters so that they too could begin to recognize symbols.

Before the evening ended, I apologized to Vittorio in advance for the descent into lesser arts that I was about to lead us into, but I told him I was curious to hear his impressions, as a Knight Templar and a Freemason, about the proliferation of popular fiction on these societies. He laughed, and confessed that he had just finished reading Dan Brown's *Da Vinci Code*, and found it quite entertaining. "The value of these books," he said, "is that at least they keep people interested and talking, and as long as people are curious they can keep asking questions." The goal, once again, was the never-ending pursuit of knowledge. "But if I had to choose," Vittorio continued after a short pause, "I would have to say that [Umberto Eco's] *Foucault's Pendulum* is in a sense more true."

Vittorio never elaborated on this hermetic comment. The two books he mentioned have a similar plot—a story of conspiracy and secrecy narrated in the genre of a mystery, although Dan Brown's (2003) is accessible to a wide audience, whereas Umberto Eco's (1988) is so thickly packed with hundreds of pages of philosophical and historical references that his fiction could hardly be described as popular. One important difference between them, however, is that in *Foucault's Pendulum* the conspiracy that was born as a hoax takes on a life of its own. In fact, it becomes real once others begin to believe in it and begin to act as if it were real all along. By the end, the conspiracy was always real.

Speculative Labor

The life-process of society, which is based on the process of material
production, does not strip off its mystical veil until it is treated as
production by freely associated men, and is consciously regulated by
them in accordance with a settled plan. ‹ KARL MARX, *Capital*›

Operative and Speculative Work

What, exactly, do Freemasons do, profane minds have inquired for three centuries. Freemasons work, that's for sure. The exact nature of Masonic work, however, is not easy to define. This is how a Maestra in the mixed-gender Grand Lodge of Italy (GLDI) once put it to me: "What do we do, you ask? Well, we build an altar to virtue and a prison for vice. That's what we do. Oh, and we do it in the name of the Great Architect of the Universe, obviously!"

With a sardonic smile and a paraphrase of Masonic teachings, the Maestra's words were intentionally elusive, and they underscored the impossibility of articulating the precise demands of a kind of labor that is more symbolic than manual in its undertakings. Building an altar to virtue and a prison for vice is an architectural metaphor for the self-cultivation path Freemasons pursue under the guidance of a nondenominational deity, the Great Architect of the Universe.

Freemasonry finds its roots in the European medieval lodges of stonemasons, who were handworkers bound to secrecy by the initiation rituals and rigid internal hierarchies of their craft guilds. As they built cathedrals and palaces throughout Europe, stonemasons' guilds were believed to carry within them old secrets of geometry, engineering, and esoteric architectural correspondences.

For reasons of economic necessity and status, by the end of the seventeenth century operative lodges of stonemasons had to start accepting nonmasons into their ranks in exchange for membership dues. These "accepted" nonmasons, in turn, were typically members of the literate classes willing to pay in order to enjoy the privileges historically reserved for guild brothers in the town life and commerce. As these upper-class nonmasons gained increasing control over the running of the lodges and over their operative brothers, Margaret Jacob writes, we can observe "the transformation of a trade guild into a gentlemen's fraternity" (1991: 38).

Although the lodges retained the symbols of the craft from which they derived—the compass and the square, geometric principles, builders' tools—the new masonry of the literate classes was philosophical in nature, and it became known as "speculative" to distinguish it from the "operative" craft of stone-masons. This is how Freemasonry as we know it—that is, *speculative* masonry practiced by "free" and "accepted" men—came into being. Instead of building cathedrals, speculative Freemasons wished to build a new society by establishing an intellectual and spiritual self-cultivation path for initiates.

The work of a Masonic lodge is thus intrinsically intellectual labor, and the esoteric rituals that are performed inside Masonic temples are aimed at facilitating what is primarily a learning path. Starting as an Apprentice and slowly advancing through the up to thirty-three degrees that comprise the expertise of a Maestro or Maestra, a Mason embarks on a life-long journey of self-cultivation through the pursuit of knowledge.

I take the practices and contents of Masonic knowledge pursuits as forms of "speculative labor" that produce symbolic capital. Pierre Bourdieu (1986) famously distinguished the form of capital most immediately recognizable in Marxian theory—economic capital—from the more subtle and symbolic forms capital can take when it is expressed as knowledge (cultural capital) or social connections (social capital). In particular, in his classic study of cultural capital, Bourdieu (1984) argued that the "distinction" of French upper classes was based not exclusively on economic resources but also on their cultivated taste for legitimated bodies of knowledge, such as European art and classical music. Taking what is often referred to as "high" culture as his point of departure, and breaking away from a Kantian aesthetics of a priori forms of beauty, Bourdieu revealed taste to be a social construct rather than a natural preference—a construct that was produced and reproduced within families and within social classes. A crucial element of Bourdieu's argument is that while taste, and especially taste for high culture, is socially and historically produced, its contingency is masked in everyday life, with the effect of naturalizing class distinctions.

Although the three forms of capital (economic, social, and cultural) are often intertwined, my focus is on cultural capital to underscore the unique processes of production that give rise to this less recognizable and yet crucial form of wealth among Freemasons. This is not to say that Freemasons do not also have important and complex relationships to economic capital or to social capital. In Italy at the time of my fieldwork, lodges continued to be the objects of conspiracy theories alleging that Freemasons used their social networks for illicit dealings and profitable criminal activities. Here, however, my intention is to analyze a form of capital of which Freemasons are not necessarily suspected, but which they produce with important consequences for the lodges' place in Italian society.

Symbolic capital is what Masonic speculative labor produces and accumulates through sometimes unconscious and sometimes self-conscious practices. Given that speculative labor, like any other form of labor, is characterized by pervasive hierarchies of difference, and given that capital results from and reproduces structural inequalities, I am interested in analyzing the social differences that are reproduced alongside symbolic capital within Masonic lodges. My contention is that the exclusion and marginalization of women from Freemasonry cannot be explained solely in esoteric terms or by reference to Masonic "tradition," as my informants believed. If sisters have elicited suspicion whenever they have taken part in the speculative labor of the lodges, it is also because the cultural capital Freemasons pursue is itself an elitist gendered discourse, one that has historically excluded women from its epistemological hierarchy of values.

Scholastic Dispositions

In the early months and years of initiation, when a Freemason is still an Apprentice, he or she is bound by the "rule of silence," unable to utter a single word inside the temple, but forced to learn to listen instead to the wisdom of those farther along the initiation path. My interlocutors usually explained the rule to me as a necessary training in humility for newly minted Freemasons who might not be accustomed to listening to others. Their explanations tended to foreground the class position and occupation of most lodge members—people who might not be used to listening to others because of their social status in their profane lives.

Francesca, for instance, told me, "There are surgeons among us, university professors, people who are not used to listening to others. . . . An Apprentice must learn humility." She was the editor of a small weekly paper, and when I met her she had been recently initiated to the second degree of Freemasonry (Fellow Mason) in the mixed-gender GLDI. When I asked her what it had been like for her to abide by the rule of silence, Francesca, who was a very chatty person, acknowledged how challenging the requirement had been for her. "It was the most difficult thing not to speak for a year," she said. "You know me! I talk a lot. There were times . . . I felt I was exploding. Because you want to say something, you want to respond to what they are saying, but you just can't."

The rule of silence, which is commonly found among initiate societies (Simmel 1906), creates the conditions of possibility for the training of neophytes. As the literature on apprenticeship has shown, various requirements and pedagogical techniques are in place not only to train apprentices in their actual craft but also to predispose them to learning (Herzfeld 2004; Kondo 1990; Lave and Wenger 1991; Maher 1987).[1] Among Freemasons, the rule of silence was specifically meant to level existing social differences among members and to turn all Apprentices into what Saba Mahmood (2001) has called "docile agents."[2]

Francesca's account instantiates precisely the pedagogical effects of the rule of silence. "When I finally became a Fellow Mason," Francesca continued, "I was allowed to speak. I could say everything I wanted. But at that point I had learned that I still had a lot to learn. I wanted to continue to listen." Despite how challenging being silent had been for Francesca during her Apprenticeship, eventually she came to appreciate and espouse the value of silence, so that by the time she became a Fellow she often chose to remain silent anyway. Francesca had become docile—in the etymological sense that she had become receptive to learning, she had become teachable, and her potential for learning was one that she herself had helped to cultivate.

The rule of silence was one of many pedagogical techniques practiced by Freemasons in an attempt to predispose neophytes to absorb and accept often unsavory or unsettling esoteric teachings.[3] Most evidently, Masonic rituals themselves were a prime pedagogical technique used by Freemasons, one that has long been shown to produce a feeling of belonging to the community of the initiated and to facilitate the acquisition of new beliefs (Asad 1993: 55–82; Luhrmann 1989; Mahmood 2005; Turner 1969).

Besides esoteric rituals and rules, however, some of the other pedagogical techniques of Freemasons were actually rather mundane, and they seemed familiar to both neophytes and profane outsiders. Unlike rituals performed donning ceremonial garments, those other techniques were so recognizably scholastic that some of my interlocutors told me that when they were first initiated into a lodge they felt they had gone back to school.

One such technique was the writing, reading, and discussion of *tavole* (lit.

"tables" or "tablets").[4] A *tavola* is a sort of research paper. A Maestra or Maestro may assign a tavola ahead of time on a particular topic to one of the lodge members, who will then be responsible for presenting his or her work at a scheduled lodge meeting. As tavole are some of the most common types of work Masons do, their content sheds light on Masonic priorities. The diversity of topics appropriate for a tavola reflects the diversity of intellectual interests represented in Masonic lodges. Some tavole might review strictly esoteric topics and principles, such as alchemy, mysticism, or the symbolism of temple architecture. Others, however, might concern current issues, such as immigration and women's rights in countries of the global South, or classical and Renaissance art and literature, such as the literary analysis of Dante's youth poetry, Aristotle's perspective on catharsis, Leonardo da Vinci's inventions, or the music of classical European composers. The literary, artistic, historical and philosophical works, which, from the ideological standpoint of Eurocentric epistemology, have been deemed to be not only cultural artifacts but the very elements of "high" culture, occupy a central position in Masonic knowledge production and self-cultivation and they were more often than not the topics of tavole.

Tavole were some of the most common pedagogical tools used in the Masonic lodges I studied. By requiring independent research and combining a variety of bodies of knowledge, they forced a studious Mason to draw connections between Masonic teachings and the profane world. They also furthered the climate of intellectual exchange that has characterized Masonic lodges since their formation, and they thus stimulated knowledge production. As didactic tools, tavole were also used to correct and to reprimand, just as a disruptive student may be assigned additional homework as a form of punishment in school. During the course of my research, I witnessed firsthand the way some Maestri and Maestre, for instance, would assign books to read and tavole to write to Apprentices whom they saw as erring. While Apprentices are not allowed to speak inside temples, they can talk during social gatherings, and those occasions provide opportunities for their training to continue.

Once, during a dinner party among members of a mixed-gender GLDI lodge, a young Apprentice—one of the few Masons I ever met who explicitly professed to be Christian, rather than spiritual, secular, or not very religious—had made some remarks about Islam that reflected dominant Western stereotypes, including some sweeping generalizations about women's oppression in Muslim countries. After some time, an older Maestro sitting at the same table intervened in the conversation by offering precise references to shari'a Islamic law and teachings, using citations from the Koran to distinguish what he considered to be the principles of a religion from their political applications in some present-day countries. After dinner, as we were all getting ready to leave, that same Maestro suggested that the Apprentice read a book on Arab perspectives on the Crusades. What was noteworthy about his "suggestion" is that it clearly carried the valence of a requirement. The Apprentice quickly pulled a piece of paper and a pen out of her purse, and dutifully copied down the reference. "Maybe you can write a tavola on it," the Maestro added casually before the Apprentice left.

When I later discussed that interaction with other Masons who had been present at that dinner, they confirmed my own reading of the event. The Maestro was correcting the Apprentice, but he was doing so discreetly enough so as not to embarrass her publicly. In turn, the Apprentice knew that she should follow her Maestro's guidance, obediently writing down the "suggested" citation in preparation for a tavola that was sure to come.

The gender dynamics at play in that scenario reflected to some degree a common pattern I observed, whereby Maestri tended to dominate conversations and embellish their speech with historical references and quotes more than Maestre did. Masonic hierarchies, however, intervened in all such profane power relations in ways that complicated significantly any simplistic gender binary. Apprentices, for instance, were typically acquiescent regardless of their gender. At that dinner party, the Apprentice's behavior therefore stood out both for the forcefulness of her opinions, which defied Masonic teachings about moderation of judgment, and for the factual errors contained in her claims. Among those present, it was the Maestro most directly responsible for the training of this Apprentice—that is, the Worshipful Maestro of her lodge—who intervened to correct her. The power dynamics at play in the profane setting of the dinner party were clearly determined by precise Masonic hierarchies.

What is worth noting about this ethnographic example of pedagogical correction is that the topic of the tavola assigned to this erring Apprentice was Islam and the Crusades from the point of view of Arabs. Freemasons' predilection for European high culture might give the misimpression that their knowledge was exclusively Western.[5] As this example shows, however, not all influences on Freemasonry were European in origin. On the contrary, the mystical, alchemic, and spiritual "traditions" that inspire the esoteric cosmology of my informants were drawn largely from a collage of times and places, ranging from ancient Egypt and Greece to Native American folklore, Islamic Sufism, Buddhist meditation, and Chinese medicine. Even in seemingly profane contexts, like the dinner party where a discussion on Islam and the Crusades led to a Maestro's reprimand of his Apprentice, Masons often revealed themselves to be quite versed in non-Western knowledges, including, in this case, shari'a law.

I am not suggesting, therefore, that cultivated Masons would be proficient only in knowledge bounded by the geopolitical limits of Europe or North America. Rather, I am suggesting that the very discourse of high culture they espoused is Occidental in the sense that it privileges and reifies selected Western-based productions, while also appropriating "other" knowledges through the discourse of an exoticizing Orientalism (Saïd 2003).[6] In this example, it was by displaying his knowledge of Islam that this Maestro could establish his own credentials as a liberal and "cosmopolitan" Occidental subject.[7]

Michael Herzfeld has suggested that a global hierarchy of values that privileges Western culture "betrays a European and colonialist origin, in that it springs from the massive preoccupation with the definition of spaces and concepts that characterized the emergence of the modern nation-state in the heyday and aftermath of colonialism" (2004: 3). As the object of Masonic tavole, high culture provided a familiar content for Masonic activities. Raised in the classical education of Italian schools, my informants valued and recognized European liberal arts as a legitimate body of knowledge. Indeed, many of them told me they were surprised to discover it in the lodges, which they had imagined to be exclusively esoteric spaces. Unlike esotericism, high culture provided a respected intellectual context that would induce neither fear nor ridicule. When studied assiduously inside lodges, through tavole and discussions reminiscent of scholastic practices, it conferred a high degree of rigor, legitimacy, and respectability to Masonic work for both neophytes and high-ranking Masons.

La cultura si fa a casa

The prestige that cultural capital can confer, however, depends not only on the quantity and quality of knowledge one possesses but also on the modes of its acquisition, and on the manner of its performance. Bourdieu (1984) recognized this very point: while formal titles bestow "cultural nobility" upon their holders, scholastic capital is merely a necessary but not sufficient component of cultural nobility.

In Italy a centralized, public, national education curriculum guarantees formal equality of knowledge to students who choose the same type of school, with an unmistakable hierarchy of prestige going from *licei* (high schools intended to prepare students for university studies) down to technical institutes and vocational schools.[8] Within this hierarchy, public schools have a definite advantage over private schools and, in an interesting reversal of values found elsewhere, the curriculum of *licei* is designed with the humanistic culture of classics, Italian literature, history, philosophy, and art history in a place of honor over the sciences. The content of the national education curriculum is undoubtedly a highly gendered, racialized, and classed knowledge formation that expresses and reproduces nationalist and Occidentalist values as canonical.

At the 2004 annual convention of the men-only Grand Orient of Italy (GOI) I attended in the town of Rimini, the Grand Maestro devoted part of his inaugural speech to defending the Italian public school system from reform bills (interestingly, sponsored by Berlusconi's right-wing coalition) that were under debate in Parliament at the time, and which seemed to favor the less prestigious private schools. The Grand Maestro insisted that unlike private schools, which often have religious denominations and are therefore socially divisive, public schools produce secular citizens, and are thus better equipped to guarantee social cohesion at a time of increasing "multiculturalism."

As the Grand Maestro's allocution underscored, the public educational system—the most obvious means for the transmission and inculcation of cultural capital—is, in turn, one of the primary institutions through which the nation-building process can occur, as students are schooled into secular citizens of the nation (Gellner 1983). The underlying humanistic values of a liberal arts education are especially dear to Freemasons, who have been at the forefront both of nation-building efforts and of the establishment of public school systems in the nineteenth century, and whose commitment to the pursuit of knowledge translated into a contemporary political commitment to free, secular, public education.

Although it is taught in schools, high culture in Italy is also largely considered to be *unteachable*—a matter of talent and predisposition, rather than application. My interlocutors shared the opinion, accepted by most in Italy, that becoming a cultivated person required more than the accumulation of knowledge about European liberal arts that schools can provide. The operative assumption was that there was something more about being cultivated—something obvious yet ineffable—than what can be measured or imparted through the devices of scholastic teaching. That air, that mannerism, that *distinction*, could be said to be a habitus, embodied and unconscious, unmistakable yet hard to pin down, developed through years of socialization within particular social networks yet unaware of its own construction.

The widespread assumption that cultivation requires more than the accumulation of knowledge is also reflected in language. There is an important distinction in Italian between the terms *cultura* ("high" culture) and *erudizione* or *istruzione* (erudition, education). While one may become highly erudite (*erudita/o*) through the syllabi of scholastic studies, there are no prescriptions or academic lessons that might make one cultivated (*colta/o*). The formal equality of public education thus reflects the nation-state epistemological hierarchy of values, inscribing inequalities within its logic of equal opportunities. Indeed, when used to describe someone, the words *erudito* or *erudita* in Italian are often a back-handed compliment, connoting a person's lack of the breadth and depth of knowledge that would constitute true *cultura*, and implying instead that the erudite only has encyclopedic, scholastic knowledge of facts and figures. As the saying goes, *la cultura si fa a casa*: culture, here in the sense of high culture, is made at home.

The dominant discourse of high culture in Italy is therefore inherently paradoxical. On the one hand, citizens are expected and required to learn its contents through a nationally mandated educational curriculum that teaches high culture's Eurocentric artifacts to all. On the other hand, high culture is also deemed unteachable through formal educational channels, which can only offer erudition but ultimately, and by definition, fall short of transmitting cultura. Although scholastically available to anybody, the discourse of high culture ensures the preservation of systems of distinction by reaffirming that only some bodies can move beyond scholastic teachings to become cultivated "at home," thanks to the social and cultural capital of their family backgrounds.

The centrality of notions of family and home, and not only of scholastic training, to the discourse of high culture in Italy makes Masonic lodges uniquely positioned to generate cultural capital through their speculative labor. Writing tavole, reading books, discussing topics of interest within lodges were all ways in which Masons could develop their knowledge of liberal arts, of Masonic history, and of the esoteric symbolism and cosmology underlying their rituals. This pedagogy certainly produced erudite people, and indeed, as a profane researcher, I could hardly ever catch up with the amount of information about Masonic history and symbolism that my informants had come to master through their speculative labor in the lodges. If they produced highly educated people, however, these scholastic techniques of Masonic pedagogy could not, on their own, produce cultivated people. To achieve cultura, the Freemasons I met relied on less formal modes of instructions.

As an institution, a Masonic lodge shares some of the same structures and pedagogies that characterize schools but also some of the relational modes typical of households and families. Freemason brothers and sisters learned together through formal and ritual practices inside temples as well as through informal exchanges and intellectual discussions in each other's company. Going to theaters, museums, vacation homes, birthday parties, and philanthropic activities, Masons effectively extended their learning space from inside a lodge to most of their social world. Thus, not only would they learn, for instance, about Egyptian fertility symbols embedded in Botticelli's art through a tavola presented by a sister during ritual work, but they would also learn *how* to comment on artwork while visiting a museum exhibit, and by observing higher-ranking brothers and sisters in action.

I would contend that this double-model, which makes Freemasonry simultaneously like a school and like a home, is crucial to its members' ability to accumulate and perform not just erudition but also cultivation, in the Italian sense that distinguishes the two. Masonic lodges could offer a continuity of exposure to the ways in which particular knowledge is performed in a variety of social contexts, and not only within the walls of the temple. For example, by observing a Maestro perform his knowledge of Islamic law during a dinner party, an Apprentice could learn how to speak of Islam with the sophistication of a cosmopolitan liberal subject. It is precisely by bridging the separation between school and home, which is also at the basis of the distinction between erudition and cultura, that the Masonic lodges I studied were in a position to produce cultivated subjects without undermining the discursive effortlessness that the cultivated habitus requires.

Bourdieu (1984) argued that the legitimacy of one's cultural capital is derived not simply from what one knows but also from one's ability to perform it. In turn, the ability to perform knowledge correctly is, for Bourdieu, predicated on the availability of a social network within which such knowledge could be practiced. In his framework, an "autodidact" would be hard pressed to achieve "distinction" for he or she would lack the social expertise required to perform knowledge successfully. For instance, one could learn from books the history of the city of Edinburgh, but without a social network with whom to practice such knowledge, one might not learn the correct pronunciation of *Edinburgh*. The very difference between erudition and cultura could then be said to depend more on the quality of the performance than on the substance of knowledge.[9]

Take, for instance, the ways in which many of my informants spoke about their hometowns, in which they took great pride. Although I worked primarily with Florentines and Romans, even dwellers in smaller and less touristy towns would show an equally passionate and informed attachment to their cities. Riding in my informants' cars from one meeting place to another, men and, less often, women too would point out to me sites of cultural importance, engaging in lengthy descriptions of their histories. As city experts, they seemed to take a special pride in showing me hidden treasures that guidebooks might have left out. Each new site, in turn, would evoke a Latin citation, a mention of forgotten historical figures, a seemingly self-confident knowledge of the line between legend ("this is what they say") and facts ("this is what they did").

Truthfully, any cab driver could probably offer a similarly ad hoc tour of the city with detailed captions of selected claims to the past, typically invoking Roman or Renaissance mythologies.[10] Love for the city, just like love of the nation, cuts across social classes. The difference, however, lies in the ease and sophistication of associations inspired by a site, an observation, or a piece of information. The distinction, in a sense, is the ability to perform connections that nonchalantly assume broader and deeper knowledge, but without necessarily producing that additional knowledge. A performance of high culture is therefore a performance of discretion. As much as it reveals, it must also hold something back to engender an aura of prestige, an "adornment" of symbolic capital around the cultivated person (Urban 2001). Too eager and drawn-out a divulgence of knowledge might seem flaunting and pedantic, like a professor lecturing a group of students or, worse, a cab driver prolonging the ride for the extra fees. The aura of the cultivated person is characterized instead by wisdom and by moderation. Knowledge of high culture must of course be revealed for the performer to be recognized by his or her peers as a cultivated person, but the revelation must come in small doses and at the right times, interjected in context and with an effortless nonchalance that is itself a reification of the natural—a performance of high culture as natural taste.

Like the difference between *erudizione* and *cultura*, it is hard to grasp and yet impossible to miss. Its obviousness to insiders is perhaps the greatest source of distinction's social power: the ability to disguise the social conditions of its existence by naturalizing its effects.

Stealing with the Eyes

The familiarity of a pedagogy based on homework-like research, oral presentations, and group discussions had helped my interlocutors make sense of Masonic activities when they were first initiated, when many of them claimed they did not know anything yet about Freemasonry. Over time, however, many of the Freemasons I met had come to value and desire a different pedagogical approach, one based on the living examples that higher-ranking Masons could provide.

When I talked with Loredana, a young Maestra in the mixed-gender GLDI, it was clear that she placed a significant but limited value on scholastic pedagogy. The responsibility of being a Maestra was something she took very seriously, even though "a Maestro is like a doctor: nowadays they let anyone do it."

Her dissatisfaction with what she saw as an overproliferation of Maestri, which she compared to the very high number of medical doctors per capita in

Italy, was as much a commentary on the decreased prestige of a previously elit-ist position as it was a statement about her own Masonic experiences. "[When I was an Apprentice] I used to hate those Maestri who would take you under their arm and would start narrating the Kabbalah to you. I know how to read it myself! The good Maestri are those who teach you by example."

Loredana's call for teaching by providing a living example, or modeling,[11] as a better pedagogical technique than lecturing reflects closely Freemasonry's stated goals: not simply to teach new information, but to fashion new (better) subjects. Since its origins in the intellectual salons of the Enlightenment, Free-masonry has pursued its philosophically revolutionary aims by means of an education path designed to better society by cultivating oneself. To achieve that goal, practice was as important as theory, and many of my informants expressed doubts about how well many Masons could live up to the standards of being Freemasons. Within the Masonic hierarchical path, Maestre and Maestri had the privilege and responsibility of guiding Apprentices and Fellows, but their guidance was to be dialogical and based on praxis. Just as they watched Ap-prentices and Fellows, third-degree Masons were also watched closely by those lower-ranking initiates whose respect and emulation they had to earn.[12]

In my time among Italian Freemasons, I noticed that both women and men seemed to look deeply into each other's eyes when they were being introduced. Long gazes were prevalent in all sorts of interactions between Masons. Mean-ingful looks and gazes were often the only means to convey discreet messages in formal occasions ("I can't stand this person," "We really need to go," etc.), which required quite a bit of diplomacy and savoir faire. I soon realized, how-ever, that Masons considered reading the eyes of others to be an art. Some of my interlocutors explicitly cited the Italian adage that "gli occhi sono lo specchio dell'anima" (eyes are mirrors to the soul) to explain to me the importance of learning how to look in order to discern another person's "essence."

The first person who mentioned watching others to me was a member of the Order of the Eastern Star. We were sitting alone for some time during a Masonic convention, and Ines had been sharing with me her impressions of Freemasonry. Although she had prefaced her opinions with the self-dismissing comments many of the women I met often used ("I'm not an intellectual . . . ," "I don't speak well . . ."), she revealed a beautifully complex understanding of Masonic beliefs and practices. The daughter of a prominent Freemason, Ines had been raised into a tacit knowledge of intuition and the importance of gazes from a very young age.

"When you meet someone," Ines explained, "you talk with them, you get to know them, and looking into their eyes you understand what kind of person they are." She spoke in a soft voice, as if revealing secrets that she shouldn't have shared. That's when she told me in a whisper about "stealing with the eyes" (*rubare con gli occhi*) loosely translatable as the ability to read people.[13] The way she described it, stealing with the eyes was the ability to appropriate (to "steal") knowledge that is not immediately available by training oneself to recognize intuitively hidden clues.

What was remarkable about my interlocutors' explanations of the importance of gazes or, as Ines and a few others put it, of "stealing with the eyes," is that they presented intuition not as an innate gift but rather as a technique that could be cultivated through practice and exercise, just as one builds muscles. In other words, intuition, unlike the intellectual knowledge of high culture, was explicitly considered to be *teachable*. Among my interlocutors, both women and men were deemed capable of intuitively stealing with the eyes. If it was a matter of distinction at all, intuition was perhaps what set Freemasons apart from the profane world rather than from each other. It was at the heart of their belief, for instance, in their uncanny ability to recognize a fellow brother or, more rarely, a fellow sister in a stranger, through a Masonic radar of sorts.

Watching each other was a prime activity within Masonic circles. More than a mode of surveillance, it was a learning technique, predicated upon a system of apprenticeship based largely on modeling. On many different occasions, I heard Masons praise the values of careful observation and the ability to "read people." Vittorio, for instance, the Knight Templar I had first met at an agape dinner and who had been a Mason all his adult life, gave me a lengthy explanation of how he had actively trained his daughters, when they were only children, to observe people. In his words, "We used to drive in the car, and I would tell [my daughters], 'I'll give a hundred liras, or ten liras—whatever it was at the time—to whichever one of you can tell me what that man on the sidewalk was doing, or who we just passed,' and that's how I taught them to pay attention."

Vittorio's and Ines's emphasis on training when it comes to "reading people" was the expression of widely shared values of Masonic pedagogy and epistemology. Paying attention was necessary for Freemasons to learn to decode the esoteric symbols scattered throughout the profane world they inhabited, and to find connections with other members of their secretive "community of practice" (Lave and Wenger 1991).

When the ability to "steal with the eyes" was applied specifically to high culture, Masons would learn from each other more than what would be available through reading books or hearing lectures. As Loredana noted earlier, she could read the Kabbalah herself with the erudition of an autodidact, but she needed her Maestra or Maestro to teach her by example, so that she could learn how to perform her knowledge in a social context. Loredana's remark about the importance of modeling was also rooted in the culturally significant distinction between cultivation and erudition. Taking modeling as a pedagogical technique, an apprentice's successful performance could then be measured by its close emulation of the Maestra's gestures. Attending museum openings, plays, classical concerts, or poetry readings, new Masons could learn from the behaviors of others how to appreciate high culture, how to perform intellectualism *correctly*. In turn, by watching others and by learning from their lived examples, a Freemason could cultivate inner sensibilities that would ultimately refashion him or her into a certain kind of person: a cultivated, cosmopolitan subject of "good character," with a taste for beauty and elegance ideologically reified through the primacy of the discourse of high culture.

Thanks to Mozart

On a Sunday afternoon a few months after I moved to Florence, I went to the main city theater, the Teatro del Maggio Fiorentino, to meet a friend for a Schubert concert. I arrived early and decided to take cover from the autumn wind inside the packed lobby, which still betrayed some of its old splendor through layers of renovations. In early November, most of the older women in the crowd had already found comfort in the warm embrace of thick brown fur coats, which seemed to form an impenetrable net of fur balls throughout the lobby, interrupted only by the occasional slim silhouette of a man in a dark suit. I was looking around for my friend, when I noticed instead a couple of familiar faces.

Standing by the stairs were two women in their late sixties, their hair dyed blond and curled around their faces. I had heard at times some of the younger Apprentices in the Grand Women's Masonic Lodge of Italy (GLMFI) joke irreverently that their Maestre must all be going to the same hairstylist. The two women were looking around, as if they, too, were waiting for someone. I had first met them in September at a white agape gala dinner organized by a men-only GOI lodge to celebrate the fall equinox and the ritual of St. John. Like many of the women at that agape, these two were Freemasons in their own right, although they had attended the event only as guests of their GOI husbands or friends, whose official policies prevented them from recognizing the validity of women's initiation.

Although we had not been formally introduced, I decided to walk over to greet the sisters. At first they did not recognize me, but then I mentioned discreetly the context of our brief acquaintance, referring to the fall equinox agape as a "dinner on September twenty-first" and calling the Grand Maestra of the GLMFI, whom I had accompanied there, by first and last name, rather than by title. Their voices immediately cheered up and we began to chat. As it turned out, they were waiting for some of their lodge sisters to arrive, and they asked me to wait so that I could greet them, too.

Within a few minutes, four sisters and their husbands—most of whom were also Masons—were standing in a circle discussing their impressions of the new orchestra director, and comparing their various experiences as seasoned theater-goers. One woman in particular, the first one I had recognized, was especially displeased with the way she had seen the Florentine theater lower its standards over the years, and remembered with nostalgia the nights she had spent at La Scala Theater in Milan. At La Scala, she claimed, women still dressed in evening gowns, whereas in Florence—she looked around at the crowded lobby, shaking her head in disapproval—"one might as well wear jeans." To her, a theater was a microcosm of its city, and she claimed that it is in the theater that one can find a city's people.

While her remark about jeans was clearly intended to be hyperbolic, as most attendees were in fact wearing business-formal attire, it is meaningful for the ways it anticipated her conclusion: that the decadence she perceived in the status of the main theater of Florence was a sign of moral decadence among Florentines. Interestingly, the discussion was not strictly about the quality of the musical performance, though there were certainly conversations about good directors "lost" to the orchestras of other cities or "stolen away." Rather, this Mason's commentary was about the state of *her* city. The suggestion that a city's people can be found in the city's theater—an untenable proposition, from a political economy perspective—is rather indicative of the particular social imaginary this Freemason held true. Assuming the high culture of classical music, especially in a venue as expensive as the city theater, to be representative of the values and possibilities of the Florentine "imagined community" is to forget the material conditions for the performance and accumulation of cultural capital.

The connection between culture and capital is made all the more evident by the woman's critique of theatergoers' attire. Her comment about the failure of Florentine audiences to show respect for high culture through their clothing assumes the prestige of classical music as much as it connects its aesthetics to an ethical sense of personal and collective responsibility. High culture is thus turned into a site for subjective refashioning—one in which the cultivation of musical taste is not independent of other bourgeois sensibilities (of dressing, posture, mannerism), whose material conditions are hidden within an ethical discourse of propriety and goodness.

Musical taste is a critical node in the production of cultural capital. Given that Western classical music was not commonly taught in public *licei* even at the time of my fieldwork, musical knowledge had to be acquired by other means, be it private lessons or concertgoings. Music therefore escaped the formal equality of scholastic opportunities and was most evidently a matter of high culture.[14] Several of the Freemasons I met, for instance, both women and men, had season passes to the *teatro*, where they regularly attended classical concerts and operas.

Although my informants' appreciation of classical music could be performed in the profane, upper-class site of the city's main theater, it was also often performed in the esoteric space of a lodge. Or, more accurately, it was also performed in those liminal sites that I have called "spaces of discretion." Those were spaces in which a Masonic public was discreetly conjured through acts and practices that while obvious to those "in the know" could nonetheless remain invisible to the profane, even and sometimes especially if those spaces were in plain sight. A coffee shop, for instance, that hosted an open lecture series on Masonic topics unbeknownst to their profane patrons, or a landscape carved with esoteric architectural references meaningless to the untrained eye, could be examples of spaces of discretion.

There were occasions in which Masonic temples themselves became spaces of discretion. A few times a year, the Masonic lodges I studied opened their doors to a profane public, albeit a carefully selected and invited profane public, for what were supposedly public cultural events, such as lectures and round-table discussions, attended not in ritual garments but rather in profane business attire. If the temple happened to be large enough for the anticipated crowd of participants, its layout would be changed, additional chairs brought in, and a technological apparatus of microphones and speakers set up on top of what used to be the Worshipful Maestra's or Maestro's seat of honor, at the Orient. Alternatively, a lodge might rent the conference room of a local hotel or the private room of a large restaurant to accommodate their curious guests. The theme for these events would be chosen from an array of intellectual topics that might interest a wider, profane audience: music, art, and literature were among the favorites.

On one of these occasions, the women-only GLMFI had sponsored a lecture inside their Florentine temple on the Masonic symbolism embedded in Mozart's music. Giorgio, the invited speaker, was an amateur musicologist who had cultivated his passion for classical music outside of his corporate engineering job. A sister I knew described him to me as "a man of letters" (*un uomo di lettere*), using a common phrase to indicate cultivation, which Giorgio derived from his knowledge of music and of liberal arts, rather than from his financially remunerative engineering job. He was also a member of the men-only GOI.

I had met Giorgio before at several of the GOI events that I had attended, and he knew about my project and about my interest in gender and Freemasonry. Although the two organizations do not recognize one another officially, personal connections between GOI and GLMFI members—as spouses, friends, or relatives—were so common that brothers and sisters were usually seen at each other's social events. It was not surprising, therefore, that a GOI brother would participate in an event organized by the GLMFI. In this case, Giorgio was a personal colleague and friend of one of the sisters who invited him to speak.

Since the event was taking place in the sacred space of a GLMFI temple, however, there was some concern among several sisters that the brother might "get in trouble" with the GOI for entering the temple of a Masonic lodge that they did not recognize. Addressing the audience before the beginning of the presentation, two sisters in charge of the event assured us that this was not a ritual activity. Nobody was wearing ritual gowns, and the compass and square that must be placed open on an altar whenever a Masonic lodge is operative were not even in the room. Giorgio was there simply as a private citizen, they informed us, just a friend, and not as a brother. Giorgio himself attested to his unofficial capacity, but added that just to be on the safe side, he would not be advertising his participation in this event back in his GOI lodge. The audience nodded knowingly.

Giorgio began his talk by describing his childhood interest in classical music, growing up deriving an inexplicable sense of understanding (*comprensione*) from the works of classical composers, Mozart above all. His talk had the mystical, soul-searching undertones so characteristic of Masonic tavole and speeches. An insatiable quest for knowledge was often the underlying leitmotif of Masonic narratives, and his was no exception. Then Giorgio paused for a moment, looked up from his notes, and added with a matter-of-fact tone something that is at the core of the relationship between high culture and Italian Freemasonry: "Many people, including myself, have approached Freemasonry *also precisely thanks to Mozart.*"

Most of those present—sisters, a few brothers from other lodges, and their profane guests—nodded in agreement, as Giorgio returned to his notes and to describing the musical passion for Mozart that eventually brought him to Freemasonry.

Giorgio played for us parts of the *Magic Flute* and of *The Marriage of Figaro*, each time focusing on the *tempo* of particular segments, pointing out how it paralleled exactly the tempo of certain Masonic rituals, down to the precise knocks of the Worshipful Master's mallet, which Giorgio held in his hand as he demonstrated the similarities, and arguing explicitly that what Mozart was depicting in his music was indeed a Masonic ritual (see also Macpherson 2008). The audience followed with interest, contributing questions and comments that betrayed a high degree of familiarity not only with the structures of Masonic rituals but also with a wide range of the works of *brother* Mozart, who had been a Freemason himself.

The audience's knowledge of nuanced elements of Mozart's work was a re-flection and an affirmation of their privileged class positions. The talk on the esoteric symbolism of Mozart's music, however, went a step further than simply reproducing class taste. By bringing together the secular and the esoteric, the talk conjured a form of intellectualism that reaffirms the primacy of European liberal arts as an exclusive and hegemonic discourse, while simultaneously as-cribing the ability to master it only to those initiates able to decode its hidden symbolism. In other words, the speaker presented Masons as better connois-seurs of high culture than similarly situated (upper-class, cultivated) profane individuals. For one would not fully appreciate Mozart if one did not also know how to listen for the esotericism contained within his music.

Ironically, this implicit claim remade high culture into a more exclusive domain of knowledge at the same time as it appeared to open it up to a wider audience at a public event, an audience that included some profane guests. Those profane individuals, who were only there as guests of some of the Free-masons present, since they could not otherwise have found out about this unadvertised public event, were potential recruits for the lodges. Claiming brother Mozart thus served a dual purpose. First, it showed Freemasonry to be a path toward high culture, which Masons were in a better position to un-derstand and appreciate than their profane counterparts. Second, it ascribed legitimacy to the Masonic path, which without the prestige and respectability of high culture could be simply dismissed or ridiculed as an esoteric, fringe cult.[15] By claiming that Mozart had influenced his decision to become a Mason, Giorgio drew an explicit connection between the cultural capital of musical taste and membership in an esoteric society that is highly suspect in Italy. His inexplicable connection with Mozart was rhetorically constructed as a natural sensibility, a matter of "taste," that was later cultivated through the speculative labor of Freemasonry. For Giorgio, high culture had worked as a password into esotericism. His desires to better understand the music of brother Mozart had first led him to seek out a Masonic initiation.

The Mozart talk showed a recurring play of gender dynamics. In this performance of high culture, it was a man who came to speak to the women's lodge about music. As was the case at several other talks I attended, the women's lodge had opted to invite a male outsider, rather than enlist a competent sister for the task—a decision that might have unintentionally reproduced at the institutional level some of the expectations on expertise and intellectual labor that I knew many of my women informants struggled with in their own homes. To be sure, however, the decision to invite an outside male speaker was also strategic. It was a way to bring members of the most influential Masonic organization in the country, the men-only GOI, into the smaller and less established women's Masonic lodge to become acquainted with the sisters and with the caliber of their speculative work. Indeed, Giorgio told me how much he admired the sisters and how impressed he was with their "excellent work." In the gendered hierarchies of Freemasonry, it was usually up to men-only lodges to validate, compliment, or otherwise assess the speculative labor of women.

Despite Giorgio's personal sympathy for the work of the women-only GLMFI, his own group was adamant about excluding women from Freemasonry as a whole, thus considering "irregular" all lodges open to women. Like several other men I spoke to in the GOI, when I asked him directly during an interview, Giorgio expressed ambivalence about the issue of women's initiation, despite the fact that he had helped the GLMFI under the table. GOI brothers often articulated their ambivalence as a tension between, on the one hand, the pull of what they recognized as a changing social world, where women's equality to men has become at least discursively normative among liberal subjects, and, on the other, the intransigence of *la tradizione massonica* ("Masonic tradition"), which they invoked as a static imperative against forces of transformation.[16]

The issue of women's exclusion from Freemasonry ran deeply through my fieldwork research as I examined the social conditions of possibility of women's initiation to Freemasonry and the sisters' enactment of fraternity not only to form solidarity with each other but also to claim a legitimate space within Freemasonry. In contrast to those esoteric and cosmological arguments for or against women's initiation that were debated explicitly within the lodges (e.g., that Freemasonry is a solar cult; that women are not free and therefore cannot be Freemasons; that women cannot keep secrets and would by nature violate the initiation oath), there was another powerful and yet unrecognized force at work in the exclusion and marginalization of women Freemasons: the gendering of the discourse of high culture. As Masonic speculative labor is essentially intellectual work, and the content of such work is often European high culture, then women's exclusion from large sectors of Freemasonry cannot be disentangled from women's exclusion from critical aspects of the production, accumulation, and performance of high culture as cultural capital.

Socrates' Wife

One evening I was invited to dinner at the house of two Freemasons. Both husband and wife belonged to Masonic lodges, the GOI and the Order of the Eastern Star, respectively. During a seemingly benign dinner conversation about pets, they asked me for the names of my many cats. One in particular caught my informants' attention—the name of what was then my youngest, Santippe (or Xanthippe, in English). As my hostess recognized immediately and with great interest, Xanthippe was Socrates' wife.

Before she could say anything else about the origins of my cat's name, her husband interjected, with an astonished look on his face: "Darling . . . have *you* heard of Socrates' wife? How do *you* know the name of Socrates' wife?"

What ensued was a perhaps too predictable scene of marital bickering, as the wife took offense at her husband's apparent lack of faith in her cultivation, and the husband continued to make matters worse by gleefully complimenting her for knowing a piece of history of philosophy that, according to him, most people would not know.

This seemingly ordinary scene of family squabbling betrays deeper hierarchies of difference within Masonic lodges specifically, and within Italian society more broadly. I relate it here as a parable about the gendering of knowledge, and about the issue of contention that I kept encountering in my fieldwork: which knowledge mattered (secretive, esoteric, profane, or otherwise), and who could make a legitimate claim to it. In this Freemason's condescending compliment to his wife, for instance, one can read not only the assumption of the wife's ignorance (and, incidentally, mine too) but, also, the affirmation of his own cultural capital, expressed through a proprietary claim to knowledge of ancient Greek history and philosophy.

Ironically, the specific case in point is centered on the controversial figure of Xanthippe—Socrates' wife, who has gone down in history as the nagging shrew who dared to question the wisdom of her husband's self-sacrifice. Famous for trying to persuade Socrates of the futility of his suicide, and for suggesting that he leave Athens instead, Xanthippe has come to represent over the centuries the quintessentially feminine inability to comprehend the masculine discourse of philosophy. As a symbol of women's ineptitude for intellectual pursuits, the figure of Socrates' wife reminds us simultaneously of the historical gendering of humanistic knowledge as masculine and of the continuing importance of humanistic knowledge as a battlefield for social equality.

During the twenty years of Fascist dictatorship in Italy, the social repercussions of this gendered hierarchy of knowledge became clear, as women were legally banned from pursuing university degrees in the humanities but continued to be permitted to study the sciences (De Grazia 1992; Macciocchi 1976). In its sexism, the Fascist ban also revealed the prevalent epistemological hierarchy of the time that placed humanistic knowledge above the sciences. Intellectual discrimination has taken more subtle forms in recent decades and through generational differences, especially as the humanities have been increasingly feminized and science and technology have risen in value in global political economies. Nonetheless, humanistic high culture continues to hold a special place in the Italian national imaginary and in everyday practices of difference. Unlike what might seem common in countries like the United States, where feminist scholarship has been deeply preoccupied with sexism in the sciences, all the while taking for granted the dominance of the sciences over the humanities, I remember my own days in an Italian *liceo*: all my science and math teachers were women, but many of the humanities instructors, and certainly all the philosophers, were men.[17]

By evoking intrinsic qualities of talent, and therefore denying the social conditions from which it arises, high culture was a contested site of knowledge claims among Freemasons too. Beneath the surface of an egalitarian system represented by the learning path from Apprentice to Maestra or Maestro, which rhetorically was said to be open to anybody, the circulation of high culture among lodge members effectively marginalized all those bodies deemed incapable of "getting it" or naturally ill-disposed to it, including women. The connection between aesthetic dispositions and race or social class has been the object of important scholarly attention (Domínguez 1986; Frykman and Löfgren 1987; Liechty 2003), and even Bourdieu's (1984) *Distinction* could be read as a helpful critique not only of class struggles but also of other forms of identity patrolling that rely on knowledge and high culture as the criteria for exclusion, such as gender.

Just like the bounded-culture concept that now causes embarrassment to most anthropologists, high culture too is often talked about as a possession.[18] It is something that some people (nations, groups) have, while others do not. Although it is often imagined as belonging to educated, upper-class citizens, high culture in Italy has historically been constituted more specifically as the property of certain classes of men. When performed by others, as in the wife who knew of Xanthippe, its appropriation is strident, noticed, and marked. In this sense, the discourse of high culture is like words in a language that resist translation. As Mikhail Bakhtin described those words, " [They] sound foreign in the mouth of the one who appropriated them and who now speaks them; . . . it is as if they put themselves in quotation marks against the will of the speaker" (Bakhtin and Holquist 1981: 293).

This may be an apt metaphor to capture some of the performative aspects of high culture. Within Freemasonry, where a Maestra's modeling should lead to an Apprentice's emulation, and the performance itself was ascribed an ontologically creative potential, then how would different bodies learn to perform high culture? The Masonic brotherhood often gave rise to a self-fulfilling prophecy of gendered intellects, expecting some men, but not women, to embody cultural nobility. In interactions among Freemason men and women that I observed, a gender-based cultural distinction, superimposed on hierarchies of seniority and class, was unmistakable. For one, many of the brothers, with the exception mainly of younger Apprentices, seemed to embrace a self-confident intellectual persona, which they displayed constantly by embellishing their conversations with sophisticated references and citations. During gala dinners, informal conversations, and open lodge meetings, men who had reached the degree of Maestro in the Masonic hierarchy would, more often than not, display their cultivated intellects for all those in the audience, including women, fellow brothers, and the profane, through acts of verbal dexterity.

Most of the sisters I met, on the other hand, would often preface their comments to me—even the most elaborate and thoughtful analyses of Freemasonry itself—with self-effacing disclaimers. In large crowds, only women who had climbed to the highest degrees of the Masonic hierarchy and had been in the path for most of their lives would display their mastery of high culture through performative acts similar to those of most men. In those cases, their intellectual observations might be met with surprise ("Darling, how do *you* know of Socrates' wife?"), admired deference (as Apprentices often showed), or awkward silences. Rarely, however, were they met with the intellectual respect that for men would lead to exchange and engagement.[19]

My observations of the ways gender "compounded with" (Weston 2002) other hierarchical relations relevant to the Masonic context are not meant to suggest too simplistic and binary a gender divide between loquacious men and quietly self-doubting women, or between intellectual men dominating the conversation and intellectual women struggling to be heard. If most Mason men performed knowledge more ostentatiously than most Mason women of equal status did, the difference is not due simply to gender ideologies prevalent in Italy. It is also because of the very gendering of high culture as a discursive play outside of material history, whose performers and audiences are assumed to be the unmarked subjects of civilization.

Within the narrative structures of high culture and its performances, the silence of many Mason women over intellectual topics at dinner tables is not an end in itself to witness and analyze. As Mary Steedly argues, the problem is not women's silence but their inability to convene an audience: "This is not, of course, simply a matter of drawing a crowd, but rather of gaining attentive and comprehending listeners, which requires *narrative plausibility* as much as *strategic self-dramatization*" (1993: 198, emphasis added).

The question of women's "narrative plausibility"—even in the case of cultivated, high-ranking Freemason intellectuals—is inseparable from the narrative conventions of high culture, which, in the European context, has developed essentially as a masculine discourse. If high culture is a gendered discourse, and its performance requires "narrative plausibility" and "strategic self-dramatization," then women's embodied performances often appeared implausible and had difficulty convening an audience.

The self-cultivation efforts of women Freemasons must be understood within the framework of this particular knowledge path, simultaneously ethical and aesthetic in its aims, historically situated in the European Enlightenment, yet grandiose in its universalistic claims. Contesting male privilege and aspiring to it for themselves, older sisters in particular performed high culture as much as their brothers did, asserting their cultural capital both in relation to men of equal status as well as in relation to lower-ranking sisters and brothers. They would therefore act as models for younger women Freemasons. In so doing, however, they were inevitably espousing a masculine discourse that effectively limits what counts as high culture to works produced by men and for men. They were not choosing, for instance, to rediscover neglected women writers or philosophers, as several Italian feminist collectives have done.[20] Instead, they were reaffirming the primacy of the European masculine high culture canon by assuming its universal relevance.

This choice need not be surprising. Coming from the upper classes, and mostly locating themselves firmly in the right wing of the political spectrum, virtually all my women informants explicitly rejected feminism, which they saw as an extremist and leftist social movement. Instead, by learning to master the canon of high culture *as is*, some Mason women embraced an empowerment strategy that could increase their legitimacy within their social class, but which would leave existing power relations largely unmodified.

Conclusion: Of Distinction and Discretion

> High culture is nothing but a child of that European perversion called
> history, the obsession we have with going forward, with considering the
> sequence of generations a relay race in which everyone surpasses his
> predecessor, only to be surpassed by his successor. Without this relay race
> called history there would be no European art and what characterizes
> it: a longing for originality, a longing for change. Robespierre, Napoleon,
> Beethoven, Stalin, Picasso, they're all runners in the relay race, they all
> belong in the same stadium. ‹MILAN KUNDERA, *Immortality*›

In my time among Freemasons, I was often under the impression that my cultural capital was being tested. This had nothing to do with my PhD in anthropology, but rather with my intellectual credentials with respect to high culture. To be sure, most people at first sight assumed I had none. Not only has humanistic intellectualism been historically presumed to be a man's activity in Italy, but it has largely been construed as the province of white men. After all, high culture is a nationalist and therefore racialized set of knowledge practices. It was only after considering that I was educated in Italian public schools that some warmed up to the idea that I might be familiar with philosophy, Italian literature, art history, or Latin (all mandatory subjects).

High culture is a uniquely generative site from which to understand my informants' self-cultivation efforts. The presence of high culture in Masonic circles was as pervasive as it was naturalized. Unlike esotericism and rituals, it was not a body of knowledge that Freemasons engaged self-consciously. None of my interlocutors ever told me that Freemasons study high culture. Yet, they did not need to say so. Every tavola I read or heard, every semipublic Masonic talk I attended, and certainly most of my informants' profane activities, interests, and hobbies betrayed to various degrees their passion for high culture. What they would say is that Freemasons pursue knowledge and ask questions. It was as a result of discourses of Occidentalism much larger than Freemasonry that what counted as a lifelong knowledge quest inevitably privileged European high culture.

It is possible, of course, that high culture was not any more discussed, appreciated, or present among my interlocutors than it would be among profane upper-class and upper-middle-class Italians more generally. Among Freemasons, however, high culture acquired additional significance beyond, for instance, its inherent nationalism and ethnocentrism, and even beyond its marking of class distinction. I found that high culture worked in practice as a password into the esoteric society of Freemasonry. My interlocutors might not have been all equally wealthy and they did not all work equally prestigious jobs, but all the Freemasons I met were *persone di cultura*, cultivated people, whose intellectual curiosity for an ideologically selective version of beauty and elegance corresponded to a moral imperative to be someone "of good character." High culture was both a precondition of Freemasons' moral refashioning, as well as its medium, through which naturalized tastes and sensibilities were cultivated into certain ways of being in the world. "Thanks to Mozart" they might be inspired to join Freemasonry, and through the speculative labor of the lodges they might in turn cultivate their belonging into an elite esoteric society. Those presumed incapable of mastering high culture were largely left out of the Masonic brotherhood, even if cultural capital was never stated explicitly as a criterion for initiation.

In his attempt to carve out an anthropological definition of "culture," Edward Sapir went to great lengths to distinguish it from its other meaning of "high" culture—the meaning that anthropologists were not supposed to be concerned with.[21] In his discussion of high culture, Sapir wrote that "the cultured ideal is a vesture and an air. The vesture may drape gracefully about one's person and the air has often much charm, but the vesture is a ready-made garment for all that and the air remains an air" (1960: 82).

To describe the cultured ideal as a "vesture," however, is to assume it to be an outer layer, rather than an internal self; moreover, it is to assume that it can be worn by different bodies with equal poise. In this chapter I have sought to highlight the production of a particular subjectivity and of particular performative acts through each other (Butler 1999; Mahmood 2005). By combining scholastic pedagogies with an esoteric training in intuition and in "stealing with the eyes," my informants' speculative labor taught them how to embody dispositions and sensibilities befitting of a Freemason so that they could ultimately remake their own subjectivities. While refined taste for high culture might be either naturalized—thus denying the labor of its production—or, alternatively, might be imagined to be learned through transparent mechanisms, such as public schooling, not every body can incorporate its value and perform it with ease. Understanding the lodges' speculative labor and the forms of symbolic capital that they engendered is crucial to understanding the persistence of patterns of exclusion among Freemasons, despite their inclusionary rhetoric.

For many older Maestre, performing high culture as much and as well as their brothers—without the self-deprecating humility of many younger sisters—was part of an intellectual project of self-cultivation. The *correct* performance of high culture, which is also a performance of discretion, has more to do with its style, with knowing how much to reveal and when to stop, than with its content. It is this discreet performance of knowledge ideologically deemed to be high culture that confers distinction upon its practitioners. Indeed, discretion and distinction are etymologically cognate, and the literal meaning of discretion is precisely the discerning power to make distinctions. Sisters knew that they had to prove the quality of their speculative labor—both in terms of esotericism and of high culture—to men who were often skeptical of women's Masonic initiation. Members of the women-only GLMFI, for instance, usually invited GOI brothers to participate in their public events, but even men's praises of women's speculative labor served to naturalize men's proprietary claims to intellectual and ritual work in the lodges. In their discreet performances of high culture, women Freemasons sometimes needed to reveal more than they concealed in order to be seen at all as legitimate members of Freemasonry and in order to achieve that distinction, which at least for older Maestri was largely uncontested. As an embodied set of practices, discretion was performed differently by differently situated bodies, and in the next chapter I will turn to the ways in which women's invisibility in Freemasonry factored into their strategic decisions about how to be discreet in response to dominant conspiracies and scandals implicating Freemasons in the darkest side of Italian politics.

In relation to high culture, however, discretion had to be used not simply to earn status or privilege but to facilitate a learning process that for my interlocutors would ultimately bring about a profound personal transformation. High culture for them was not simply a "vesture" to wear cynically or pragmatically, but rather a sign of an inner disposition that merged ethics with knowledge and aesthetics, and which would remake, in turn, their own selves through a path of self-cultivation. Ultimately, Masons' pursuit of knowledge was never for knowledge's sake but in the name of a salvific project of social goodness. And if the notion of the "new world order" has fallen in disrepute in our times of late capitalism, the *novus ordo saeclorum* of Masonic prophetic dreams for my interlocutors continued to be a universalistic and humanist vision of social progress, rooted in a profoundly Occidentalist repertoire of values and knowledge, and often unaware of its own contingent histories.

In the everyday lives of the Masons I met in Italy, a set of practices of knowledge accumulation and embodied performances came to define and to reify what it meant to be "a Freemason within," and high culture was a powerful but unrecognized site for such subjective refashioning. In the face of the profound rift between Freemasonry and much of Italian political and civil society, however, not even the distinction conferred by high culture, with its attachments to nationalist and Occidentalist mythologies and its assurance of class privilege, could shield the brothers from pervasive suspicions about their sources of social and economic capital.

PASSWORD III

———— * ————

In Masonic terminology, an *agape* (pl. *agapi*) is a banquet. After the end of a formal meeting, especially on celebratory occasions, the members of a lodge would share a meal together. This fraternal feast, as they often described it, follows specific, codified rituals that regulate the consumption of food, wine toasting, and the role of the participants. Although ritual agapi were reserved for the initiated members of a lodge, "white" agapi (*agapi bianche*) were open to profane guests as well.

Like many other Masonic customs, white agape dinners could appear, at the same time, curiously familiar and yet rather uncanny. Their explicit purpose was to extend the gift of fraternity beyond the doors of the temple, outside the lodge and its members. It was a practice that brought Masons and non-Masons together into a space that was neither entirely esoteric nor unequivocally profane. What might have appeared, at first sight, to be simply an elegant group dinner had more to it than the opulence and aesthetic cultivation of a gala. To be sure, the settings (and probably most of the participants) of the agape could have been the same at an upper-class, profane gala dinner. Yet, there were clues and markers that made it noticeably different. The topics of conversation, for instance, included discussions of numerology (or alchemy or the Egyptian pantheon) that evoked esoteric forms of knowledge, in addition to repertoires common to many middle-aged, upper-class individuals in Italy. During one of the agapi sponsored by the Grand Women's Masonic Lodge of Italy (GLMFI), for instance, a major preoccupation among some of the participants was a soccer match taking place that evening. After receiving frequent, whispered pleas for updates, the waiters swirling around tables had simply begun to serve updated information about the ongoing game with every new course. White agape feasts therefore represented one of the most experience-near contexts in which the Masonic and the profane were revealed as a mutually constitutive dyad rather than two ontologically separate worlds. Both participants and practices of the agape feast brought together elements of the Masonic and of the profane that reconfigured each other in the process.

This was the case that night. The invitation had been printed on thick parchment and showed a picture of a painting by Leonardo da Vinci. On the bottom, below the announcement of the ritual, it read "white agape will follow—RSVP requested." We followed seating charts to find our table among the beautiful frescos and golden-framed mirrors of the baroque hall, where attentive waiters served us a five-course meal and ensured our wine glasses were always full. Despite its spectacular display of wealth and social and cultural capital, however, the agape was not simply a gala dinner.

Standing around looking for their seats, many of the guests were half-jokingly complaining about their assignments, not at all because of the company, but rather because of their table number. Right before dinner, Valeria told me they had had to make some last-minute changes and asked me if I would mind moving from table 3 to table 2. When I told my previous tablemates, some of whom I knew quite well, that I would have to leave them, they politely expressed their disappointment, but also added that they felt sorry for me, since I was clearly headed to a worse table. I was not sure what they meant. In the geography of the hall, table 2 was closer to table 1, where the Grand Maestra was sitting. Moreover, those sitting at table 2 were fellow sisters and some of the honorary guests. I simply could not understand why table 2 would be any worse than table 3 with respect to either location or occupants.

One of the sisters I had worked with closely over the course of my research was quick to put my doubts to rest. It was not a statement about the company I would find at table 2, she assured me. She did not even know who was sitting at table 2. It was just that the number of the table, 2, was not as good as theirs, 3. The men and women next to her were nodding in agreement, and one continued to explain that the symbolic meaning of the cipher 2 is not quite like the meaning of 3. I stood there for a few minutes, as my former tablemates engaged in a discussion of numerology with one another. I knew that numerology was one of the many kinds of esoteric studies cultivated within Masonic Orders and, especially, within Rites. To see numerology being applied to as mundane a context as the table assignments of a gala dinner in an antique hotel in the center of Florence, however, was yet another instantiation of the porous boundaries between the profane and the Masonic.

The most significant ritual performed during an agape was always the toast. To be exact, the seven toasts. Toward the end of dinner, as desserts were being served, we filled our glasses with champagne and followed the Grand Maestra in the execution of the seven toasts, each dedicated to a celestial body and to its human counterpart.

It's a Masonic tradition to make seven ritual toasts.

Sisters, brothers, welcome guests, please stand:

The first toast was dedicated to the Sun, king of nature, center around which all celestial bodies gravitate (raise your goblet), and we address the first toast to the Head of the State, may he always ensure our peace.

Fire!

The second toast was dedicated to the Moon that guards mysteries most secret in its pale light, and we address it to the Order's governing board, the Grand Women's Masonic Lodge and the Federal Council that protect the order and guide it wisely, thanking especially the former Grand Maestra and the former Federal Council for their work.

Fire!

The third toast was dedicated to Mars, who presides over both councils and battles, and we address it to the honor of our most respected Grand Maestra, whom we freely chose as our guide. We drink to her health and that of her family, to the success of her projects, her works, and the achievement of her ideals.

Fire!

The fourth toast was dedicated to Mercury, whom the Egyptians had named Anubi—or the Ever-Watchful God. We address it to the Senior and Junior Warden, who keep order and watch over the instruction of all sisters.

Fire!

The fifth toast was dedicated to Venus, goddess of generation, and we address it to our newly initiated sisters. They follow bravely the initiation path and they apply themselves diligently to become perfect Masons. We wish them health and perseverance in their quest for truth.

Fire!

The sixth toast was dedicated to Jupiter, also known as Xeno, god of hospitality. We dedicate it to our welcome guests, Grand Maestre, and Grand Officers of the Orders that have honored us with their presence. We drink to their health, to the prosperity of the lodges they represent, and to the fraternity that should unite all lodges in the world.

Fire!

The seventh toast was dedicated to the planet Saturn, whose immense orbit seems to embrace the whole world. We dedicate our seventh toast to all sisters and brothers scattered throughout the world, wishing wisdom and moderation to those who are powerful, and wishing health and the return of good fortune to those who suffer illness or misfortune. Finally, to those who are about to leave us and who are preparing themselves to undergo the ultimate initiation—that which the profane know as death—we wish courage and strength to face the Eternal Orient.

Fire!

After each toast, we shouted "Fire!" (*fuoco*), as if firing cannonballs in celebration. The toasts were formulaic, repeated as part of a codified ritual, rather than being an impromptu expression of sentiments. In the white agapi of other Masonic lodges, I had witnessed the same seven toasts being performed, and except for a few slight modifications (e.g., toasting to a Grand Maestro instead of a Grand Maestra), they were essentially very similar. Indeed, the earliest codifications of the seven ritual toasts in a Masonic lodge date back to early eighteenth-century England (Mainguy 2004: 374). At the beginning of the twenty-first century in Italy, those earlier texts had clearly been adapted to the current political context, and the first toast to the sun, for instance, had been dedicated to the office of the president of the Republic of Italy, the head of state, so that he may "always ensure our peace."

That very first toast was also the most remarkable in that it was an explicit gesture of embrace toward the profane world. Toasting to the sun and to the head of state implied recognition of the authority of the Italian state, embodied in the figure of its president. The first time I heard it, I had been very surprised. Because of the separation of church and state in Italy, religious spaces, which are primarily Roman Catholic, are usually devoid of any explicit symbols of the state. For instance, unlike many religious institutions in the United States, churches in Italy do not typically display the national flag or make any reference to government offices.[1] Although Freemasonry is not considered a religion, its spiritual and esoteric endeavors inside temples devoted to the Great Architect of the Universe make it nonetheless a spiritually driven institution. It was therefore surprising for me to discover that the ritual works of a lodge always begin with the singing of the Italian national anthem, and that the Italian flag is often displayed inside Masonic temples, and that the first ritual toast, to the sun "around which all celestial bodies gravitate," is not dedicated to the Grand Maestra, supreme head of the Order, or to the deity of the Great Architect of the Universe. Instead, it is dedicated to the head of state, the profane figure presiding over the country. Such nationalist symbols are conspicuously absent even from many sites of Italian civic institutions, let alone religious ones (unless, of course, the World Cup is on).

The fact that Freemasons would place so much emphasis on nationalist symbols is in part a relic of their nation-building histories. In the twenty-first century, however, the dedication of the first ritual toast to the president as the first and highest authority also served to assert Freemasons' loyalty to the Italian state. It affirmed symbolically that Freemasons do not operate outside the law of the state but, rather, within it, respecting it and cherishing it. In the context of longstanding accusations against Freemasons as subversives undermining the state's democratic processes, this toast carries quite a laden set of meanings, and it anticipates some of the wishes contained in the final toast, for the powerful in the world to be wise and moderate and for the suffering of many to be appeased.

While the first toast was dedicated to a profane office, most of the others celebrated various Masonic figures working within the GLMFI as well as guests from other lodges, and brothers and sisters "scattered throughout the world." The rhythmic poetry of the toasts, spoken aloud and performed by the participants through repetitive bodily acts, gave solemnity to a ritual that could seem out of time and out of place. In the urban center of Florence, amid profane waiters and hotel personnel assisting customers at what might appear to be a gala dinner, seven toasts to Jupiter, Mars, or the moon, to the Grand Maestra, the Wardens, or to those who have undergone their last initiation to the Eternal Orient—the term Freemasons used to refer to the afterlife—might seem bizarre. The seven ritual toasts made during agape dinners were a prime example of the inextricability of profane and Masonic practices.

To be sure, some self-censorship happened at times among Masons facing profane crowds. When I had heard the seven toasts in other agapi, for instance, some times they had omitted any explicit reference to the planets. Some of my informants had explained that erasure to me as a precaution, insisting that they had used "discretion" because the restaurant waiters and other customers could have overheard them. Even when planets were omitted from the performance of the ritual toasts in white agapi, however, several other elements of the feast might have raised suspicions among profane strangers, leading to the perception that something was quite weird.

A white agape required a good amount of discretion. To host an agape a Masonic lodge needed to confront the public space of a profane service industry, including restaurant waiters, hotel receptionists, managers, and other strangers whose beliefs about Freemasonry were, at best, unknown. While I attended white agapi inside a Masonic temple or even in my informants' homes, most took place in public venues. The choice of location often required some research. In the case of that particular GLMFI agape, the designated hotel halls and catering services had already been used by the GOI earlier that year. In general, my informants would propose venues where they personally knew the owner or that had been recommended to them. In most cases, these were rather upscale locations, revealing my informants' own positions and networks within the social hierarchies of the profane world.

White agape dinners were more often than not at locales in which the performative display of opulence unfolded against a backdrop of nationalistically rich histories, in Renaissance buildings or baroque restaurants that a lodge splurged to rent for the occasion. For a profane person considering being initiated to a lodge, these agapi were often the first points of contact with a wider group of Freemasons, giving all parties an opportunity for a mutual exploration of fit in a public location, separate from the hidden temples. The agapi's spectacles of wealth contributed to an image of Freemasonry as firmly elite, and thus consumeristically more desirable. At the same time, their opulence, which effectively framed the agapi as gala dinners, also provided a sugar coating to the perhaps less palatable aspects of Masonic practice a neophyte would be confronted with: the eccentric rituals and sinister practices so often associated with Satanism and fringe cults. Hints of esotericism could thus be dropped in a nonthreatening form, like seven ritual toasts to celestial bodies made with champagne in crystal flutes, or a solstice celebrated inside a baroque ballroom. Each instance represented a discreet revelation of Masonic rituality, open but immediately closed again, to elicit desire but not to fulfill it.

Transparent Conspiracies

Citizens have the right to form associations freely and without
authorization for those ends that are not forbidden by criminal law.
Secret associations and associations that, even indirectly,
pursue political aims by means of organizations having a military
character shall be forbidden. ‹ *Article 18, Italian Constitution* ›

You study Freemasons? Really? They should all go to jail for
what they did. ‹ *A left-wing law student in Florence* ›

One fine morning in September 1993, Gianna woke up to a startling discovery.
Her husband's name was in the newspaper. There was no mistaking him, even
though she kept wishing that it could all be just one big misunderstanding.
Gianna told me that she stared at the page in front of her as if in a trance. Along
with her husband's first and last names, the newspaper had also printed his date
of birth, place of birth, occupation, and current city of residence: "Rossi, Mario.
Born 2 February 1942 in Prato, FI. Bank employee. Rome."

Next to his biographical information, one additional entry completed the
listing: her husband's Masonic Order of affiliation, the Grand Orient of Italy
(GOI). On that same page, as on many pages before and after, Gianna read row
after row of other names—many friends, acquaintances, and relatives—listed in
black and white for there to be no mistaking them. The newspaper that morning
had published the membership lists of the major Masonic Orders in Italy.

Gianna's voice still trembled many years later, in 2006, as she and I sat together in her living room, right outside the center of Rome, revisiting the experiences of the previous decade. She recalled how sick she had felt, viscerally, physically sick, as her finger had run through the pages, reading all the names and birthdays published in that paper, and then in other daily and weekly newspapers, national and local presses, over the following weeks, as more and more lists had gone public. Leaning back on her sofa, she rested her head on the palm of her hand as she shared her memories with me. All these years she had kept the publications tucked away in the back of a shelf behind some encyclopedias. She showed them to me as we spoke, insisting that I had to see them with my own eyes if I wanted to understand the anger and disbelief in hers.

Between September and October 1993, some of the most widely acclaimed and respected national and local Italian newspapers published lists of any men currently or previously affiliated with the major Masonic organizations in the country, including the men-only GOI and the mixed-gender Grand Lodge of Italy–Piazza del Gesù (GLDI). The lists had presumably been leaked to the press by Italian secret services, following over a decade of intensive surveillance of the lodges suspected of subversive activities against the state. With thousands of names to publish, some newspapers had to devote most of their pages to the lists, while others had to publish them in installments over a few issues. For instance, *L'Unità*, the newspaper founded by Antonio Gramsci and still a bastion of left-wing information, published an entire separate booklet on Tuscan lodges, included free of charge with the daily issue. Over the course of a few weeks, the papers published over twenty thousand names like that of Gianna's husband, sorted by geographic region and listed in alphabetical order.

Many of my informants in Florence still had copies of that booklet in their personal libraries. Often I happened to be at someone's house for a late afternoon tea when something in the conversation or something in the daily news brought up memories of the early 1990s, the "dark times." They would ask me if I had ever seen the "blacklists" before, and then they would fetch the booklet or an old newspaper from a bookcase—knowing exactly where it was. Over ten years later, my interlocutors were able to talk about it with some degree of humor. "Look, my fifteen minutes of fame, as Andy Warhol said!" one man told me. Often, though, their accounts were still permeated by a deep sadness. Whenever I asked them if they knew anybody else on that list, their answer was always the same. They knew plenty of other people whose lives, just like their own, had been affected by the lists. It was a public "outing," as Masons called it, using an Anglicized word they borrowed from the Italian gay rights movement. It was a forcible coming out that exposed thousands of Freemasons to ridicule and to persecution in the name of transparency, security, and the public's right to know.

One glaring omission, however, marked the lists of Italian Freemasons: women were missing. Gianna's own name was not published, and neither were the names of her sisters, the many women Freemasons who have long populated women-only and mixed-gender lodges, but who continue to be virtually invisible in mainstream representations of Freemasonry as a brotherhood of men. The blacklists of Italian Freemasons, published in the name of transparency to eradicate the secrecy of the lodges and thus to undermine their power, would appear to have missed entirely women's existence.

In this chapter I explore women's absence from the blacklists as a striking example of the limits and contradictions of transparency itself. The legal and political discourse of transparency has gained popularity in societies across the globe, where transparency is increasingly used as a measure and signifier of good governance and democratic values. Recent studies of transparency, however, have situated its rise within neoliberal ideologies, and they have shown the uneven, contested, and at times impossible applications of transparency claims in practice (Garsten and De Montoya 2008; Hood and Heald 2006; West and Sanders 2003). For women Freemasons, the state-sponsored deployment of transparency that left them largely invisible was a reminder of their ongoing invisibility within Freemasonry, even as they struggled to effect their own self-cultivation project: to become women Freemasons and therefore genderless brothers.

Deployed against Freemasons through the spectacle of the lists, transparency was a multivalent political tool, one that Freemasons themselves eventually reappropriated. In an ironic twist of political history, some Masonic Orders in the early twenty-first century decided to go "transparent" as part of a publicity campaign to rehabilitate the name of Freemasonry. This ethnographic case therefore raises crucial questions about both the paradoxical workings of transparency within liberal democracies and the unanticipated uses of transparency as a tool of subversion by social actors who find themselves under surveillance. How does transparency's promise of an all-seeing eye work in practice to reiterate dominant structures of difference, such as gender? How does transparency as a technique of governance manage to conjure new subjects into being, under the guise of simply exposing existing ones? In turn, how do these "transparent subjects" appropriate the tools of transparency deployed against them to soften the duress of their predicaments, and what acts of subversion might be possible from the blind spots?

Reviewing my informants' practices of transparency, always carefully enacted with "discretion," I suggest that a feminist anthropological study of the political and legal discourse of transparency can help elucidate the workings of transparency as a gendered discourse deployed in complicity with other ideologies of difference, which inevitably mediate its uneven effects on different bodies.

Freemasonry and Terror

Unlike Masonic lodges elsewhere, Italian lodges of the early twenty-first century largely continued to operate in secrecy, hiding their temples and activities in undisclosed locations. Lodges typically hid behind façade organizations, in whose names they rented out office spaces that they were actually using for their temples. Moreover, with the exception of the Grand Maestre and Grand Maestri—the national leaders of Masonic organizations—who are public figures, the lodges with which I worked guarded carefully their membership lists. Most of my informants negotiated very cautiously their self-presentations in the profane world outside of Freemasonry. Many of them were not out to any of the non-Masons in their lives, including their profane family members. Among those who told their relatives, some had faced a profound rift in familial relationships, while others had found support, understanding, or at least denial. One of my interlocutors, a woman in her late thirties who was the Worshipful Maestra (the leader) of her local lodge of the mixed-gender GLDI, told me, for instance, about the knowing silence between her and her profane father about Freemasonry. Even though they did not discuss the topic explicitly, she sensed that her father had come to some peace about it over the years, "now that he has seen that I didn't turn out to be a right-wing terrorist after all."[1]

This last comment, self-evident to an Italian audience, might seem odd. A father's fear that his Freemason daughter will turn out to be a right-wing terrorist might sound especially foreign to a North American audience used to the presence of Masonic lodges as a staple of small-town living. In Italy, the association of all things Masonic with a dangerous elitism was fairly common, and popular representations of the lodges attributed to them powers that were extraordinary, if mostly nefarious. This father's fear for his daughter reflects popular portrayals of Freemasonry in Italy as a sinister brotherhood, a second state within the state, whose powerful members infiltrate networks of power and run the country from behind the scenes. In other words, as nothing short of a terrorist organization.

Before the term *terrorist* was co-opted as a signifier of a Muslim/Arab/jihadist brown or black other in much of the world in the early twenty-first century, it used to evoke quite a different image in Italy. Black or red, Fascist or Communist, the figure of the terrorist crystallized in the 1970s and 1980s, during the period known as the Lead Years (*Anni di Piombo*), when bullets and bombs brought the country to chaos. In those years, the fight for political control played out as much in official campaigns as in the violent confrontations between far-left revolutionary groups, such as the Red Brigades, and far-right neo-Fascist militias. A string of bombings of streets, trains, and train stations, mostly attributed to right-wing groups, killed and injured hundreds of people, producing a state of generalized insecurity in the country. At the same time, political attacks culminating in the kidnapping and murder of Italian prime minister Aldo Moro in 1978, attributed to the Red Brigades, attempted to paralyze the state's political machinery.[2]

The role of Freemasonry in the terrorist acts of the Lead Years has been a profoundly controversial subject, debated in Italy's highest judicial courts' rulings. Popular representations of the Lead Years have suggested that state intelligence agencies worked with parastate actors and, allegedly, with Freemasons to create the conditions of possibility for a far-reaching repression of leftist organizations. While Masonic lodges have not been legally convicted of any crimes, individual Freemasons have been repeatedly under investigation for political corruption, for nepotism, and for their alleged involvement with the Mafia. The self-evident association between Freemasonry and right-wing terrorism continues to prevail not as a fringe conspiracy theory but rather as a popular common sense, espoused by mainstream news outlets, left-wing politicians, and ordinary citizens. Many in the Italian Left and Center have long suspected the lodges of being behind the "strategy of tension" of the Lead Years.

Consider, for instance, the words of two judges who presided over the initial trials for the Bologna train station bombing of 1980—a terrorist attack that left eighty-five dead and over two hundred injured, and of which two neo-Fascist militants were eventually convicted:[3]

> An *invisible power* has established itself in Italy, and as it is connected at the same time to both organized crime and terrorism, to political-military environments, secret services sectors, and *Freemasonry*, and as this power moves simultaneously on all these levels, it has been able to take control of institutional mechanisms to such an incredible extent as to become its own *state within the state*. (Cited in Bollini and Rossi 1994: 5, emphasis added)

Inscribed in the official records of the court proceedings of the trials for the terrorist attack in Bologna is the specter of a vast conspiracy. As themselves agents of the state, the judges in that case sanctioned the popular view that

Freemasons are traitors to the state and are guilty of failing their own citizenship in the most violent ways. In this quote, however, Freemasons are also equated metonymically with the state itself, and they are called a "state within the state," a phrase that echoes common attributes of the Mafia (Schneider and Schneider 2003).

The discursive merger of organized crime, Freemasonry, and the state found in the judges' words, as well as in popular conspiracy theories about Freemasonry, posits the state not simply as a static arbiter and enforcer but, more significantly, as itself an object of mistrust. The state here appears infiltrated, compromised, and thus delegitimized. Paul Silverstein (2002) has suggested that conspiracy theorizing, at least in the context of the Algerian Civil War, is a multivalent tool capable of reinforcing the dialectical structure of hegemonic processes. He has argued that rather than attributing conspiratorial thinking only to marginalized or resistant factions of the political spectrum, conspiracy theorizing should be recognized as a shared tool of political culture (Silverstein 2002). In Italy too, where conspiracy theorizing is a style of political engagement readily available to all ideological sides, conspiracies about Freemasons have the effect of both strengthening and weakening the state. Conspiracies that portray Freemasonry and the state as simultaneously oppositional and metonymical have the effect of casting a shadow of doubt on the integrity of both.

Such representations are not unique to Freemasonry, but they are instead part of a wider political lexicon used to articulate tensions among the state, organized crime (e.g., the Mafia, the Camorra, and other similar groups), Vatican influences (e.g., Opus Dei, Catholic parties), and ideologically divided party politics (Galt 1994; Herzfeld 2009; Jacquemet 1996; Kertzer 1980; Però 2007; Schneider and Schneider 2002). It is therefore helpful to recognize the representations of Freemasonry in Italy not as exceptional but, rather, as indicative of broader ideological tensions that structure Italian politics. In so doing, conspiracy theories must be recognized as legitimate forms of political knowledge production.

Many anthropologists working on state terrorism and counterterrorism have highlighted the problematic position of an often anthropomorphized state, itself implicated in conspiratorial practices (Aretxaga 1997) and producing dangerous citizens through the terrors of its democratic enforcements (Greenhouse, Mertz, and Warren 2002; Panourgiá 2009; Taussig 1986). In Western Europe and the United States , however, the dominant self-congratulatory discourse of liberal democracies makes the equation of state and terror appear oxymoronic, with the result that conspiracy theories are often relegated to the delusions of paranoia (Marcus 1999). In the United States , for instance, to call a political opinion a conspiracy is often to dismiss it as invalid, thus delegitimizing its proponents. Moreover, the information system underlying state secrecy is articulated through a technocratic apparatus of clearances, hierarchies of access, and bureaucratic procedures designed to legitimate state authority even in its most conspiratorial moments, and not to undermine it (Masco 2006).[4]

The Italian state is somewhat at the margins of these Euro-American political imaginaries of governmental efficiency and legitimacy. A general mistrust of the state's effectiveness characterizes Italian political common sense so pervasively that conspiracy theories are in fact, more often than not, mainstream theories, just as they are in many parts of the global South. Conducting fieldwork in Italy, I needed to take conspiracies seriously not in the sense that their content must necessarily be true, but in the sense that, as a form of political knowledge production, conspiracy theories can prove just as revealing or concealing, and just as ideologically informative, as news reporting, political speeches, or state archives. In other words, I take conspiracy theories seriously in the context of Italian fieldwork because to dismiss them tout court would be to participate in another kind of ideological work: one meant to instill blind faith in a democratic state.

Freemasons in Italy were not only the objects of conspiracy theories, but they also constructed their own conspiratorial ideations about the state and about Catholic and Communist forces in the country. Many of my informants, for instance, often complained that "only in Italy" could such displays of anti-Masonic sentiments occur. Cristina, a Maestra in the Grand Women's Masonic Lodge of Italy (GLMFI) who had traveled to Masonic conferences in different countries compared her experiences to those of her European and American brothers and sisters, concluding that in those "truly democratic countries" Freemasons did not need to be as secretive. We laughed together about how absurd it would seem in Italy to list a Masonic temple in the phone book, even though that is precisely the case in many other countries. Cristina felt very strongly that only in Italy did lodges need to be as secretive as they were in order to protect themselves. She was worried about being unjustly harassed by state officials, but she was also worried about acts of interpersonal or terrorist violence because of how many people in Italy loathe Freemasonry. Her concern with issues of safety echoed those expressed by many other Freemasons who had asked me in all seriousness, what if a madman decides to leave a bomb outside the temple?

Freemasons participated in the same conspiratorial theorizing that many in Italy deployed against them, expressing fear of terrorist acts by political enemies and of persecution by state agents, such as the police. Unlike left-wing conspiracies, which in Italy mostly suggest a fear of a state viewed as corrupt, the Masonic conspiracies I heard from my informants mostly indicated fear of enemy political forces—of Catholics and Communists above all. Despite these differences in attributions, both transparency demands and conspiracy theorizing operated as multivalent tools, used by differently situated actors in the Italian polity to further radically different ideological stands. In other words, conspiracy theorizing, just like transparency, was a broad style of doing politics in Italy that cannot be attributed only to a particular marginalized group or to a particular state agenda. While the Freemasons I met usually attributed their ongoing "persecution" to the undue influence of the Catholic Church on Italian politics and to the dominance of left-wing parties on politics and media, much of the public attributed Freemasons' ongoing impunity to their social connections.

To be sure, there are valid reasons for the resilience of anti-Masonic conspiracy theories in Italy. In the 1980s, Masonic lodges, which were already suspected of being behind many of the terrorist attacks of the Lead Years, were thrown into the middle of one of the most infamous and spectacular political scandals in Italian history: the P2 case. Much too entangled in a web of Orwellian proportions to recount fully here, the P2 case required a congressional investigation and an eleven-year trial in the Supreme Court (Rossi and Lombrassa 1981).[5] To many, it provided irrefutable confirmation of the nefarious truth about Freemasons. I briefly recount it here because during my own fieldwork it became clear that the P2 case was still referred to by Freemasons and by the profane alike as the main reason for the continuing surveillance of Italian Freemasons into the present.

Propaganda 2, or P2 for short, was the name of a covert Masonic lodge operating within the men-only GOI, the largest and oldest Masonic Order in the country. In the pyramidal structure of Freemasonry, a covert lodge operates as a secret society within a secret society. Its existence was known to the Grand Maestro, but not to any of the other lodges within the same organization. Although the history of the P2 dates back to the nineteenth century, the lodge appears to have operated with increasing autonomy in the 1960s under the leadership of its Worshipful Maestro, Licio Gelli, who has since become a household name in Italy. In 1976, after growing internal tensions, the Grand Maestro of the GOI finally revoked the P2's charter, thus officially dismantling the lodge. From that moment on, it appears that the P2 continued to operate as a secret criminal society, no longer under the purview of the GOI.[6]

According to the records uncovered by police and secret services, the P2 lodge counted over a thousand members, including ministers and members of parliament, supreme court justices, military generals, bankers, secret service agents, journalists, and even allegedly one media tycoon, and later Italian prime minister Silvio Berlusconi (Guarino 2001).[7] When the existence of the P2 was revealed to the public, what emerged was the specter of an organized network of powerful men plotting right-wing coups, terrorist acts, and multimillion-dollar bank fraud throughout Italy, Europe, and Latin America. The P2 was therefore the very embodiment of long-held fears about Freemasonry: a brotherhood of men conspiring to bring about a new world order through oligarchic control of the financial markets, the media, the military, and the governments of individual countries.

The consequences of the P2 scandal were devastating for Italian political life and for Freemasonry. In the years that followed, as some of the members of the P2 were tried for crimes ranging from embezzlement of public funds to criminal conspiracies, treason, and attempted coups, the police and secret services continued to search Freemasons' homes and temples all over the country. It was as part of the ongoing surveillance of Masonic lodges by Italian authorities that in 1993 the membership lists of all major Masonic organizations in the country were confiscated and then leaked to the press.

In The Name of Transparency

In September 1993 the DIGOS, an elite branch of the Italian police fighting terrorism, political crimes, and organized crime, with the help of secret services, stormed into Masonic lodges all over the country. The large-scale, coordinated police raids took place almost simultaneously all over Italy. Some brothers were brought back to the precincts for questioning; others were arrested. Homes and temples were searched; all membership lists were confiscated. During my fieldwork, between 2004 and 2006, I heard many of my informants remember the events of those "dark times," as they often referred to the early nineties. Gianfranco, for instance, a Maestro in the men-only GOI, told me about the day the DIGOS came into his lodge and took away their lists along with one of his brothers. Later in the day, he received a phone call from an old friend of his, a magistrate who had reviewed the evidence brought back to the precinct. "Gianfranco, do you know your name is on these lists?" His friend had asked him. "Yes, I am aware," Gianfranco had answered. Incredulous, his friend the magistrate went on. "Do you know who else is on these lists? The most respectable [per bene] people in [our city] are all on these lists!" "Yes, I am aware of that too," Gianfranco had told his friend, and looking at me, all those years later, he added: "In our province, there were nineteen thousand registered members of the Communist Party then. It was a Freemason hunt [*caccia al Massone*]. A few days later the lists were published by the papers."

My informants' memories echoed each other very closely—including police searches, bugs found in temples, personal threats at work and at home, and the certainty that both Catholic and Communist forces were to blame. One of my informants in the mixed-gender GLDI was Ornella, a woman in her late sixties whose warmth and great sense of humor in the face of personal adversities made her very likeable. I knew that many of her lodge sisters and brothers had a profound respect for her. During a small gathering with some of her Mason friends that I attended, the conversation happened to turn to the lists and the scandals. It was striking to watch this kind, cheerful woman I had come to know suddenly be overtaken by anger and hurt at the mention of those events.

Ornella told us she could not breathe when she first read her father's name in the newspaper. She liked to say that she had grown up in Freemasonry, knowing pretty much everyone and anyone from a young age. So that morning she recognized virtually everyone in the published lists of Freemasons living in her city. When she came across her father's name, however, she became very worried. He was old and his health was not good. She feared that his high rank within the GLDI could make him an easy target of public attacks. Ornella composed herself enough to call him immediately, at 6:00 a.m., still holding the paper in her hands. She said her father answered the phone after a few rings. He sounded unusually cold. "They are already here," he had told her with an unnatural calmness, and then he had hung up the phone before she could ask for more. Ornella rushed to her father's house, but by the time she arrived, police investigators had already torn it apart. The police had come banging on the door at 5:00 a.m., search warrant in hand. As she told us her story, Ornella kept cursing under her breath the name of the prosecutor responsible for those investigations—he had become famous in Italy, advancing his career through the trials of Freemasons. By midmorning, she continued, memories of a lifetime were scattered all over the place in the house of her childhood that Ornella said was never quite the same to her. Nonetheless, her family had been "lucky," she conceded. One of the other sisters in her lodge, she told me, was still waiting for the police to return her family jewels, which they had confiscated from a safe-deposit box in 1993.

One of Ornella's guests asked me if I had seen what was in the papers just that week. Yes, I had. She was talking about news stories pointing to Freemasons in the latest political corruption scandal. In the scheme of things, and given the recursivity of Italian scandals, those had been minor stories.

"Yes," I answered. "And I saw that the GOI issued a statement denying . . ."

Ornella cut me off abruptly. "Denying? I'm sorry."

I wasn't sure if she was sorry for cutting me off or for what she was about to say next.

"Scusami, eh, ma che cazzo nega il GOI?" ("I'm sorry, but what the fuck can the GOI deny?"). Ornella continued without taking a breath: "They [the GOI] are the ones who did the P2, and they deny, but in the mean time we all have to pay for what they did."

She blamed the GOI for the wrongdoings of the P2, despite the fact that the deviated lodge had no longer been authorized to operate under the GOI's charter by the time it began its criminal activities. Nonetheless, the GOI bore moral culpability in her eyes for not stopping the P2 sooner, for not seeing what was about to happen. And two decades later, as unspecified "Masonic influences" continued to be attributed by Italian media to most political scandals, regardless of whether actual Freemasons were involved in the specific case at hand, she blamed the GOI for that too. She blamed the GOI for turning *Massoneria* into a dirty word.

Meanwhile, I knew from GOI brothers like Gianfranco that by now, whenever "something happens" (a scandal potentially involving Freemasons), the local chief of police would call their headquarters for help. They are on very good terms, the brothers had assured me. In Gianfranco's words, the police and the GOI had been working together in the interest of justice. When I had talked to him, he had told me that the GOI, rather than the state, had done the right thing.

"Ultimately," Gianfranco had told me, "we were the only ones who condemned the P2. What did the state do? Nothing. We put them [Freemasons involved with the P2] on trial, we found them all guilty, even the ones who didn't go to jail." As a Freemason, Gianfranco didn't have any more faith in the Italian justice system than many profane citizens did. In his mind, the GOI had at least made sure some justice was done. Freemasons who had been involved in the P2 were all sentenced to death and expelled from the GOI after undergoing a Masonic trial, which he insisted was more than could be said for the Italian state. From that moment on, the GOI had led the way in doing a lot of *pulizia interna*, internal cleaning of the lodges, becoming transparent and cooperating with law enforcement.

Before I turn to an analysis of those practices of transparency that the GOI spearheaded and that other lodges followed, it is worth noting the blame game in which many of my interlocutors participated. Like Ornella, who blamed the GOI as much as a career-driven prosecutor for the suffering of her family, many of my interlocutors suspected other lodges and other Freemasons of bearing responsibility for Freemasonry's bad reputation.

Good Masons, Bad Masons

As an older Maestra once patiently explained to me, there were "good" Masons and "bad" Masons. Good Masons believed in the principles of equality, fraternity, and freedom that were at the basis of the path. They wanted to pursue knowledge to become better people and to improve society. Bad Masons, on the contrary, had joined a lodge in the hopes of finding material gain, motivated by greed and desire for personal profit. These bad Masons had many names in my informants' parlance. Some referred to them as *bottegai* (shopkeepers), *affaristi* (businessmen), *furbi* (crafty ones). Whatever the word, it typically emphasized material, pecuniary motives and led to an unabashed condemnation of bad Masons as a disgrace to Freemasonry. It was never clear, however, who these bad Masons were or where they could be found. Everyone knew they existed, although nobody seemed to know one personally.

Most of my informants agreed that "business" did happen inside Freemasonry, but insisted that neither they nor their friends had ever been involved. The content of such business—what, exactly, was being transacted, if anything— and its frequency were also confusing matters. Angelo, the young Apprentice in the men-only GOI whom I met in Florence, put it rather theatrically. "You know, even if they do sometimes exchange favors, it's not like they say . . ." He hunched forward and faked a Sicilian accent to parody the sound of an elderly *mafioso* trafficking in the most coveted contracts and permits of the time. "'I'll give you that bridge and you'll give me that new high-speed train line.' No, I never saw anything like that!"

Several Masons felt offended at the suggestion that they might be conducting illicit affairs inside lodges. Most Freemasons I interviewed generally located the sites of business in other lodges. For instance, Chiara, a woman in her early forties who was an Apprentice in the mixed-gender GLDI, insisted that Freemasonry would in no way aid her in her career as an architect. On the contrary, because of Freemasonry's reputation, she had to keep her affiliation a secret from her coworkers at the firm where she worked. "If a young lawyer," she told me, "wanted to build his career through this [Masonic] path, he would not come to us [GLDI], because we do not have the power that the GOI has. If your objective is to see an improvement in your career, you wouldn't come to us." Most of the Freemasons I met had a similar way of dispelling any doubts regarding their integrity, while still acknowledging that some "business" might be going on among other Masons—"bad" Masons—in other lodges. Often, such instances of blaming mapped onto existing rivalries among groups, such as between the mixed-gender GLDI and the men-only GOI, which represented the two largest Masonic organizations in Italy. Chiara's words attributing to the GOI a tempting potential for career advancement, and simultaneously denying such capacity to the GLDI, echoed those of some of her lodge brothers and sisters. The GLDI, though, was not the only lodge to shift blame elsewhere. Members of the women-only GLMFI shared similar concerns about the illicit activities of bad Masons and how they would impact Freemasonry's reputation. Most of the sisters I met, however, insisted that their organization was simply too small and certainly not important enough for any "business" to occur. It was among the men, many suggested, that such transactions could take place, in the GLDI or in the GOI. Some of the members of the Order of the Eastern Star (ES)—the auxiliary organization for female relatives of the GOI—felt a strong allegiance to their GOI relatives, and told me explicitly that they believed business transactions occurred most frequently in the GLDI, whose members, some claimed, were not worthy or respectable people ("non sono persone valide").

One evening, when I was at a GLMFI lodge waiting for the start of one of their public talks, I struck up a conversation with a GOI Maestro who was also waiting around. I was curious to hear his opinion on the matter of illegal affairs within Freemasonry, particularly because he belonged to the very organization that had produced the P2. I fully expected him to shift the blame onto the GLDI, but Paolo instead gave me a sardonic smile and began to talk the cryptic talk of so many Freemasons: "You see, all Maestri are equal. But some Maestri are more equal than others. Have you read Orwell?"

He was sitting at the desk of what was technically the antechamber of the temple, but that night it was just a convenient place to sit without being in the way of the sisters preparing their event. Paolo's dark suit jacket was unbuttoned to allow more room for his protruding stomach, a physical characteristic rather typical of older male Freemasons, and which they sometimes attributed to all those agape dinners they had to attend. He was playing with his tie and clearly waiting for me to say something about his Orwellian reference. He reminded me of the Cheshire cat, with a complacent smile to oblige my curiosity. I decided not to press him, however. I had learned that an interested look could be more inquisitive than ten questions, and that my informants' disclosures were inversely proportional to my inquiries. So I sat quietly with notebook in hand, waiting for him to continue when he was ready. Sure enough, after a short pause Paolo decided to satisfy my curiosity. "Let me explain myself," he began.

Paolo told me that he was a Maestro, and therefore in the third degree of

Freemasonry. "Freemasonry has three degrees, Apprentice, Fellow, and Master, everyone knows that. The rest is nonsense [*stupidaggini*]." He was referring, of course, to the distinction between Orders and Rites. A Masonic Order contains the three degrees of Freemasonry. Once a Mason becomes a Master, however, he or she can potentially enter a Rite, an additional hierarchical path that leads from the fourth up to the thirty-third degree of Masonic enlightenment. Since the Order and the Rite operated independently of each other in the GOI, inside a particular temple on a particular night it should not make a difference whether a Maestro was a third-degree Maestro or a thirty-third-degree Maestro.[8] Those hierarchies should not overlap. Paolo's point, however, was that despite the official wisdom claiming that all Maestri are equal, some Maestri (those in the Rite) were more equal than others (those in the Order). That is why he had never wanted to be initiated into a Rite: he was a third-degree Freemason, and the rest was "nonsense."

The Rite maintained a code of secrecy much stricter than the Order. To enter a Rite, a third-degree Freemason could not apply, but rather had to be tapped from above.[9] Furthermore, members of the Rite were explicitly forbidden to out themselves, though I met several who did so anyway. Before I learned how secretive Rites were, and how discreet I should be about them, I asked a Maestra in the GLMFI directly whether she was also in the Rite. Her answer was a simple riddle: that she was not allowed to answer my question, and that therefore, by virtue of that answer, I should be able to guess the answer to my question.[10] The argument in favor of such secrecy was, ironically, a democratic argument. As several GOI brothers who were in the Rite explained to me, when they participated in the activities of the Order it was important to maintain equality among all Maestri. By disclosing their status within the Rite they would risk imposing a hierarchy that did not belong to the Order, and they might risk trumping the spirit of equality that should reign among Maestri in a lodge operating at the third degree. The mixed-gender GLDI, the only Masonic organization that united Order and Rite in one continuous hierarchy, made the exact opposite claim regarding secrecy, and found that their own system was much more democratic because it did not conceal the Rite from the Order.

According to Paolo, the transparency campaign undertaken by the GOI under the leadership of its Grand Maestro represented a position of overture embraced by the Order, but not by the Rite. "It's in the Rite," he insisted, "that you can find all the shopkeepers [*bottegai*]." Even in the United States, Paolo continued, where Masonic lodges are public knowledge, a recent president like George Bush Sr. was a thirty-third-degree Freemason. He asked me if I didn't find that interesting. Wouldn't that suggest, he asked me, that even in the United

States it is the Rites, and not the Orders, that keep all the secrets? Paolo was not the first of my interlocutors to speculate that even in the United States, where Masonic Orders are considered harmless and ultimately not that relevant to national politics, there might be powerful secrets traded inside Rites.

Regardless of their accuracy, Paolo's claims echoed a view held by a large part of the scholarly literature on Freemasonry. That is, despite the intentions or values of the institution as a whole, and perhaps despite the intentions of most of its members, the very structures of secrecy and hierarchy that characterize the lodges provide fertile ground for the development of secret societies *within* Freemasonry. Chiara, the Apprentice Mason in the mixed-gender GLDI, who had shared with me her conviction that an ambitious young professional would seek initiation in the more powerful GOI to forge connections, also admitted that sometimes she wondered about what goes on "up high" [*nei piani alti*] in her own Masonic group.

> My children sometimes hear something at school or in the news, and they ask me if I'm sure of the people [Freemasons] I know. I tell them, "You know them, Aunt Silvia, Uncle Francesco." That reassures them. The people I know, I would trust them with my life [lit. "I would put my hand over fire for them," *ci metterei la mano sul fuoco*]. To be honest, though, I have no way of knowing what happens on top of the pyramid, up high.

The narratives of blame and suspicion that Freemasons threw around toward other lodges and sometimes toward higher-ranking Masons in the Rites had a double purpose. First, they obviously ensured the innocence of the speaker, who had no direct knowledge of any wrongdoing, and whose own brothers and sisters were all "good" Masons. Second, however, such narratives also kept alive the dominant representation of Freemasonry as a powerful society where "business" was sure to happen. It is highly remarkable that my interlocutors, all of whom could easily have subscribed to a "party line" denying that anything at all inappropriate occurs in any Masonic lodge, were so invested instead in reproducing the dominant mythology of Freemasonry as a powerful network of secret-keepers, even if they were careful not to implicate themselves personally. "Interpellated" (Althusser 2001) as powerful subversives by media and bureaucratic state institutions, Freemasons attempted to resignify what it meant to be a Freemason, highlighting all their positive contributions to Italian society and denying that they had anything to hide. At the same time, however, my interlocutors could also play with the seduction of the limitless power attributed to them.

It was only after I developed enough "cultural intimacy" (Herzfeld 2005) with my informants that I began to hear some of my interlocutors admit, usually with embarrassment, that there was a curious appeal to the image of Freemasonry thrown around in the media.[11] They knew that image to be hyperbolic, of course, and insisted that they never would have chosen to be initiated if they had seriously believed that right-wing terrorists populated the lodges or that satanic rituals took place in the temples. Nonetheless, they found something intriguing, some confided to me, about the seemingly formidable organization that the state spent so much energy trying to defeat, and that was enough to spark their curiosity. Where state ideological apparatuses might have hoped, presumably, to instill unequivocal repugnance toward Freemasonry, the effects on the ground, within the concealment of intimacy, were in some cases quite opposite. Even among those who did not believe the publicly circulating narratives about Freemasonry, those narratives could nonetheless elicit, at least for some, an embarrassing desire for the power ascribed to it. One of the unintended consequences of the state's anti-Masonic campaign, which culminated in the publication of the blacklists in 1993, was the sharp increase in requests for new initiations that most lodges received shortly after the scandal erupted. Some of the sisters I interviewed who had been initiated in the mid-1990s credited the blacklists for making them aware of how many people they already knew were Freemasons, and for leading them right into the belly of the beast.

Transparency's Blind Spots

When I met Gianna, the Maestra whose story opened this chapter, for tea at her house, it had been almost thirteen years since the publication of the lists. She was a petite woman in her fifties, and for much of our conversation she had struck me as rather strong and confident, though her tone changed suddenly when we began talking about the 1990s. She told me about both her past and her current fears. She and her husband were both Masons, although working in different lodges. He was a member of the men-only GOI, while she had been initiated in the women-only GLMFI. That morning in September 1993, in which Gianna first woke up to the discovery of her husband's name in the paper, she also discovered something equally troubling. As she read through the pages and pages of names of outed Freemasons, she realized her own name was missing. Gianna was a Maestra, a third-degree Mason, just like her husband. And yet, neither her name nor the names of any of her lodge sisters had been printed in the newspapers. Women, it appeared, had been forgotten.

Gianna's account was not significantly different from the stories I heard from others. Yet our meeting was marked by warnings I had been given about her. As lodges had officially embraced the politics of transparency, they increasingly engaged in institutional and interpersonal practices of monitoring their own members. When they found out that I was going to meet Gianna for an informal interview, some of her sisters encouraged me to take her with a grain of salt, claiming that her approach to Freemasonry was a little more esoteric than some of the others were comfortable with. "Gianna is into magic, the occult, you know, those kinds of things," I had been warned. Some of the sisters were concerned that she might give me the wrong impression about Freemasonry—an impression, that is, more in line with conspiracy theories portraying Freemasonry as a cult, and less with the sanitized image they were trying hard to convey of a nonprofit, benign cultural association. I had also been warned not to disclose too much personal information to Gianna about my own research or my contacts because, some of the others suggested, she is "someone who asks for favors" ("una che chiede i favori"). This last concern was also clearly tied to larger considerations about Freemasonry's public image, specifically trying to fight the common view of it as a network of corruption and favoritism.

Gianna liked to say that she was a direct person, not afraid to talk about what Freemasonry gave her as much as what it took from her in terms of time, energy, and patience, especially dealing with some of her sisters. Though she did not get into too much detail, I knew her lodge had gone through some troubled times because of internal disagreements. At several parties and dinners, I had noticed that Gianna seemed to keep somewhat in the margins of the festivities, and indeed we had scheduled this appointment when I found her sitting by herself during one of those events. Although the sisters' concerns turned out to be unfounded—Gianna did not talk much about esotericism, nor did she ask me for any favors—they are highly revelatory of the ongoing operations of image control and reciprocal surveillance within Masonic circles.

As we sat in her living room sipping our teas in 2006, I asked Gianna to remember how she had felt in 1993 upon realizing that her own name was not on those lists. I asked her if she felt relieved that at least she and her sisters had not been outed in the papers along with their men. It could be argued that the pervasive invisibility of women in Freemasonry had for once worked in their favor, potentially shielding them from harm. Despite the presence of women in Masonic lodges since the eighteenth century, and their ongoing struggle for equality and recognition, it would appear that not even the transparency campaigns to out every Freemason in Italy had succeeded in exposing the simple fact of the existence of women Freemasons.

The irony of their predicament did not escape my interlocutors, the women in mixed or women-only lodges who talked to me about those "dark times." It was with sarcastic resignation that many of them acknowledged to me that they clearly "did not exist." Some members of the women-only GLMFI assured me that back in the early 1990s, when the lists were published, their organization was already legally registered with the authorities. The police, in other words, already knew that their Masonic Order existed. It was therefore even more shocking to them that their membership lists had not been confiscated and leaked to the press along with the men's. Emma, one of the older members of the GLMFI, one of Gianna's sisters who had long held leadership roles within the women-only organization, told me that in the aftermath of the publications she had personally phoned the local branch of the DIGOS, the special police, to offer her lodge's collaboration. "When I called them to say that we could register our lists with them if there was a need for it, they told me, 'Don't worry, we already know who all of you are. We are watching you.'" As this experience shows, the mechanisms of state surveillance that led to the outing of thousands of men Freemasons were also in place with regard to women, although with different effects.

Gianna told me that she had not felt fortunate at all. Even though her own name did not appear on the list, her husband's did. Freemasonry tends to run in families. Virtually all the women Freemasons to whom I spoke told me they had male relatives, or at least close male friends, whose names were published. "[Because of the newspapers] everybody knew now," Gianna told me, "that my husband was a Freemason, even if they didn't know that I was one too. So what's the difference?"

Many of my interlocutors had explained to me what it meant to be known as the wives or daughters of Freemasons. Throughout my fieldwork, I heard women talk about the effects of Freemasonry's sinister reputation on their own lives as mediated by their relationships to suspected men. As I sat in Gianna's living room, I remembered, for instance, the words spoken by an Eastern Star sister when I first began my project: "People think we are the wives of murderers." She had said it as a matter of fact, as if the truism of Freemasonry's significance in Italy would be self-evident to all. So what is the difference, Gianna asked me rhetorically, between being a terrorist, a criminal, a Mafioso, or a crook, and being his wife? "It's easy enough to laugh at it now, more than ten years later, but at the time I was so scared, I was so scared I would lose my job."

Gianna began to tell me about proposed legislation, at both city and national levels, which would have banned Freemasons from public office. Public office, she specified, would include teaching in public schools or working for city offices, not only holding political positions. It became a human rights case, she told me, referring to the 2001 European Court decision that eventually ruled in favor of Freemasons, condemning anti-Masonic Italian legislation as discriminatory (European Court of Human Rights 2001). After the lists were published, for a long time Gianna had continued to worry about both her own job and her husband's. He kept finding threatening notes on his desk at work, on his car, and even in their mailbox at home. Legally, they could not fire him, she told me, but Gianna was certain that the reason he had never received a promotion after 1993 was that his name had been on those lists. She told me that in the public *liceo* where she taught, they made her life very difficult, too. For months she had faced her colleagues' stares and the hate mail, "as if my husband had murdered somebody," and she believed that the principal and the other faculty were hoping she would quit her job. Gianna, however, never quit her job. "All things considered," she told me, "we were much luckier than others." She was referring to those who lost their jobs or the respect of their friends, or who faced legal prosecution.

The women Freemasons whose male relatives were outed in the lists were caught in an ideological paradox. On the one hand, as wives, daughters, or mothers of outed Masons, many of them had experienced open hostility and disdain in their workplaces, for their association with Freemason men made them culpable too, in the eyes of those who loathed the brotherhood. On the other hand, women Freemasons, unlike men, were not considered dangerous or threatening themselves. In my conversations with many profane people who were suspicious, to say the least, of the lodges' activities, I often heard women described as brainwashed for their choice to participate, even if only as wives, in the Masonic family. Even some of my informants' own relatives, the profane family members who knew about their aunts' or mothers' or sisters' Masonic affiliations, often spoke to me of women Freemasons as naïve and misguided. Many of those relatives held serious reservations about Freemasonry, and some of them expressed their concerns to me that women Freemasons might simply be too trusting of the men in their lives, and might not realize fully the kinds of dangerous power games that, in these relatives' opinions, must surely go on in Masonic lodges.

In other words, women Freemasons, including the highest-ranking Maestre I met, might be naïve or brainwashed in the eyes of others, but they could not possibly pose a serious threat. They might be married to dangerous men, complicit in the nurturing of subversive politics, and thus culpable by association, but not dangerous subjects themselves. What is remarkable about these portrayals of women Freemasons is that they leave intact the dominant representations of Freemasonry as a dangerous and subversive organization of men.

The existence of women Freemasons does nothing to mitigate the truism that Freemasonry is a dangerous society. At the same time, their involvement in the lodges is not enough to remake naïve women into potentially dangerous citizens. Dominant gender ideologies thus remain intact, with men Freemasons posing a threat to the polity, and women standing by their side, either as victims or unwitting fools.[12]

The reluctance to see women Freemasons as a threat while simultaneously perceiving Freemasonry as a dangerous organization underlined dominant stereotypes of Freemasonry as a powerful society of men. The notion of a woman Freemason seemed oxymoronic in most sectors of Italian society, where people were seemingly oblivious to the very possibility of that subject position: a woman and a Freemason.

In noting how gender affected the publication of the lists, I use gender here as a compound of subject positions (Butler 1999; Weston 2002). The women Freemasons among whom I conducted fieldwork had been invisible certainly because of their marginalized status within Freemasonry. The dominant image of a Freemason is still masculine. Women Freemasons, however, could also arguably remain invisible to the state, not raise red flags, and not seem to pose a security threat not because of their marginalization but rather because of their privilege. After all, how else could we understand the glaring omission of virtually all women from the lists of Freemasons? Are we to conclude that the same secret services capable of hunting down the Masonic membership records of important male government officials were simply eluded by almost all of the women? What would have stopped editors of newspapers throughout Italy, and their secret services informants, from disclosing women's names? Gianna conceded that it probably never occurred to the editors of those newspapers compiling the lists for publication that there were women Freemasons, too. But wouldn't have they seen women's names on the lists?

When Italian state authorities wished to expose Freemasons in the public forum of mass media, they did not simply list the names of a few public figures, which might have been sufficient for a journalistic scoop. The publication of the lists demonstrated instead a zealous commitment to a comprehensive exposure, capable of capturing as many individual Freemasons as possible, regardless of space constraints, even at the cost of publishing the lists in installments or in separate booklets offered to readers as complimentary additions to their daily papers. It is precisely the comprehensiveness of these efforts to turn mass media and secret services into all-seeing eyes for the state that makes the erasure of women Freemasons all the more significant.

Italy saw its share of female terrorists during the Lead Years—among both the

Red Brigades and neo-Fascist groups (see Braghetti and Mambro 1995; Glynn 2009)—but those terrorists were usually militant young activists, not middle-aged ladies. My informants were mostly upper-middle-class, well-educated, professional, white, heterosexual women with impeccable manicures and designer clothes who embodied bourgeois respectability and espoused a secular, right-wing morality. It was therefore a particular combination of marginalization within Freemasonry and privilege within Italian society, I would argue, that erased women from the blacklists of Freemasons. Their class and gender positions compounded to make women Freemasons irrelevant. Gianna, for instance, was in her late fifties when we met. A *liceo* teacher with a PhD in Italian literature, she was married to an economist who worked as a financial advisor for a bank. The kind of women my informants were simply did not register as a threat in the state bureaucratic logic of security, nor in the media-driven conspiracy theories about who is supposed to be driving the course of this new world order.

The publication of the lists provided a rare opportunity to intervene, potentially, on the ideological representations of Freemasonry in Italy. In the name of transparency, and in light of the evidence collected by the police, Freemasons could have been exposed as women, as public school teachers, or as housewives. They could also have been exposed as female politicians, lawyers, doctors, and journalists. They could have been exposed as multigenerational dynasties, since Freemasonry often runs in families, rather than as a horizontal oligarchy of men united only by their greed. Thinking about a number of possible alternative representations that might have been possible under the rhetoric of transparency and its attending structures of anti-Masonic surveillance might help to denaturalize the singular image that emerged from the published lists.

By taking seriously the erasure of women's names from the blacklists, I contend that such erasure cannot be properly understood as simply an accidental omission. Rather, this type of ignorance—one that is predicated, in this case, on prevalent ideologies of gender—is structural to the very deployment of transparency, and should be recognized as strategically motivated (see also McGoey 2012). As scholarship has already shown, transparency is a discourse produced within the context of neoliberalism and its attending ideologies (Garsten and De Montoya 2008; Strathern 2000). Transparency cannot therefore exist independently of the field of power within which it is inscribed. It is not possible to demand transparency from corporations or individuals, for instance, without already conceiving of corporations or individuals as given subjects, which, in turn, is only possible within a modernist logic of subjectivity (Foucault 1978). Feminist scholarship is especially helpful in demystifying political representation as a process that calls new subjects into being within the logic of democratic governance. As Butler has suggested, "the domains of political and linguistic 'representation' set out in advance the criterion by which subjects themselves are formed, with the result that representation is extended only to what can be acknowledged as a subject" (1999: 4).

The processes of subjectification underlying the construction of social and political life condition the possibility of any deployment of transparency as well. If Italian state officials demanded that Masonic lodges be transparent, the very expression of that demand was predicated on the intelligibility of Freemason as a subject category produced within uneven structures of power, including gender structures. The state's interpellation of Freemasons—both in the judicially authorized searches for their membership lists and in their subsequent outing in the newspapers—had the effect of not merely bringing to light those lurking in the shadows, but of producing the very political subjects they claimed to be searching for. In other words, only masculine subjects, perceived to be capable of being Freemasons and of being dangerous, were pursued and unmasked as Freemasons.

What is most striking about the published lists of Freemasons is therefore not what they revealed but what they obfuscated in their ostentatious refusal to make visible the very subject(s) they claimed to be exposing. By including only men, the lists represented Freemasonry as a masculine organization, reinforcing the idea that secrecy is only dangerous if gendered as masculine. Against all evidence to the contrary, the lists thus reified the very subject they claimed merely to expose, and confirmed what common sense had already told us: Freemasons were the usual suspects; the usual suspects were Freemasons.

Becoming Transparent Subjects (with Discretion)

Visibility is a trap. ‹MICHEL FOUCAULT, *Discipline and Punish*›

At the beginning of the twenty-first century, reeling from years of political and legal battles, the most prominent Masonic organization in Italy, the men-only GOI—the same organization that had produced the P2 in the first place—made a radical decision. In a highly controversial move, Gustavo Raffi, the elected Grand Maestro, decided to embrace the rhetoric of transparency that had been used against Masonic lodges up to that point. The formerly secret society thus decided to go transparent.

Under Raffi's leadership, the GOI began to expend an extraordinary amount of resources on in-house press rooms and PR offices charged with developing a new image for the brotherhood. The GOI started to host public events, such as lectures and receptions, to which they would invite members of the press, law enforcement, and city officials.[13] They built a website, providing information on the history of the Order, its values, and its mission. They became publicly involved in charitable projects, such as hospitals, homeless shelters, and programs for orphans, to show that Freemasons cared not only about Italy's cultural patrimony, as evidenced by the topics of their sponsored public talks, but also about their fellow citizens.

The lodges' attempts to improve their public image involved efforts to reach out to the profane world as well as increased control over their own members. Many of my informants told me that the lodges did a lot of "internal cleaning" as a result of the scandals. All the lodges I worked with now checked prospective Masons' police records before initiating them, and some even modified certain aspects of their rituals to counter the impression that they were a satanic, occult sect. The GOI, for instance, replaced its ritual garments—black hooded robes—with more palatable simple white aprons embroidered with Masonic symbols, which the brothers could wear around their waists over elegant business suits. The aprons were often the target of sexist jokes made by members of other Masonic groups at the GOI's expense ("look at those grown men with their ridiculous little aprons!"), but with their gendered connotations the new garments were effective in making the brothers appear harmless. More significantly, the GOI also modified the wording of its initiation ritual, replacing the Apprentice's oath, which carried the threat of a very painful death if ever broken, with a more somber "solemn promise."

"We have nothing to hide," Grand Maestro Gustavo Raffi claimed at a public allocution I attended in 2004 in a convention center the GOI had rented out for the occasion, in front of an audience that included Freemasons as well as city officials, law enforcement, and members of the press. "And we have no debts to pay to the justice system." Other Masonic organizations started to follow the GOI's example, and by the time of my fieldwork they already had a web presence and annual open receptions. "So people can see," in the words of another of my informants, "that we don't eat children and we don't sacrifice virgins." As Masonic lodges in Italy have taken extraordinary measures to prove to public authorities that they are not a secret society, my informants would often point to all of these strategies of transparency, and ask me, rhetorically, "How could we be more public than this?"

Anthropologists and other scholars working on transparency in recent years have shown the global resonance of this term (Florini 2007). The wide variety of case studies available in the literature on transparency, including analyses of governmental institutions, civil society, elected officials, corporations, and media, are a testament to the diversity of transparency's enactments and circulation. Throughout these varieties, however, a few patterns appear to emerge. First, regardless of whether transparency can be thought of as a "new" political and legal discourse, it can be linked to modernist desires for a democratic rationality expressed in the name of an underlying public, even if its actualizations might be characteristic of the "postmodern" (Schumann 2007; Vattimo 1992). Second, regardless of whether transparency is imposed on private citizens and institutions by a democratic state or, on the contrary, required of state apparatuses to be accountable to the people, the circulation of transparency implies, in most cases, some degree of duress that makes transparency discursively inseparable from surveillance and discipline (Finel and Lord 2002; Foucault 1979; Strathern 2000). Third, transparency, as an optical metaphor, is politically and morally contrasted to the opacity of secrecy, corruption, and subversion, despite the fact that such distinctions are historically and ethnographically untenable (Mazzarella 2006; West and Sanders 2003).

Within Masonic circles, the transparency campaigns I observed in my fieldwork were explicit strategies, carefully concocted within "closed chambers," as particular kinds of conspiracies to counter anti-Masonic state narratives. Masonic strategies of transparency drew from the power of positive self-stereotypes to refashion a new image for Italian Freemasonry. Often those strategies relied on Freemasons' historical contributions to the nation and to the making of its heroes and artistic patrimony, highlighting the lives of famous Freemasons like brother Garibaldi, brother Voltaire, or brother Mozart (Gnocchini 2005). Although transparency was a Masonic plot, it was not an antidemocratic conspiracy any more (or any less) than the transparency strategies designed in the press rooms of business corporations are understood to be antidemocratic conspiracies.

Freemasons' strategies of transparency were predicated on their active engagement in a discursive play that followed the rules of state bureaucratic logics. Lodges played within state ideologies, rather than without them, pouring extensive resources of media savvy and legal counsel onto communication technologies aimed not at subverting the state but rather at essentializing themselves in positive ways that would thus oblige the state. Freemasons' practices of transparency, received with great skepticism by some sectors of the profane public, were therefore in a profound way democratic conspiracies that enacted transparency with the full-blown honesty of its paradoxical and contradictory outcomes.

In the "cultural intimacy" of a trusted encounter (Herzfeld 2005), however, many Freemasons were willing to express views on their politics of transparency more complex than a simple espousal. Some members of the mixed-gender GLDI, for instance, found it dreadful that the GOI had caved in to political pressures to the point of changing their ritual. Ornella, for instance, the GLDI Maestra who blamed the GOI for the aftermath of the P2 scandal, said, "They [the GOI] now promise; they make a promise. I didn't promise anything. I took a solemn oath!" The GLDI had uncompromisingly maintained its rituals, including the long, hooded black robes donned by its members in the temples. Their decision—arguably a brave one in the political context in which it occurred— came from a refusal to accept the terms of the discourse of transparency and rationality used against them in the mass media. Like my informants in other lodges, members of the GLDI insisted that they had nothing to hide. Since they kept no secrets, in the profane sense of the word, they did not need to change their rituals to make amends to the state. It was the state, many would argue, that had unfairly persecuted them.

Virtually all my interlocutors recognized transparency as a legitimate democratic principle, but they often questioned the fairness of what they saw as selective applications of transparency to Freemasons. For instance, Margherita, a cofounder of the GLMFI who had shared with me the history of the women's lodge, once pointed out that all social organizations, including Catholic parishes, must be transparent to the state to some extent. "Of course, if there is a court order, then the president [of the Masonic association] can provide the documents, but honestly not even parishes post a list of their members with everyone's addresses to their doors, so why should we?"

This type of comment was meant to question the excesses of a discourse of transparency, and it underscored the difference between transparency as an abstract ideal and as a set of daily practices resulting from complex negotiations of privacy rights and notions of fairness and justice. Margherita reminded me that Freemasons are bound by oath not to disclose the identity of other Freemasons, to protect their privacy. "We have to be very cautious for the sake of those who work in a field where it might be very difficult to explain. If there's a scandal in the papers, it's immediately linked to Freemasonry, but Freemasonry has so many particles and little groups that do all sorts of other things. We are not given the chance to explain and say, 'Look, I'm not with them!' They judge us all by the actions of some." That is why, Margherita concluded in a familiar refrain, "we have to be discreet."

This comment reveals the complexities of a logic of transparency to which my informants ascribed but only, in their own words, with some *discretion*. Their fears for their safety, instantiated by concerns about possible attacks to the temples, and their fears of persecution by state agents meant that while the lodges might not have anything to hide, individual privacy had to be protected. Indeed, my interlocutors often evoked the notion of "privacy" to legitimate their discretion.

As I have defined it, discretion, unlike secrecy, is characterized not by an exclusive preoccupation with concealment, but rather by a careful balance of both concealments and disclosures. Among Freemasons, being discreet meant knowing just how much to reveal, to whom, and in what context. Discretion was used to explain to me the choice of concealing one's own Masonic identity from coworkers or not revealing that of a fellow brother or sister. Discretion had to be used in our e-mail communications, during phone calls that might be tapped, or during meetings in cafes or restaurants whenever a waiter might be within earshot of a conversation about Freemasonry. The paranoia that alimented my interlocutors' discretion, as much as it alimented anti-Masonic sentiments in Italy, was founded on Italy's political history. Whether or not my informants' phones were still tapped in 2006 at the time of my fieldwork, many of them certainly had been in the 1990s. Some of the Freemasons I met continued to suspect the state of violating their privacy rights. During a phone call, for instance, a Maestra in a mixed-gender GLDI lodge was sharing with me some of her personal thoughts on the administration of her particular lodge, and asked me not to name any names or report any of the details of the information she had given me in my research. Suddenly, she grew very concerned. "You are not tape-recording this phone call, are you?" she asked me out of the blue. I assured her of my ethical commitment to respect her confidences, and that I would certainly not tape-record any of our interviews without her consent. "Oh well," she joked, sounding more comfortable. "I'm sure the police are listening in anyway. Good morning, officers!"

For my informants, rationality was not on the side of the impossible version of transparency demanded by Italian state officials, but rather on the side of their own moderate practices of transparency. With discretion, they could perform an obliging docility, while also retaining a sense of personal dignity. Discretion was the set of practices through which they could enact transparency in ways that they thought just, equitable, and reasonable, and therefore they saw no contradiction between being transparent and being discreet. To the excessive, uneven, and unreasonable demands of the state, my informants countered a self-imposed version of transparency rooted in their rationality as liberal political subjects of a democracy, entitled to dignity, privacy, and freedom.

Although the GOI's overtures have mostly been met with support in Masonic circles, as evidenced by Grand Maestro Raffi's re-election to two subsequent terms, some of my interlocutors remained deeply skeptical. For instance, Francesca, a Fellow in the mixed-gender GLDI, viewed with some concern the GOI's attempts at disclosure. She was herself the editor of a small weekly paper, and she suspected that no matter how many convention centers the GOI could rent to host public talks with mayors and police chiefs, "transparency is fine, but nothing will ever be enough . . . how can I put it? . . . the more they [the GOI] open up, the more others will want to know. . . . There is no end to it."

Francesca's astute remarks were not alone among those of my interlocutors. The concerns she raised about the never-ending demands of transparency match the insights derived from scholarship on secrecy and on transparency. The power of the secret lies in its incommensurability. Even if a secret is revealed, others may always be lurking in the shadows. In fact, more often than not, the disclosure of a secret has the paradoxical effect of casting further doubts on the trustworthiness of the secret keeper (Simmel 1906). Haridimos Tsoukas, for instance, has argued that "the paradox is that the more information on the inner workings of an expert system observers seek to have, the less they will be inclined to trust its practitioners" (1997: 835), leaving a system of governance based on transparency impossible to fulfill by definition.

Francesca went further in her critique, questioning the GOI brothers' true motives for their sudden turn to transparency.

I am afraid that they are only trying to clean up a little bit of dirt that people put on us [Freemasons], and mostly gain some publicity. In the past people used to build towers—my tower is bigger than your tower, right? Now the thing to do is "I communicate more than you!" It's [an approach] born out of ignorance of the medium of communication. I don't think they know what it is they want to communicate. They don't have a long-term plan of what they'd like to say. They are just trying to make their presence known, and that's not a good thing.

In addition to questioning the logic of openness of a strategy of transparency, some of my interlocutors also questioned the risks that transparency posed for differently situated social actors. Teresa, an older member of the women-only GLMFI, pointed out to me that their organization did not have anywhere near the financial, legal, and media resources of the men-only GOI. Counting only a few hundred members, as opposed to the GOI's fifteen thousand, or even the mixed-gender GLDI's nine thousand, her own group could not afford, she told me, to fight expensive legal battles to defend its name, were they to be under attack. The sisters therefore needed to be much more cautious than the GOI. "There is a great cost in going public," she warned me. "There are risks one must be prepared to take." For the women of the GLMFI, being transparent thus also required discretion, but their discreet enactments of transparency, their own practices of revelations and concealments, had somewhat different purposes. Whereas the goal of the GOI was ostensibly to rehabilitate an already compromised public image, the goal of a women-only organization like the GLMFI was to make themselves to some extent publicly visible and recognized as members of the brotherhood of Freemasonry.

Ironically, the GLMFI had in a sense gone "public" much earlier than the GOI, registering their association with the proper authorities long before the scandals of 1993. The sisters had already made their existence known voluntarily to the state's bureaucratic apparatus of surveillance. They had a taxpayer ID number and had been "regularized" (*regolarizzate*) as a nonprofit association long before the GOI changed its ritual garments or its initiation oath. As we saw earlier, with the example of the apparent disinterest of the special police in women Freemasons ("we already know who you are"), my interlocutors had already complied with the technical and legal requirements of transparency as a form of governance. They had been so transparent, in fact, as to preempt the need and justification for police searches of their own lodges. More importantly, they had adopted a tactic of transparency that allowed them to satisfy bureaucratic controls without entering the debates about Freemasonry held in the court of public opinion. Unlike the GOI, which has sought to use the press to influence the public image of Freemasons, the GLMFI practiced a kind of discreet transparency that mostly allowed its sisters to remain exactly where they had been: in the shadow of dominant discourses on Freemasonry.

In the false dichotomy of visibility and invisibility, transparency and opacity, discretion mediated the self-constructions of both men and women Freemasons, who had different stakes in the spectacle of Masonic scandals and wished to control their public representations to become the *right* kind of visible. For women, both in the large, mixed-gender GLDI and in the smaller, women-only GLMFI, the historical struggle to become more visible was tempered by the risks all of my informants associated with becoming *too* visible. The publication of the lists had been an act of exposure, rather than controlled publicity, an indiscretion with long-lasting effects on Masonic experiences in Italy. By choosing to embrace transparency with discretion, my interlocutors relied on a multivalent tool of political culture that, just like conspiracy theories, concealed knowledge at the same time as it revealed it.

Conclusion: The Limits of Transparency

The publication of the lists of Freemasons followed a fairly typical ritual of exposure that often accompanies political scandals (see Apostolidis and Williams 2004). Often taking the form of media spectacles, those scandals hide much more than they reveal, including the workings of power that gave rise to them in the first place. Whether the scandal is about a corruption ring, or a politician having an affair, or about Italian Freemasons being powerful men hiding in plain sight, the "discovery" is hardly a surprise. As William Mazzarella asked, "Is it possible to cause a sensation by revealing something that everybody already knows?" (2006: 473).

That seems to be what transparency often does. As much as transparency is a kind of optics, its political promises mostly fail to acknowledge that, by definition, what is transparent may be seen through. Just as illuminating an image can wash it out to the point of rendering it unrecognizable, so the pressures of transparency might also have the unintended effect of making invisible the very objects that they are trying to expose. Blindness, in other words, can sometimes be induced by an excess of light, rather than by its absence. It is this process of obfuscation inherent to practices of transparency that the blacklists of Freemasons reveal—an obfuscation that is ideological rather than accidental.

While transparency typically provides information (names, dates, places, and numbers), it is not capable of offering knowledge, let alone wisdom. The lists of Italian Freemasons published in 1993 ran for pages and pages of newspapers, and their effects seemed for a moment to shake both Italian politics and civil society to the core. The lists, however, did not teach us anything we did not already know or suspect. The published information did not offer any new knowledge.

This ethnographic case serves as an important reminder of the internal limits of the discourse of transparency itself. In political and legal arenas, transparency is often hailed as the antidote to the opacity of corruption, secret dealings, unfair trades, and antidemocratic conspiracies. However, the case of Italian Masonic lodges confirms that transparency's promise of an all-seeing eye works in practice only to refuel a self-referential system of surveillance, which is ultimately impossible to fulfill. The circulation of information about Freemasons appears to have led to more doubts and suspicions, rather than fewer. Even Freemasons' subsequent attempts to remake themselves into transparent subjects have been met with suspicion by a profane audience skeptical of their motives. The predictably disappointing conclusion of this spectacle of transparency and exposure may then be that nothing seems to change. And yet, what is at work, and what emerges from the blind spots of the lists of Freemasons, is the painstaking labor of spectacle necessary to maintain and to reproduce the status quo.

The experiences of women Freemasons, oxymoronic both inside the lodges and in the profane world, have the potential to cause a rupture in the gendered representation of Freemasonry, and could also serve to cast a radical doubt against the efficacy of a system of transparency that failed to identify an entire gender of suspects. The ethnographic facts of this case, however, show that neither dominant gender ideologies nor popular depictions of Freemasonry were significantly altered by the "discovery" that there are women in the lodges. Like racial profiling, which is not only racist but also ineffective, a logic of counterterrorism or anticorruption centered on transparency has yielded very little in terms of change or justice in Italy.

Italy's political dramas, unfolding with dialectical urgency through the recursivity of scandals and conspiracy theories that make up the status quo, have prompted Andrea Aureli to notice that "the institutional continuity and the recycling of elites are among the key features of Italian conspiracies" (1999: 214). Transparency, just like conspiracy, seems to produce yet again a predictable set of outcomes. Masonic scandals and spectacles did not change in meaningful ways the course of politics in Italy and instead fit easily into it. Long after the publication of the lists, men Freemasons were still the usual suspects of political crimes, and while my interlocutors still felt—and, to some extent, arguably were—recurrently persecuted by state forces, an alleged P2 member has been prime minister, and the profane public has watched in dismay a corrupt, impotent, and always already sold-out state unable to defend itself (and from whom?), scandal after scandal, about which nothing could be done short of putting all political ruling classes in jail.

Could women Freemasons then perhaps be the wild cards in the discursive game of transparency in Italian politics? It is tempting, although irresponsible, to cast women Freemasons as the unwitting heroines of a counterstrategy that relies on bodies so irrelevant, so oxymoronic, so invisible, as to elude the panoptic power of state surveillance even as they stand in plain sight. For instance, one could read in women Freemasons' experiences the potential for resisting the demands of transparency by learning to occupy its blind spots. However, women Freemasons were not invisible to the state thanks to any successful resistance tactic of their own, and resistance is itself an overly romanticized concept (Abu-Lughod 1990). They were invisible, rather, simply because of their discursive irrelevance to the political games in which transparency engages—

an irrelevance further confirmed and reiterated by women's absence from the published lists of Freemasons, which reified Freemasons as dangerous men.

The circular logic of the reproduction of the status quo is what drove the spectacle of the lists and their aftermath, not any movement for change or resistance. It is more useful, I would suggest, to recognize transparency's promises of better justice, accountability, and democracy as mythologies of governance predicated on highly suspect notions of "change" and "progress" (Weston 2002). In this sense, transparency may be understood as a form of political engagement that, in certain contexts and after the 1990s, has come to replace conspiracy theorizing as a shared tool of political culture, available to a wide range of political actors, including formerly secret societies.[14] It is in the moments of greatest exposure, moments coded as scandals like the publication of the lists of Freemasons, that transparency reveals itself as an ideological discourse that fails its own promises.

"The DIGOS, the secret services, they are all trying to discover the secret of Freemasons," Gianna said to me in her living room, after we finished reliving the political dramas of the previous decades. "But do you know what?" She leaned forward in a conspiratorial posture, and took my hands into hers. "The biggest secret is still that we women are here too, and even that is not really a secret. . . . It's just that people don't want to know about it, and perhaps it's really better this way, don't you think?"

A Profanation

In this sense, we must distinguish between secularization and profanation.
Secularization is a form of repression. It leaves intact the forces it deals with
by simply moving them from one place to another. [. . .] Profanation, however,
neutralizes what it profanes. Once profaned, that which was unavailable and
separate loses its aura and is returned to use. Both are political operations: the
first guarantees the exercise of power by carrying it back to a sacred model;
the second deactivates the apparatuses of power and returns to common use
the spaces that power had seized. ‹ GIORGIO AGAMBEN, *Profanations*›

The last white agape I attended was on June 24, 2006, the day of St. John,
three days after the day conventionally marked as the summer solstice. I knew
then that my time in the field was almost over. By mid-July most city dwellers
would begin their yearly "exodus," as news media usually labeled the massive
departures from urban centers toward holiday destinations on the Italian shores
or abroad. By August, the depopulation of Italian cities would be complete,
in celebration of some of the most generous workers' vacation policies in the
world. Most lodges would close their ritual works for the summer and reopen
just in time for the autumn equinox. The summer solstice agape was therefore
going to be my last chance to see many of the Freemasons I knew all together
in a group setting.

Apparently, my interlocutors thought so too. As we hugged and kissed that
night—with three kisses on the cheeks, to signal at least symbolically my inclusion in their fraternity—the tone was nostalgic and commemorative. We
remembered how we met, how that year had flown by us, and how it seemed

only yesterday that I had been introduced as a researcher from North America wanting to study women Freemasons. The Worshipful Maestra of one of the lodges of the Grand Women's Masonic Lodge of Italy (GLMFI) with which I had worked more closely called me aside at the end of the agape dinner. Was there anything that I still needed for my research? Did I talk to everyone I wanted? I mentioned I had some more interviews to do, and that I was still trying to coordinate with some sisters whose schedules were especially full. The Worshipful Maestra looked suddenly very worried. "Who?" she asked me with a concerned tone. "Who hasn't made themselves available to you?" ("chi è che non ti ha dato la disponibilità?").

I reassured her that all the sisters had been more than generous with their time, and that I had felt they were very open to meeting me and talking with me. My assurances seemed to put her at ease, and after giving me another hug she walked me back to my table, where I said good-bye to a few others. Nonetheless, the Worshipful Maestra's momentary expression of concern was indicative of the efforts many lodges put into controlling their public image as nonprofit associations with nothing to hide. As everyone put on their jackets, Teresa, one of the sisters I had come to know best, stopped on her way out a few feet away from me. She looked back at me, and with a smile she said loudly enough for all to hear, "Lilith, we gave you everything. *Adesso mi raccomando!*"

Adesso mi raccomando. Be careful now, do a good job now, pay attention now, take care now. There is no direct English translation for this common Italian expression. Literally, it means, "Now, I recommend myself," but it has the volition of a command. Even when left as a fragment, as in this case, *mi raccomando* is understood to be followed by an exhortation to act well and carefully, to ponder one's acts, to be judicious. The particular topic of the recommendation, such as driving safely, being home in time for dinner, or carrying a glass vase without breaking it, is not as important as the sentiment underlying the request. The recommending speaker has something at stake, something she cares about, and by making the recommendation she is entrusting someone else with herself and her own desires. *Mi raccomando* signals both personal care and the release of control on the part of the speaker. Like the English "take care," it can function without mention of a specific object to care for, but as an expression of love and concern for the other. *Mi raccomando*, for instance, is how old friends would say good-bye to me before I would board a plane. It was as if they were asking me to carry their concern with me and take good care of myself as a result.

When spoken by a Freemason on the eve of my departure from the field, *mi raccomando* showed a certain intimacy between us. Teresa had come to know me and to care about me, and she wanted to wish me the best. At the same time, however, and precisely because it was left hanging open-ended, her recommendation also contained the ambiguity of all her unspoken concerns. By inviting me to "take care," in a sense, she left open multiple interpretive possibilities of what she wanted me to care for. "We gave you everything," Teresa said, as I was about to leave the field to go write about her experiences and those of her sisters in Italian Masonic lodges. "Now, please take care." In the act of recommending herself to me, Teresa was expressing a concern shared by many of the others: could I be trusted with something so dear to them? Could I take good care of their experiences and their stories?

When I first began this project, I was often told that I was welcome to study Freemasons because "we are transparent" ("siamo trasparenti") and because I seemed "discreet." The policies of transparency implemented by the men-only Grand Orient of Italy (GOI), by the women-only GLMFI, and to a lesser extent by the mixed-gender Grand Lodge of Italy (GLDI) were rhetorically based on the premise that there was no secret there. Freemasonry was not a secret society, there was nothing to hide, and everything was public. Yet these policies could only be effective in redeeming Freemasons' public image if they were practiced carefully and with *discretion*, mediated by PR offices dedicated to cultivating a suitable image and controlling information circulating about Freemasonry. As the P2 scandals of the 1980s and 1990s had taught them, the wrong public image could have devastating consequences for the personal lives of Freemasons. I knew that the fact that they allowed a profane researcher to study their organization would in itself constitute evidence of their transparency. In a literary landscape, however, where most profane writers wrote condemnatory works on Freemasonry, my credentials were carefully examined.

The "burden of representation" in this case is different from the one described by many anthropologists and feminist scholars. It was not my task to give voice to the voiceless, or to educate Euro-Americans about the customs of "other" people. As highly educated European citizens, my informants could represent themselves, and indeed much of the literature on Freemasonry is written by Freemasons. Yet my scholarship would insert itself in a highly divided field, where most works are either apologetic of Freemasonry or denunciatory (Ciuffoletti and Moravia 2004). Teresa's concern, in other words, was about my own production of knowledge about Freemasonry, about her sisters, and about her. In letting go of epistemological control and trusting me, a profane, to carry out independent research, my informants had taken a calculated risk. As I walked away with a treasure chest full of knowledge, they could only hope the risk would pay off.

The sense of persecution my informants described was at first very dif-

ficult for me to represent. Those suspected of being Freemasons were typically university presidents, members of parliament, medical directors, news
anchors, judges, or media moguls. Although those representations exaggerate
somewhat the wealth of Freemasonry, virtually all the Freemasons I met came
from the upper and upper-middle classes. They were not, in other words, the
oppressed, subaltern subjects that much of Marxist, postcolonial, or feminist
studies have focused on. The plight of a misunderstood elitist organization that
still discriminated against vast sectors of the population was not what I had set
out to study. Personally and politically, I wanted to understand how alternative
forms of gender-based social movements could be born out of premises that
were neither feminist nor reactionary, and how a particular articulation of an
allegedly unmarked brotherhood could bring about material and corporeal
transformations in both subjectivity and sociability. I had certainly not expected to encounter "social suffering" in the midst (Kleinman, Das, and Lock
1997).[1] In fact, it was not until I moved to Florence to begin fieldwork, and
I started listening to some of my informants' stories—their voices trembling,
their tearful eyes looking down at the floor, a mixture of sadness and anger in
their tone—that I realized the importance of suffering to their life experiences
as Freemasons in Italy.

To take seriously Freemasons' intimate narratives of fear and loss is to extend
a phenomenology of suffering to the study of the material and political conditions within which subjects emerge in relation to oppressive nation and state
formations. Being attuned to the suffering of my informants, thinking through
it rather than dismissing it a priori, is not only an exercise in the complacent
empathy of the adage that even the rich cry. More importantly, it provides
an analytical lens to examine how social suffering is produced by conflicting
claims to citizenship and belonging among differently situated subjects of a
nation-state imaginary.

To be sure, I am not excusing the complicity of the privileged in the subordination of others. Nor do I wish to deny the material effects of a global hierarchy
of suffering on the living conditions of those whom Chandra Mohanty (2003)
has called the "two-thirds world"—even though the very concept of a "hierarchy of suffering" is itself suspect. In a time when historically privileged groups
increasingly claim oppression as a political status for themselves, challenging
the fairness of measures of redress like affirmative action or "pink quotas" in
the name of liberal individualism and historical amnesia, the anthropology
of European elites must not be apologetic of privilege. In taking the social
suffering of Italian Freemasons as a case study for the violence of citizenship
building, and for the violence of liberalism and Occidentalism even against

privileged European bodies, I am therefore not suggesting that Freemasons should be considered "oppressed" in a Marxian sense, or "burdened" in the racist logic of colonialism, or that their suffering is any more significant than the daily oppression faced by many others. Freemasons themselves would be unlikely to ascribe to the political identity of "the subaltern" in their everyday lives, since much of their sense of self was derived from helping "those less fortunate" through philanthropic and charitable activities, which, in turn, ensured performatively my interlocutors' own elitism. Freemasons' narratives of persecution and injustice emerged specifically in relation to state actors, such as the police or left-wing parties in power, as well as in relation to those institutions of civil society they saw as directly influenced by mainstream Italian politics, including schools and mass media.

My aim in attending to Freemasons' experiences of suffering in this book has rather been to question the democratic ideologies on the basis of which Italian Freemasons, as well as other groups perceived as threats to the state, can become objects of political repression in the liberal countries of the global North. In the name of security and in the name of transparency, a formidable apparatus of surveillance and discipline can be deployed against a variety of subjects to make them "other." Those usual suspects of terror—indigenous guerrillas, Muslims, insurgents, students, antiglobalization activists—have often received the sympathy of academic writers, who have been able to expose the structural inequalities of a system that induces fear in order to fabricate its enemies. But what about anthropology's "other others?"[2] What about the unsympathetic subjects of ethnographic studies, whose right-wing or religious views on gender, class, race, sexuality, labor, nationalism, or the military, for instance, might push anthropologists to the limits of our own cultural relativism?

There are many among the Italian Left who would like to see Freemasons in jail, or at least banned from public office, and who would certainly like to see Masonic lodges dismantled under Article 18 of the Italian Constitution, the one that bans secret societies. To that end, many leftists have condoned or even applauded the unequal treatment Freemasons have received over the years whenever they have been suspected of this or that scandal. As a profane who came to political consciousness within the Italian Left, I find it especially alarming to hear left-wing voices sound dangerously like Mussolini, who was after all the only one to ever succeed at banning Masonic lodges in Italy. To recognize the workings of an apparatus of surveillance and discipline not only when it is deployed in the name of security against sympathetic "others" but even when it is deployed against those "other others" of ethnographic studies that we, too, might find "repugnant" (Harding 1991) is to expose the relentless power of a disciplinary system without falling into the temptation of believing that perhaps, just this one time, against this one group, we should condone its effects. This was precisely Antonio Gramsci's point in 1925, when he spoke to Parliament in defense of Masonic lodges not because he supported Freemasonry's bourgeois interests, but because he foresaw the expansion of a Fascist logic of governance, if left unchecked (Gramsci and Mussolini 1997).

I stated in the introduction that this book is neither an apology for nor a condemnation of Freemasonry, but that it is instead a "profane ethnography" of Italian lodges and, more specifically, of that biggest secret of Freemasonry, as Gianna called it: women Freemasons. It is a profane ethnography not only in the sense that it was written by a profane, with all the resulting epistemological and methodological considerations that accompany the subject position of the profane ethnographer (Mahmud 2013), and that it is driven by the ethnographic principle of making the strange and exotic seem familiar and intelligible. It is also a profane ethnography in the sense that as much as it represents the world of Freemasonry, it does so by engaging in an act of what Giorgio Agamben (2007) has called "profanation," which is an act that demystifies the workings of power by neutralizing some of its apparatuses and returning them to common use.

Despite all the sensationalist portrayals of the lodges throughout the last three centuries, and despite the lodges' own spectacular use of rituals, Freemasons only make explicit the otherwise unrecognized patterns of subject formation, social organizations, and power relations that characterize the imaginary of European liberalism more broadly. Both in their experiences of persecution at the hands of the democratic state and in their own labor of self-cultivation within a highly exclusive path that was ostensibly open to anybody, my interlocutors' engagements with secrecy and fraternity reveal a laborious struggle to reify their subject positions as democratic citizens. An ethnographic study of Freemasonry can therefore serve as a profanation of the workings of power and privilege that reproduce the hegemonic common sense of what it means to be a liberal subject in the democratic countries of the global North, by exposing the labor of that reproduction.

One of the devices of power that are made explicit in the case of Freemasons is the secrecy that pervades the deployment of contemporary ideologies of democratic governance, as they are enacted, contested, or appropriated by state actors, citizens, and institutions. The very notion of a modern democracy as we know it, founded upon the principle of a public to whom the state is accountable, was born out of a necessary contradiction. As Habermas and others have shown (Dean 2002; Habermas 1989; Jacob 1991), modern liberal governance was born in secret through the conspiratorial plots of enlightened revolutionaries, most of whom were Freemasons. Dominant representations of Freemasons in Italy have condemned their secretive practices, attributing to their secrecy a malevolent disregard of democratic values. Although some of those accusations find a reasonable ground in criminal acts that have shocked the country, dominant representations of Freemasonry fail to take note of the ways in which secrecy characterizes not only the lodges but also the democratic ideologies used against them. Secrecy has pervaded the workings of modern democracies since their inception.

If they were not so hurtful, discourses of transparency and security could be laughed off as utterly idiotic, given how ineffectual they have proven themselves at achieving their stated goal of "keeping us safe." For instance, the Italian state's call for transparency against Freemasons failed to "discover" the simple fact of the existence of women Freemasons. Those discourses of transparency and security, however, have a secret too, which is that their ideological blind spots are highly effective at achieving other unstated goals, such as the construction of internal and external enemies—something that has been shown to be necessary to the functioning of modern nation-states (Aretxaga 2003; Mosse 1988). This is not to excuse what some deviated Masonic lodges have done in Italy or elsewhere, and it is not to discount the formidable potential for subversion in the coming together of members of the upper-classes in a somewhat secretive association with a long history of carrying out revolutions. However, it is to recognize that the opposition between democratic transparency and corrupt oligarchic secrecy is itself a myth of liberal governance. If democratic states are inherently secretive and violent, as many commentators have suggested, then Freemasons' experiences are a case in point for how those seemingly abstract discourses of democracy, transparency, publicity, and good governance rely on secrecy for their everyday operations.

Examining the dialectic of secrecy and transparency as organizing modes of power, I have focused on Freemasons' reliance on "discretion" to conceal and reveal their subjectivities in an often hostile profane world. Discretion, however, is not the prerogative of Freemasons. My informants cultivated it, labored at it, and embodied it to such a degree that "discretion" became an inevitable category of study for me, but once again they only magnified patterns found among other social groups and even among state institutions. When Margherita suggested that, although the state has a right to ask for transparency, "not even parishes post a list of their members with everyone's addresses to their doors," her comment pointed to the state's own use of discretion: when and from whom and in what form to demand transparency.

Far from being merely a shield against undue pressures, the practice of discretion was first and foremost a serious "game" of knowledge and expertise, just as relevant to negotiations of transparency as to the mysteries of initiation or to discussions of profane high culture, where a casual Latin citation can mark the status of the speaker, redraw intersubjective boundaries, and kindle the audience's desire to know. The practice of discretion was a knowledge-making technique that would enchant the world and would render it meaningful in special ways to the community of discreet practitioners trained to read the signs. Learning how to be discreet, knowing when to keep knowledge secret and when or how much to disclose, was key to Freemasons' ability to assert power. The *discretion* with which they would share knowledge was thus also a sign of their *distinction* (see Urban 2001). By revealing an interpretive layer inaccessible to profane eyes or even to the eyes of a lower-ranking brother or sister, they could remind the audience that there is always more to be seen, and that the Masonic path provides a lens to see the fine grains and contours of what was previously assumed to be a transparent reality.

For sister Masons, whether in women-only or mixed-gender lodges, certain practices of disclosure were aimed at proving their legitimacy and belonging in an esoteric world materially and rhetorically dominated by men. The GLMFI, for instance, enacted policies of transparency that rivaled the GOI's. And yet, the sisters' attempts at making themselves public, *indiscreetly* phoning the local police or inviting GOI brothers to be guests in their temples during special events and partially open rituals, were met with either indifference or, at best, with the brothers' condescending praises, which reinforced over and over again men's ultimate authority over Masonic work. When the sisters were guests at GOI's events, for instance, at times when the brothers performed part of a ritual publicly, the sisters were never in a position to compliment GOI brothers on how well the latter had followed the codified rules of Masonic rituals. The use of discretion had uneven consequences for differently positioned subjects.

If women Freemasons continue to occupy a subject position that is by definition oxymoronic, it is because of the discursive power of fraternity, a structurally masculine notion defined by its universal promises. The discourse of fraternity is one of the most resilient devices of power, one that the ethnography of Freemasonry ought to expose and to profane. As a guiding principle of liberal humanism, fraternity has been both an end goal and a presupposition of modern democratic governance. Postcolonial, feminist, and subaltern studies scholars have long decried the failures of humanist fraternity, its false promises that never seemed to apply outside of a privileged European white masculinity. It is as if humanist fraternity, imagined to have started out in Europe, could not travel very far or very fast away from the center of its production; and when it did, it arrived at the periphery of empire already too diluted to heal any wounds, and too marked by its own foundational imprinting for its inclusionary promises to be believable. Perhaps it was a problem of scale (from particular to abstract) or a problem of distance (from Europe to the colonies), or a problem of sexism (women cannot be brothers), but the humanism of fraternity certainly sounded cynical: all brothers are equal, but some are more brothers than others. Nonetheless, the rallying cry of fraternity has continued to move peoples throughout the world, inspiring countless social struggles for freedom and equality. Fraternity might have been a broken tool of liberalism, but most emancipatory movements have attempted to repair it and to reclaim it, so that it could apply to *all* at last.

In a sense, what women Freemasons were doing was not that different from what many others have done with fraternity: holding it accountable, demanding more of it, and, most of all, desiring it with a fervor so ardent and committed that repeated disappointments and failures could only be oil poured on fraternity's fire. Their own subject positions as privileged white European women also meant that my interlocutors could have expectations about fraternity applying to them that perhaps other subjects might not have dreamed to have. If humanist fraternity is imagined to be a product of enlightened liberalism, then women Freemasons could certainly be imagined to have it within their reach.

The problem with such an approach, however, is that it inevitably reifies the existence of a center of authenticity (a white, male, upper-class, European authenticity) where brothers can just be brothers, and humanist fraternity applies effortlessly, *the way it was meant to*. By explaining that women cannot be brothers because of sexism, or that colonized subjects could not be brothers (and therefore not fully human) because of racism—both absolutely true statements—one runs the risk of believing, by contrast, in fraternity's literalism for some people somewhere else. My contention has been instead that although fraternity is a sexist (and racist) construct, it is not actualized anywhere, not even inside Masonic lodges that "invented" the Enlightenment, not even by men Freemasons in Europe, and that to concede to some (white, male) Europeans a primal authenticity over the embodiment of fraternity's promises is to fall into fraternity's trap: that is, to forget that all along it was just a promise, nothing more and nothing less, and that it takes an extraordinary amount of work to make it look possible to keep it.

Insofar as being capable of fraternity has been a measure of humanity and of political subjectivity (those who were not deemed capable of being brothers were not fully human), performing fraternity brings about a great degree of privilege. An analysis of fraternity is therefore also an analysis of power. Feminist scholars know well that privilege in all forms (e.g., white privilege, class privilege, male privilege) works in part by appearing like a natural given, when in fact it must be actively maintained. Cultural capital is a prime example of what seems to be natural, like taste, and yet is the product of symbolic labor to naturalize class privilege. The fetish of Occidentalism takes labor to maintain, like all other fictions. The anthropology of Europe, and especially of European "elites," can and should make visible the labor that goes into reproducing the privilege of Occidentalism within the geopolitical limits of Europe (Carrier 1992; Coronil 1996).

The self-cultivation work that takes place inside Masonic lodges exposes the labor of fraternity's production even within one of its supposedly "authentic" sites. Becoming a cultivated person, a reader of fine arts and literatures that have come to define European civilization, a spiritual but not dogmatic believer who cherishes the separation of church and state, a cosmopolitan and well-traveled citizen, a philanthropist, a well-spoken rational agent: that is the Occidentalist aspiration of the lodges; that is what it means to become a brother. Of course, the subject I just described could be a Freemason, or an academic, or a liberal, or most of the readers of this book, or my friends, or me. Freemasons make explicit the labor of production necessary to engender the "culture" of Europe not as a real place but as an Occidentalist aspiration. It is because my interlocutors, both women and men, worked so hard at it that they made it seem easy.

Women Freemasons deconstructed themselves in order to become brothers, but in doing so they exposed the labor that men Freemasons did, too. Derrida noted in his analysis of democratic fraternization that the demand of a fraternal democracy to come is deconstruction at work. "There has never been anything natural in the brother figure. . . . Denaturalization was at work in the very formation of fraternity. [. . .] The relation to the brother engages from the start with the order of the oath, of credit, of belief and of faith. The brother is never a fact" (2005: 159). To understand how such deconstruction was technically possible, how it was engendered through a labor of self-cultivation, is to profane the device of Occidentalist power that is fraternity.

Ethnographically, I saw that fraternity operated not only to constitute a particular community of practice within a lodge, but also, and more pervasively, to put forth an imaginary of civil society and of civilization. For the scale of fraternity to change from the particular (brothers and sisters) to the generic (fraternity in its meaning of agape), my interlocutors engaged in techniques of liberal abstraction such as philanthropy, mobility, and knowledge cultivation. Those were techniques for the enactment and embodiment of fraternity, which, in turn, was a cultivation of privilege.

For them, however, just like for many postcolonial subjects struggling for equality, the pursuit of fraternity was a profound source of meaning and purpose in their lives. Instead of dismissing fraternity as a convenient lie that colonizers told, we must recognize fraternity as an intentional project, something never quite achieved, but powerful precisely because of the unfulfilled potential with which it seduces people into devoting their lives to its pursuit. And when occasionally fraternity does make an appearance, as a feeling, as a sensory experience, or as an egregore conjured via a group ritual, that embodied experience of fraternity can be so exhilarating and life-affirming that a world without it would seem painfully imperfect indeed.

And that is the real secret of Freemasonry: an incommunicable experience of fraternity. The Freemason and famous lover Casanova revealed in his memoirs the secret guarded in the lodges:

> Those who become Freemasons only for the sake of finding out the secret of the order, run a very great risk of growing old under the trowel without ever realizing their purpose. Yet there is a secret, but it is so inviolable that it has never been confided or whispered to anyone. Those who stop at the outward crust of things imagine that the secret consists in words, in signs, or that the main point of it is to be found only in reaching the highest degree. This is a mistaken view: the man who guesses the secret of Freemasonry, and to know it you must guess it, reaches that point only through long attendance in the lodges, through deep thinking, comparison, and deduction. He would not trust that secret to his best friend in Freemasonry, because he is aware that if his friend has not found it out, he could not make any use of it after it had been whispered in his ear. No, he keeps his peace, and the secret remains a secret. (2007: 57)

To profane the secret of Freemasonry—not the salacious secrets that Italian authorities have been after, but the secret of fraternity at the heart of humanism—has been the aim of this ethnography. May we deactivate its apparatuses of power, and may fraternity be returned to common use.

NOTES

Introduction

1. In addition to Anderson's *Constitutions*, Masonic lodges rely on landmarks and "Old Charges" to delineate rules of conduct and expectations. The landmarks are an unwritten list of principles, which may vary from lodge to lodge. Some of the most widespread landmarks include the injunctions to profess faith in a higher being, to be a free person of good character, and to believe in the immortality of the soul. The "Old Charges" were a series of manuscripts compiled between the fourteenth and eighteenth century and mostly now lost, which detailed the workings of operative guilds of masons as well as a history of the speculative craft of Freemasonry connected to alchemic pursuits and biblical stories. Anderson's *Constitutions* were partly intended as a replacement of the "Old Charges." For a lengthier discussion of textual sources of authority for Masonic lodges, see Irène Mainguy (2004) and Patrick Négrier (2006).

2. For a selected bibliography of the history of Freemasonry in Italy, please see Ciuffoletti (1989); Ciuffoletti and Moravia (2004); Conti (2003); Conti (2007); Dito (1905); Esposito (1956); Mola (1992).

3. In some contexts, and especially within Francophone lodges, Freemasons have done away with the requirement to believe in a higher being. Such debates over the

liberty of conscience, including the liberty not to believe, however, were not common among my interlocutors in Italy.

4. Before the P2 scandal, other organizations had been rumored to have gone underground inside Masonic lodges. From the Knights Templar excommunicated in the fourteenth century to the Illuminati in the eighteenth century, the U.S. KKK in the nineteenth century, and even the Mafia and the *carboneria* in nineteenth-century Italian history, several groups have supposedly found refuge in the pyramidal structure of Freemasonry (Esposito 1956; Mola 1992).

5. Throughout this book, I choose to use the Italian words *Maestro* (masculine) and *Maestra* (feminine) instead of the English *Master* to call attention to the gender of these terms.

6. The relationship between Orders and Rites is quite complex, and is beyond the scope of this research. Some Freemasons believe that "true" Freemasonry should only have three degrees. For the most part, the hierarchies of Orders and Rites existed in parallel to one another and had different leaders, so that members of the Rite could not make any hierarchical claims over the Order. In at least one of the groups I worked with, however, the mixed-gender GLDI, the Order and the Rite were part of the same path. This meant that the head of the Rite (the Sovereign), was the same person as the Head of the Order (the Grand Maestro).

7. The GOI actually lost the endorsement of the UGLE in 1994, but GOI members at the time of my fieldwork suggested that the status loss was temporary, and they were confident they would eventually regain the UGLE's support. This example shows how precarious treaties of Masonic friendship can be, and how hard it is to define which groups are or are not legitimate Masonic lodges.

8. Both the GLMFI and the GLDI were members of an international organization called CLIPSAS. Membership in CLIPSAS has become a de facto source of legitimacy for lodges worldwide that are not recognized by the English UGLE. The GLMFI was also a member of the CLIMAF, a similar umbrella organization specifically for women-only lodges.

Chapter One

1. With the exception of the leaders of Masonic organizations, who are considered public figures, all names and identifying characteristics of individual Freemasons have been changed to protect my informants' privacy. The names of the Masonic Orders and Grand Lodges are real names.

2. Throughout this book I follow my informants' usage of the word *profane* in contrast to *Mason* to designate people, such as myself, who have not been initiated to Freemasonry.

3. The strong reactions many people had to my project were not atypical. Anthropologists of Italy studying secretive and criminalized organizations, such as Mafia or Camorra, have often had to negotiate their informants' trust while also mitigating the suspicions and concerns of state institutions and general populace (Jacquemet 1996; Schneider and Schneider 2003).

4. Although Angelo became a good friend and informant, the sexualized and racialized readings of my presence in the field that this ethnographic moment illustrates characterized many of my interactions with male informants in Italy. Some women Freemasons told me about their own negotiations of some brothers' sexual innuendos or outright harassing behaviors. At times, in group settings, sisters also protected me and shielded me from some of the men. Overall, my interactions with male Freemasons in both the GOI and in the mixed-gender GLDI remained respectful and professional. There were a few times, however, when I decided to give up potentially useful research contacts as a result of the discomfort that I felt, and which, more broadly, women anthropologists sometimes have to contend with in our fieldwork encounters with male informants.

5. The invisibility of Italians of color is part of a larger misrecognition of racialized and non-Christian communities in Europe who continue to be excluded, by definition, from the discursive construction of Europeanness (Asad 1993: 239–268; El-Tayeb 2011; Najmabadi 2006).

6. The name of the "institute" has been changed.

7. Personally, though, I also found it hard to let go of my own sensibilities and dispositions toward Freemasonry, which were structured within dominant public discourses in Italy. When I had started this project, I had felt the "repugnance" theorized in anthropology about ethnographic engagements with unsympathetic subjects (Harding 1991). It was only through the social intimacy of the fieldwork encounter that I came to feel affection and sympathy for my informants and for some of their struggles. Even though it is not a path for me, I learned to appreciate and respect why the Masonic path could give meaning to many.

8. My interlocutors' fears were rooted in Italy's violent political history, which up until the 1990s had seen the far Left and the far Right fighting each other through terrorism and assassinations. Expressing concerns about their own safety, however, Freemasons turned upside down popular representations of violence in Italy, which depict them as perpetrators rather than victims.

Chapter Two

1. In Italy, the Ancient and Accepted Scottish Rite, the Symbolic Rite, and the Rectified Scottish Rite were the most prevalent Rites available to Maestre or Maestri wishing to continue their training beyond the third degree.

2. Following Sherry Ortner, I take subjectivity to mean "a specifically cultural and historical consciousness" that does not negate the unconscious dynamics of structuring processes, but which "is always more than those things" at both the individual and collective levels (Ortner 2005: 34).

3. Within medical anthropology in particular, subjectivity has been tied not to ontological questions but to moral and ethical dramas unfolding on the uneven playing field of global inequalities: people's experiences of small- and large-scale structures of suffering and violence that are necessarily "intersubjective" (Biehl 2005; Biehl, Good, and Kleinman 2007; Desjarlais 1997; Kleinman, Das, and Lock 1997).

4. Some Freemasons had explicitly told profane family members that they had been initiated into a lodge. Those were *Massoni dichiarati*, which literally means they were "declared" Freemasons, but to be "declared" (*dichiarato*) in Italian, especially in a queer sense, means to be "out." Most, however, negotiated their Masonic identities with their profane loved ones very discreetly, typically resorting to a tacit understanding that was neither stated nor denied.

5. As anthropologists have found elsewhere (Steedly 1993), during my fieldwork in Italy I realized that my informants' narratives were not often linear. The history of the construction of the GLMFI was one I had to recreate by piecing together interviews and oral histories.

6. Gender differences in employment opportunities are found even among the upper classes. Many of the older women with whom I worked were employed in middle-management positions or as teachers, rather than as architects, lawyers, or doctors. These latter professions, which were common among Freemasons overall, were typical of the younger women Freemasons I met.

7. Several scholars have studied food consumption practices to gain insight into experiences of social class, community building, identity, or nationalism (Bourdieu 1984; de Certeau, Giard, and Mayol 1998). In the Italian context, Carole Counihan's (2004) ethnography of Tuscan cuisine is an interesting study of gender, power, and family. Agape dinners were prime sites for Masonic community formations.

8. Despite the rich variety of lodges operating in Italy, each with a distinctive philosophy, history, and membership, the dominant image of Freemasonry all over the world remains singular, thus reifying an institution that is not otherwise there. There are Masonic lodges, each bound by complex treaties and systems of mutual recognition, each attracting different members as a result of social pressures, systems of exchange, and personal histories colliding to create the conditions of possibility for an initiation. There is, however, no institution of "Freemasonry," despite the fact that my interlocutors too partook in this reification.

9. In describing Masonic subjectivity as intersubjective, I do not mean to downplay the radical individualism of the humanist ideology Freemasons ascribe to. As a product

of European modernity, the fraternity of Freemasons is universalizing precisely because it finds humanity in the specificity of the inner (masculine, European) rational, and individual self (Kant 2002).

10. Not unlike writers from the colonies, advocates for the rights of women in Europe since at least the eighteenth century (see Mill 1989; Wollstonecraft 2004) have similarly positioned the "woman's question" as the condition of an internal other. Simone de Beauvoir famously defined woman as "the Other in a totality of which the two components are necessary to one another" (1989: xxvi). Mimicry and alterity have been crucial terms in the development of a European liberal subjectivity and of its (many) others.

11. Ann Stoler (1995), for example, has argued that the bourgeois discourses of sexuality that have been taken to be characteristic of European modernity (Foucault 1978) in fact emerged through a mutually feeding relationship with the racial and sexual anxieties of the colonies. Her corrective argument is one effort in a larger scholarly project of provincializing Europe (Chakrabarty 2000; Herzfeld 1987; Holmes 2000) and questioning its normative centrality to discourses presumed to have later traveled to other locales.

12. The self-congratulatory claims of secularism and liberalism that many nations in the global North make are often deployed ideologically to mark others (other nations, immigrants, et al.) as different and backward. Such claims are therefore less representative of actual Euro-American sensibilities and lived experiences, and more indicative of ongoing Orientalist depictions of non-Western subjects (Fernando 2010; Jakobsen and Pellegrini 2008; Scott 2007).

13. Unlike in the mimicry Homi Bhabha (1994) describes, potentially menacing also because of the language of revolutionary mockery, and unlike in the "parodic performances" in drag that Butler (1999) is concerned with, enveloped in the irony of "subversive laughter," I found no irreverent intentionality or disavowal in women's claims to Freemasonry. Although the women I met were certainly outspoken in their critiques of the sexism they encountered in the lodges, and had no illusions about how much work needed to be done to make Freemasonry truly equal, they nonetheless espoused overall the same masculine terms of the discourse as men Freemasons.

Chapter Three

1. Interrogating the affect of modernist political subjects, Anderson (1991 [1983]) famously asked not only how people can feel love for the abstraction that is the nation but also why they are willing to die for such limited imagining. Feminist and postcolonial scholars of nationalism have gone further in examining the specific dynamics of nationalist love, and their patterns of gendering and sexualizing a motherland, fatherland,

and a beloved country (Chatterjee 1993; Kaplan, Alarcón, and Moallem 1999; Parker 1992; Ramaswamy 1997; Visweswaran 1996). More recently, love itself has begun to be examined as a governing affect in relation to empire and transnationalism (Hardt and Negri 2009; Maira 2009; Povinelli 2006).

2. For instance, feminist and abolitionist Olympe de Gouges, better known for authoring the "Declaration of the Rights of Woman and of the Female Citizen" in 1791 to denounce the limits of the French Revolution and of the 1789 "Declaration of the Rights of Man and of the Citizen," was a Freemason.

3. The injunction against nepotism in liberal modern democracies is so pervasive that Michael Herzfeld called it "the political equivalent of the incest taboo" (2001: 120). As a sign of the corruption of politics, an inappropriate comingling of private and public, nepotism serves as an ideological indicator of backwardness and incivility, positing "traditional" societies organized around kinship structures against the Euro-American "modern world," where bureaucratic structures sustain imaginaries of proper governance, regardless of the actual political practices found in the global North (Herzfeld 2001).

4. The Anglophone feminist notion of sisterhood has been strongly criticized for its inevitable exclusion of some groups of women by others, such as women of color from white sisterhoods or lesbian women from heterosexual feminist groups (Lorde 1984; Mohanty 1988; Moraga and Anzaldúa 1981). Despite some attempts to rehabilitate sisterhood within feminist circles (hooks 1984), the term has lost much of its earlier currency in favor of models of alliance and solidarity more attuned to power differentials among women (Carrillo Rowe 2008) and better able to address local experiences of gender in relation to "scattered hegemonies" of transnational oppression (Grewal and Kaplan 1994).

5. In an insightful critique of feminist ethnography, for instance, Judith Stacey (1988) argued that, as a result of notions of sisterhood, "feminist researchers are apt to suffer the delusion of alliance more than the delusion of separateness" in relation to our subjects of study. See also Kamala Visweswaran's (1994) engagement with Stacey's work.

6. In an interestingly similar context, sociologist Lisa Handler investigated the concept of sisterhood as a form of conservative gender strategy in U.S. college sororities (1995). She argued that the notion of sisterhood underlying sorority life is different from the notion of sisterhood found in many feminist discourses. Unlike the latter, based on a shared experience of gender oppression, she argues that the sisterhood of sororities is based on stereotyped views of womanhood, harbored in a markedly heterosexual context (238).

7. For selected exemplars of the rich and diverse revisionist literature on kinship, please see Borneman (1996); Collier, Yanagisako, and Bloch (1987); Franklin and Ragoné

(1998); Kahn (2000); Krause (2005); Paxson (2004); Schneider (1980); Strathern (1992); Weston (1991); Yalman (1967).

8. Anthropologists have well documented the mutual influences of family and business models (Kondo 1990; Marcus and Hall 1992), especially in the Italian context (Goddard 1996; Yanagisako 2002). Taking the lodges as socioeconomic organizations, I find that the familial relations among members are neither surprising nor unusual.

9. The transnational quality of Freemasonry has historically positioned the lodges as precursors of globalization (Harland-Jacobs 2007). In the early twenty-first century, Freemasonry' transnationalism is still predicated upon the privilege and cosmopolitanism of its members, who hold passports and resources to travel flexibly for business and leisure (see Ong 1999).

10. As part of a new trend toward studying unsympathetic groups in anthropology (see Harding 2000), some critics have suggested that feminist ethnography should broaden its scope to explore nationalism and state forms of power as sites of conservative women's activism outside the rubric of feminism (Visweswaran 1997).

11. The often uneasy connections between feminism and leftist movements, especially Marxism, has been well documented even outside Italy, and the transnational flow of feminist scholarship and experiences has made for several instances of cross-fertilization on this subject (see Dalla Costa and James 1973; Sargent 1981; Young 2000).

12. Teresa de Lauretis (1994) has offered a countercritique of the common North American feminist critique of essentialism, and Gayatri Spivak (1993) has been among those insisting on the "strategic" value of a gender essentialism in certain political contexts (see also Schor and Weed 1994). Nonetheless, it is fair to generalize that gender essentialism has been more prevalent among Italian feminist organizing than among North American feminisms of the last four decades.

13. Sometimes I also heard members of the GLMFI and the GLDI tell homophobic jokes at the expense of GOI brothers because of their stubborn refusal to allow women in their lodges.

14. Many of my informants told me explicitly that they vote for right-wing parties and that most other Masons they know "sono di destra" ("are right-wingers"), although they could point me to some whom they knew to be socialist. The few sisters or brothers I met who identified as socialists felt very much that they were a political minority within their lodges, but their views of feminism were not significantly different from those held by right-wing Masons. It is perhaps important to notice that the Italian Socialist Party has split in recent years into two political forces, one on the right and one on the left of the political spectrum. Since Italian Fascism emerged from the ranks of the Socialist Party of the time, being a socialist in Italian politics is not as tied to the historical Left as being a member of the Communist Party is. For a discussion of the Left in Italy, see also Kertzer (1980) and Però (2007).

15. Especially in the context of Muslim and Middle-Eastern societies, a postcolonial and post-Orientalist generation of feminist anthropologists has sought to examine the everyday tactics of resistance enacted by subaltern, gendered agents (see Abu-Lughod 1986; Ahmed 1992; Altorki and El-Solh 1988; Boddy 1989), without necessarily misattributing to them a "feminist consciousness" that they might not experience (Abu-Lughod 1990: 47).

16. This is not to say that such critiques did not exist earlier. Suffice it to recall Sojourner Truth's famous speech, "Ain't I a Woman?" bringing an abolitionist perspective to a "women's" suffrage movement dominated by white women (hooks 1981).

17. However, in Italy too there has been an increase in volunteerism that has coincided with a neoliberal restructuring of the public sector and a decrease in workers' protections (Molé 2010; Muehlebach 2012).

18. Derrida recognizes fraternity's affinity to a history of ascension when he defines fraternity as "not a progress but an elevation, a sublimation, no doubt in affinity with what Kant defines also as the stellar sublimity of the moral law . . . the profound height, the altitude of the moral law of which fraternal friendship would be *exemplary*" (2005: 271).

19. Berlant argues that "the vague futurities of normative optimism produce small self-interruptions as the utopias of structural inequality" (2006: 35). It is both because of fraternity's utopian longings and its everyday reliance on structural inequalities that I consider my informants' attachment to it as a kind of "cruel optimism."

Chapter Four

1. Dorinne Kondo (1990), for instance, studied the construction of "disciplined selves" in Japanese employer-sponsored work ethics programs. She found that "it is by first keeping the rules which define the form, even if one's understanding is incomplete or one disagrees with them, that a sincere attitude is eventually born" (107).

2. Mahmood emphasizes that docility and agency are in a mutually constitutive relationship when she writes that "although we have come to associate docility with abandonment of agency, the term literally implies the malleability required of someone to be instructed in a particular skill or knowledge—a meaning that carries less a sense of passivity and more that of struggle, effort, exertion, and achievement" (2001: 210).

3. Tanya Luhrmann (1989) has described the process by which neophytes come to believe in the cosmologies of an occult or magic group as an "interpretive drift," slowly replacing earlier skepticism with the increased acceptance of unorthodox beliefs and tenets. The suspension of disbelief, Luhrmann argues, is a necessary precondition for the espousal of beliefs that might be controversial or on the fringe of mainstream society. The rule of silence is but one technique used to engender a docile disposition.

4. Contemporary English-language Masonic writings usually refer to *tavole* simply as "papers" and only occasionally as "tablets." The word derives from the Latin *tabula*, which signifies a stone or wooden surface inscribed with writings. I retain the Italian term, which is as obsolete as its English equivalent would be, to follow my informants' usage. The word *tavola* reflects Freemasons' genealogical attachment to an imagined tradition of writing and research evoking past centuries and millennia as well as the geometric tools of stonemasons.

5. Indeed, the high culture that Masons celebrated was by definition Western. Although in some cases it could be interpreted as more narrowly Italian—such as Roman antiquity or Florentine Renaissance, appropriated post facto as Italian by the new nation-state—it was typically Occidental, as in Mozart's music crossing the boundaries of the nation-state to stand in for European civilization. A particular relation to the past is central to the constitution of high culture, and in the case of European high culture it is inseparable from the shifting imaginaries of space and time concomitant with nation-state processes of the eighteenth and nineteenth centuries (Anderson 1991 [1983]; Gellner 1983; Mosse 1988; Saïd 2003). Edward Sapir acknowledged the centrality of an invented past to performances of cultivation when he remarked that "perhaps the most extraordinary thing about the cultured ideal is its selection of the particular treasures of the past which it deems worthiest of worship" (1960: 82).

6. The names of some of the lodges I worked with are illustrative of this point. The Grand Orient of Italy and the Order of the Eastern Star, for instance, betray an Orientalist sensibility with their names.

7. As Caren Kaplan (1996) and Inderpal Grewal (2005) have noted, many diverse subjects, including postcolonial and diasporic subjects, have been cosmopolitan; nonetheless, the association of cosmopolitanism with imperial power and privilege has served to represent Europeans as world citizens.

8. Italy is similar to other European countries that guarantee formal equality of education through a system of prestigious, public schools. Despite such formal equality, however, differences in opportunities and mobility, particularly along class lines, are maintained through more or less subtle discriminatory processes on the ground (Willis 1981).

9. In his ethnography of French magicians, Graham Jones (2011) also found that magicians' knowledge was characterized not by their technical understanding of secret tricks, but, rather, by their ability to perform them. As he writes, "Magicians do not merely *know* secrets; they embody secrets as *know-how*" (6). It is that embodied performance, produced for particular audiences and cultivated within a community of practitioners, that ultimately asserts the magician's legitimacy.

10. These processes of selective reinvention of the past are certainly not an Italian or Masonic prerogative, but are rather an integral element of nationalist imaginings

and of the construction of what counts as cultural patrimony. Looking at Greece, for instance, another country located at the margins of European power and influence, James Faubion (1993) has made the compelling case that Athens accumulates cultural capital of nationalist significance (archaeological sites but also museums and important universities) to accrue its prestige as first city of the nation. In this project of achieving distinction, Athens' multiple pasts are inevitably reduced to an overly simplistic and singular tale of history that is essential to the establishment of Greek prestige in the eyes of other European countries (91–103; see also Herzfeld 1987).

11. I choose to use the word "modeling," instead of the perhaps more commonly used "role-modeling," to avoid the simplistic singularity implied by the notion of a "role" (see Connell 1987).

12. In his classic text, *Pedagogy of the Oppressed*, Paulo Freire (2000) similarly theorized that the kind of education that would serve revolutionary purposes ought not to be based on the prevalent "narrative" model of an omniscient teacher narrating knowledge to listening students, but instead on a dialogical model of pedagogy. As he wrote, "Education is suffering from narration sickness" (71)

13. The concept of "stealing" and specifically of "stealing with the eyes" appears repeatedly in the literature on apprenticeship, especially in Southern Europe (Grasseni 2007; Herzfeld 2004; Jones 2011; Maher 1987).

14. Musical taste was also a particularly important site of class distinctions in Bourdieu's (1984) argument. He noted that because music was not a commonly taught subject in French schools at the time of his research, the cultivation and naturalization of musical taste occurred within certain classes and families.

15. This attempt to legitimize Freemasonry through a reclaiming of famous historical figures is reflected in several books describing the biographies of famous Masons (see Gnocchini 2005).

16. This too is an "invented tradition" (Hobsbawm and Ranger 1983), since historical records suggest that women have been present in Masonic lodges in various forms since their beginnings (Jacob 1991; Leuci and Vatri 2003; Vigni and Vigni 1997). At the very least, Masonic historiography reveals that the issue of women's initiation is not at all a "new" controversy brought about by recent societal changes, but rather, it is as old as Freemasonry itself. The exclusion of women from men-only institutional spaces in the name of "tradition" is a well-documented phenomenon, occurring in a variety of settings. See, for instance, Laura Brodie's (2000) study of women's struggle for inclusion in a U.S. military academy.

17. My memories of my own *liceo* experience in the 1990s are of course only anecdotal, and the faculty composition of other schools might have been different. Nonetheless, it was only after I moved to the United States that I learned about the dominant stereotype according to which girls and women are supposed to be bad at math.

18. On the culture debate, see Abu-Lughod (1991), Brumann (1999), Clifford and Marcus (1986), Gupta and Ferguson (1997b), and Steedly (1996).

19. The gender divide surrounding high culture in Italy is reminiscent of the tropes of honor and shame in classic anthropological literature on the Mediterranean (Pitt-Rivers 1966), whereby the moral system of "men of honor" would be based on the protection of women from shame. Criticized for its overly simplistic and essentializing assumptions, this model has been reformulated to various degrees by several commentators (Davis 1987; Delaney 1987; Herzfeld 1980). In the gender struggles inherent to Freemasonry in Italy, high culture would seem to represent a predominantly masculine site, so that those known as "men of culture" or "men of letters" (*uomini di cultura, uomini di lettere*) might enjoy a privileged social status not unlike that of "men of honor."

20. In the national curriculum of Italian education in Latin literature, Italian literature or philosophy, virtually every author is a man, with the notable exception of the Greek poet Sappho. To counteract the masculine discourse of valued knowledge in Italy, several collectives of leftist feminists since the 1970s have established research institutes, bookstores, and libraries of women's works throughout Italy. Women Freemasons who perform Italian high culture to affirm their social position in a male-dominated institution are clearly choosing a different strategy of self-cultivation.

21. The fact that the other meaning of culture has received so little attention in anthropology is a sign of how marginal the study of elites has been to anthropological projects, despite Laura Nader's (1972) call for "studying 'up,'" and despite some notable exceptions (see Marcus and Hall 1992; Pina-Cabral and Lima 2000; Shore and Nugent 2002) that are becoming increasingly more prevalent in the discipline.

Password III

1. David Kertzer has long made the point that Catholic ritual symbols structure ritual space even among nominally atheist Communists in Italy (see Kertzer 1980, 1988, 1996). What I observed among Freemasons was the infringement of nationalist, secular motifs—flags, anthem, etc.—into a quasi-religious ritual space that was constructed as predating the Italian nation-state. This infringement is especially remarkable given the long-standing tensions between Masonic lodges and political institutions in Italy.

Chapter Five

1. There are interesting parallels to draw between Freemasons' subjectivity in Italy and the insights derived from queer theory (Decena 2008; Sedgwick 1990). For my informants, being a Freemason was a core identity, but one that they had to manage in a context that felt hostile to them.

2. For a deeper discussion of the history of the Lead Years, please see Aureli (1999) and Antonello and O'Leary (2009). Pierpaolo Antonello and Alan O'Leary write that "although some have claimed that there has been an overemphasis on the role and presence of political violence in those years, it is a statistical fact that between 1969 and 1980 there were more than 12,000 incidents of politically motivated violence (an average of 100 incidents per month, three per day): 362 people were killed, 4,500 were injured, 597 terrorist groups, of both left and right, were counted" (2009: 1).

3. The case of the Bologna train station bombing is unique among the Lead Years terrorist acts in that two Fascist militants were found guilty of the crime: Valerio Fioravanti and Francesca Mambro, a husband and wife. The two have maintained their innocence, garnering some support even from the Red Brigades (Braghetti and Mambro 1995), and many in the association of family members of the Bologna victims continue to suspect that the "real" culprits were never found. The conspiratorial consensus in the Left is that it was members of the deviated Masonic lodge P2 who commissioned the bombing of the train station.

4. And yet, as Joe Masco suggested in his study of the production of classified information about U.S. nuclear power and intelligence, with the proliferation of technocratic practices of state secrecy, (re)deployed differently in different political times, all knowledge has become increasingly suspect in "the secret society that is the state" (Masco 2010: 456).

5. For additional information on the P2, please see also Cecchi (1985), Galli (2007), and Mola (2008).

6. When the P2 scandal went public, the GOI "sentenced to death" (i.e., expelled) brother Licio Gelli, and it has since maintained that the criminal activities of the P2 occurred without the knowledge or authorization of the GOI. To all my informants, even those who belonged to other Masonic organizations, including the GLDI and the GLMFI, the P2 was a case of deviated Freemasonry (*Massoneria deviata*), which was no longer Freemasonry at all, and for which they would not and should not be held accountable.

7. Although his name appeared on the membership list of the Masonic lodge P2 uncovered by secret services, Silvio Berlusconi has repeatedly said in his defense that he did not know he had been listed as a member (Guarino 2001).

8. While the GOI and the GLMFI separated Order and Rite hierarchies, the mixed-gender GLDI united the two under a single leadership in a single path.

9. Different Rites had different admission requirements, but most did not allow prospective initiates to apply directly.

10. Whereas the head of an Order, the Grand Maestra/o, is a public figure, the identity of the head of the Rite, known as Sovereign, is usually kept quiet. It was only

after over a year of fieldwork, for instance, that I finally found confirmation that the person I had suspected of being the Sovereign of the Rite in the women-only GLMFI was, in fact, the Sovereign.

11. Herzfeld (2005) discusses cultural intimacy specifically in relation to nation-state formations, arguing that the collective secrets of an "imagined community" (Anderson 1991 [1983]), those embarrassing group traits to be recognized only among insiders, are what ultimately secures people's nationalist loyalty. By applying cultural intimacy to my argument, I not only intend to emphasize its methodological impact on field research, but I am also drawing an analogy between the homogenous, horizontal comradeship of nation-state imagined communities and the universal fraternity of Freemasonry, both produced discursively within the same historical context of post-Enlightenment European modernity.

12. Scholars have noted these gendered patterns in relation to the politics of nationalist and conservative movements, which often cast women as mere symbols or victims of a masculine organization (Chatterjee 1993; Ramaswamy 1997). As an organization often suspected of right-wing subversive politics, Freemasonry in Italy can be analyzed productively in the context of literature on nationalism.

13. The intellectual topics that would serve as a theme for these public talks were almost always drawn from the nationalist body of high culture, such as Verdi's music or Botticelli's art. In these public talks, high culture served a double purpose: it affirmed Masons' ties to the nation through its heritage, and it conferred "distinction" (Bourdieu 1984) upon Masons, thus giving them legitimacy as upper-class citizens. Letting the audience know about famous historical figures who were Masons, such as "brother Mozart" or "brother Garibaldi," Masons would attempt to reclaim their contributions to Italian history, which textbooks had effectively erased (see Gnocchini 2005).

14. George Marcus and Michael Powell have also noted that "conspiracy theories and transparency issues have developed in overlapping but sequential order. In the 1990s, one heard about the prominence of paranoid social thought, but not about transparency issues from cultural analysts. In this decade, one hears about transparency issues, but not so much about conspiracy theories" (2003: 325).

Coda

1. Kleinman et al. (1997) argue that social suffering is to be found everywhere, in high-income as in low-income societies, but that it affects disproportionately "those who are desperately poor and powerless" (ix). In this book, I have extended their framework to the context of elite Masonic organizations in Italy because a phenomenological approach rooted in the social conscience of material struggles of the kind

they propose can potentially yield a more sophisticated understanding of the workings of power from above.

2. I am using Mary Steedly's term for those unsympathetic or unusual subjects of ethnographic research that, like Freemasons, have rarely been the object of anthropological studies (personal communication).

WORKS CITED

Abu-Lughod, Lila
  1986   *Veiled Sentiments: Honor and Poetry in a Bedouin Society*. Berkeley:
            University of California Press.
  1990   "The Romance of Resistance: Tracing Transformations of Power through
            Bedouin Women." *American Ethnologist* 17(1): 41–55.
  1991   "Writing against Culture." In *Recapturing Anthropology*, ed. Richard G.
            Fox, 137–162. Santa Fe: School of American Research Press.

Agamben, Giorgio
  2007   *Profanations*. New York: Zone Books.

Ahmed, Leila
  1992   *Women and Gender in Islam: Historical Roots of a Modern Debate*. New
            Haven: Yale University Press.

Ahmed, Sara
  2010   "Killing Joy: Feminism and the History of Happiness." *Signs* 35(3):
            571–594.

Althusser, Louis
  2001   *Lenin and Philosophy, and Other Essays*. New York: Monthly Review
            Press.

Altorki, Soraya, and Camillia Fawzi El-Solh, eds.

1988   *Arab Women in the Field: Studying Your Own Society.* Syracuse: Syracuse University Press.

Anderson, Benedict R.

1991 [1983]   *Imagined Communities: Reflections on the Origin and Spread of Nationalism.* London: Verso.

Anderson, James, Lionel Vibert, and Freemasons

1924   *Anderson's Constitutions of 1723.* Washington, D.C.: Masonic Service Association of the United States.

Antonello, Pierpaolo, and Alan O'Leary, eds.

2009   *Imagining Terrorism: The Rhetoric and Representation of Political Violence in Italy, 1969–2009.* London: Maney Publishing.

Apostolidis, Paul, and Juliet Williams, eds.

2004   *Public Affairs: Politics in the Age of Sex Scandals.* Durham: Duke University Press.

Aretxaga, Begoña

1997   *Shattering Silence: Women, Nationalism, and Political Subjectivity in Northern Ireland.* Princeton: Princeton University Press.

2003   "Maddening States." *Annual Review of Anthropology* 32: 393–410.

Asad, Talal

1993   *Genealogies of Religion: Discipline and Reasons of Power in Christianity and Islam.* Baltimore: Johns Hopkins University Press.

Aureli, Andrea

1999   "The Usual Suspects." In *Paranoia within Reason: A Casebook on Conspiracy as Explanation*, ed. G. E. Marcus, 197–224. Chicago: University of Chicago Press.

Bacchetta, Paola, and Margaret Power, eds.

2002   *Right-Wing Women: From Conservatives to Extremists around the World.* New York: Routledge.

Bakhtin, M. M., and Michael Holquist

1981   *The Dialogic Imagination: Four Essays.* Austin: University of Texas Press.

Balibar, Etienne

1994   "Racism as Universalism." In Balibar, *Masses, Classes, Ideas: Studies on Politics and Philosophy before and after Marx*, 191–204. New York: Routledge.

Beauvoir, Simone de

1989   *The Second Sex.* New York: Vintage Books.

Bellman, Beryl Larry

1984   *The Language of Secrecy: Symbols & Metaphors in Poro Ritual.* New Brunswick, N.J.: Rutgers University Press.

Berlant, Lauren

2006   "Cruel Optimism." *Differences: A Journal of Feminist Cultural Studies* 17(3): 20–36.

Bhabha, Homi K.

1994   *The Location of Culture.* London: Routledge.

Biehl, João Guilherme

2005   *Vita: Life in a Zone of Social Abandonment.* Berkeley: University of California Press.

Biehl, João Guilherme, Byron Good, and Arthur Kleinman, eds.

2007   *Subjectivity: Ethnographic Investigations.* Berkeley: University of California Press.

Birnbaum, Lucia Chiavola

1986   *Liberazione della donna: Feminism in Italy.* Middletown, Conn.: Wesleyan University Press.

Boddy, Janice Patricia

1989   *Wombs and Alien Spirits: Women, Men, and the Zar Cult in Northern Sudan.* Madison: University of Wisconsin Press.

Bollini, Paolo, and Cesare Rossi

1994   *I Giorni della strage.* Bologna: Clio.

Bono, Paola, and Sandra Kemp, eds.

1991   *Italian Feminist Thought: A Reader.* Oxford: B. Blackwell.

Borneman, John

1996   "Until Death Do Us Part: Marriage/Death in Anthropological Discourse." *American Ethnologist* 23(2): 215–238.

Bourdieu, Pierre

1977   *Outline of a Theory of Practice.* Cambridge: Cambridge University Press.

1984   *Distinction: A Social Critique of the Judgement of Taste.* Cambridge, Mass.: Harvard University Press.

1986   "The Forms of Capital." In *Handbook of Theory and Research for the Sociology of Education,* ed. J. G. Richardson, 241–258. New York: Greenwood Press.

1990   *The Logic of Practice.* Stanford: Stanford University Press.

Braghetti, Laura, and Francesca Mambro

1995   *Nel cerchio della prigione.* Milan: Sperling & Kupfer.

Brodie, Laura Fairchild

2000   *Breaking Out: VMI and the Coming of Women.* New York: Pantheon Books.

Brown, Dan

2003   *The Da Vinci Code: A Novel.* New York: Doubleday.

Brumann, Cristoph

    1999   "Writing for Culture: Why a Successful Concept Should Not Be
           Discarded." *Current Anthropology* 40(S): 1–26.

Butler, Judith

    1990   "Performative Acts and Gender Constitution: An Essay in Phenomenology
           and Feminist Theory." In *Performing Feminisms*, ed. S. E. Case, 270–282.
           Baltimore, Md.: Johns Hopkins University Press.

    1993   *Bodies That Matter: On the Discursive Limits of "Sex."* New York: Routledge.

    1999   *Gender Trouble: Feminism and the Subversion of Identity.* New York:
           Routledge.

Calzolari, Silvio, and Vittorio Vanni, eds.

    2001   *Iniziazione femminile e massoneria: Saggi sull'esoterismo massonico.*
           Montespertoli, Italy: MIR Edizioni.

Caracciolo, Sebastiano

    2004   *L'iniziazione femminile in massoneria: Il problema dei problemi.* Florence:
           Libreria Chiari; Firenze libri.

Carrier, James

    1992   "Occidentalism: The World Turned Upside-Down." *American Ethnologist*
           19(2): 195–212.

Carrillo Rowe, Aimee

    2008   *Power Lines: On the Subject of Feminist Alliances.* Durham: Duke University
           Press.

Carsten, Janet

    1997   *The Heat of the Hearth: The Process of Kinship in a Malay Fishing Community.*
           Oxford: Oxford University Press.

Carter, Donald Martin

    1997   *States of Grace: Senegalese in Italy and the New European Immigration.*
           Minneapolis: University of Minnesota Press.

Casanova de Seingalt, Jacques

    2007   *The Memoirs of Casanova.* Vol. 2, *To Paris and Prison.* Teddington,
           Middlesex, U.K.: Echo Library.

Cecchi, Alberto

    1985   *Storia della P2.* Rome: Editori riuniti.

Chakrabarty, Dipesh

    2000   *Provincializing Europe: Postcolonial Thought and Historical Difference.*
           Princeton: Princeton University Press.

Chatterjee, Partha

    1993   *The Nation and Its Fragments: Colonial and Postcolonial Histories.* Princeton:
           Princeton University Press.

Ciuffoletti, Zeffiro

    1989   *Le origini della massoneria in Toscana*. Foggia: Bastogi.

Ciuffoletti, Zeffiro, and Sergio Moravia, eds.

    2004   *La massoneria: La storia, gli uomini, le idee*. Milan: Oscar Mondadori.

Clawson, Mary Ann

    1989   *Constructing Brotherhood: Class, Gender, and Fraternalism*. Princeton: Princeton University Press.

Clifford, James, and George E. Marcus, eds.

    1986   *Writing Culture: The Poetics and Politics of Ethnography*. Berkeley: University of California Press.

Collier, Jane F., Sylvia J. Yanagisako, and Maurice Bloch, eds.

    1987   *Gender and Kinship: Essays toward a Unified Analysis*. Stanford: Stanford University Press.

Connell, R. W.

    1987   *Gender and Power: Society, the Person, and Sexual Politics*. Stanford: Stanford University Press.

Conti, Fulvio

    2003   *Storia della massoneria italiana: Dal Risorgimento al fascismo*. Bologna: Mulino.

    2007   *La massoneria a Firenze: Dall'età dei lumi al secondo Novecento*. Bologna: Mulino.

Coronil, Fernando

    1996   "Beyond Occidentalism: Toward Nonimperial Geohistorical Categories." *Cultural Anthropology* 11(1): 51–87.

Counihan, Carole

    2004   *Around the Tuscan Table: Food, Family, and Gender in Twentieth-Century Florence*. New York: Routledge.

Dalla Costa, Mariarosa, and Selma James

    1973   *The Power of Women and the Subversion of the Community*. Bristol, U.K.: Falling Wall Press.

Davis, John

    1987   "Family and State in the Mediterranean." In *Honor and Shame and the Unity of the Mediterranean*, vol. 22. ed. D. Gilmore, 22–34. Washington, D.C.: American Anthropological Association.

de Certeau, Michel

    1984   *The Practice of Everyday Life*. Berkeley: University of California Press.

de Certeau, Michel, Luce Giard, and Pierre Mayol

    1998   *The Practice of Everyday life*. Vol. 2, *Living and Cooking*. Minneapolis: University of Minnesota Press.

De Grazia, Victoria

1992   *How Fascism Ruled Women: Italy, 1922–1945*. Berkeley: University of
        California Press.

De Lauretis, Teresa

1994   "The Essence of the Triangle; or, Taking the Risk of Essentialism
        Seriously: Feminist Theory in Italy, the U.S., and Britain." In *The Essential
        Difference*, ed. N. Schor and E. Weed, 1–39. Bloomington: Indiana
        University Press.

Dean, Jodi

2002   *Publicity's Secret: How Technoculture Capitalizes on Democracy*. Ithaca:
        Cornell University Press.

Decena, Carlos

2008   "Tacit Subjects." *GLQ* 14(2–3): 339–359.

Delaney, Carol

1987   "Seeds of Honor, Fields of Shame." In *Honor and Shame and the Unity
        of the Mediterranean*, vol. 22, ed. D. Gilmore, 35–48. Washington, D.C.:
        American Anthropological Association.

Delaney, David

2002   "The Space That Race Makes." *Professional Geographer* 54(1): 6–14.

Derrida, Jacques

2005   *Politics of Friendship*. London: Verso.

Desjarlais, Robert R.

1997   *Shelter Blues: Sanity and Selfhood among the Homeless*. Philadelphia:
        University of Pennsylvania Press.

Dito, Oreste

1905   *Massoneria, carboneria ed altre società segrete: Nella storia del Risorgimento
        italiano*. Torino: Casa editrice nazionale Roux e Viarengo.

Domínguez, Virginia R.

1986   *White by Definition: Social Classification in Creole Louisiana*. New
        Brunswick, N.J.: Rutgers University Press.

Eco, Umberto

1988   *Il pendolo di Foucault*. Milan: Bompiani.

El-Tayeb, Fatima

2011   *European Others: Queering Ethnicity in Postnational Europe*. Minneapolis:
        University of Minnesota Press.

Elyachar, Julia

2011   "The Political Economy of Movement and Gesture in Cairo." *Journal of the
        Royal Anthropological Institute*. 17(1): 82–99.

Engels, Friedrich

1978   "The Origin of the Family, Private Property, and the State." In *The Marx-Engels Reader*, 734–759. New York: Norton.

Esposito, Rosario Francesco

1956   *La massoneria e l'Italia dal 1800 ai nostri giorni.* [Rome]: Edizioni paoline.

European Court of Human Rights

2001   Grande Oriente d'Italia di Palazzo Giustiniani c. Italia. Ricorso numero 35972/97. In Vincent Berger, *Case Law of the European Court of Human Rights*.

Evans-Pritchard, E. E.

1976 [1937]   *Witchcraft, Oracles, and Magic among the Azande.* Oxford: Clarendon Press.

Fanon, Frantz

2008   *Black Skin, White Masks.* Rev. ed. New York: Grove Press.

Faubion, James D.

1993   *Modern Greek Lessons: A Primer in Historical Constructivism.* Princeton: Princeton University Press.

Fausto-Sterling, Anne

1993   "The Five Sexes: Why Male and Female Are Not Enough." *Sciences* (March/April): 20–25.

Fernando, Mayanthy

2010   "Reconfiguring Freedom: Muslim Piety and the Limits of Secular Law and Public Discourse in France." *American Ethnologist* 37(1): 19–35.

Finel, Bernard I., and Kristin M. Lord, eds.

2002   *Power and Conflict in the Age of Transparency.* New York: Palgrave Macmillan.

Florini, Ann, ed.

2007   *The Right to Know: Transparency for an Open World.* New York: Columbia University Press.

Foucault, Michel

1978   *The History of Sexuality.* Vol. 1, *An Introduction.* Translated by Robert Hurley. New York: Vintage Books.

1979   *Discipline and Punish: The Birth of the Prison.* Translated by A. Sheridan. New York: Vintage Books.

Franklin, Sarah, and Helena Ragoné, eds.

1998   *Reproducing Reproduction: Kinship, Power, and Technological Innovation.* Philadelphia: University of Pennsylvania Press.

Freire, Paulo

2000   *Pedagogy of the Oppressed.* New York: Continuum.

Frykman, Jonas, and Orvar Löfgren

1987   *Culture Builders: A Historical Anthropology of Middle-Class Life.* New
        Brunswick, N.J.: Rutgers University Press.

Gable, Eric

1997   "A Secret Shared: Fieldwork and the Sinister in a West African Village."
        Cultural Anthropology 12(2): 213–233.

Galli, Giorgio

2007   *La venerabile trama: La vera storia di Licio Gelli e della P2.* Torino: Lindau.

Gallucci, Carole

2002   "She Loved Mussolini: Margherita Sarfatti and Italian Fascism." In
        Right-Wing Women: From Conservatives to Extremists around the World, ed.
        P. Bacchetta and M. Power, 19–28. New York: Routledge.

Galt, Anthony H

1994   "The Good Cousins' Domain of Belonging: Tropes in Southern Italian
        Secret Society Symbol and Ritual, 1810–1821." *Man* 29: 785–807.

Garsten, Christina, and Monica Lindh De Montoya, eds.

2008   *Transparency in a New Global Order: Unveiling Organizational Visions.*
        Cheltenham: Edward Elgar.

Gellner, Ernest

1983   *Nations and Nationalism.* Ithaca: Cornell University Press.

Gilroy, Paul

1993   *The Black Atlantic: Modernity and Double Consciousness.* Cambridge, Mass.:
        Harvard University Press.

Ginsberg, Elaine K., ed.

1996   *Passing and the Fictions of Identity.* Durham: Duke University Press.

Ginsburg, Faye D.

1998   *Contested Lives: The Abortion Debate in an American Community.* Berkeley:
        University of California Press.

GLDI

2012   *I principi: Leggi fondamentali.* http://www.granloggia.it/GLDI/default
        .aspx/1271-leggi_fondamentali.htm, accessed on August 28.

Glynn, Ruth

2009   "Writing the Terrorist Self: The Unspeakable Alterity of Italy's Female
        Perpetrators." *Feminist Review* 92(1): 1–18.

Gnocchini, Vittorio

2005   *L'Italia dei liberi muratori: Brevi biografie di massoni famosi.* Milan: Mimesis.

Goddard, Victoria A.

1996   *Gender, Family, and Work in Naples.* Oxford: Berg.

Good, Byron
  1994   *Medicine, Rationality, and Experience: An Anthropological Perspective.*
          Cambridge: Cambridge University Press.

Gordon, Linda
  1990   *Women, the State, and Welfare.* Madison: University of Wisconsin Press.

Gramsci, Antonio, Valentino Gerratana, and Istituto Gramsci.
  1975   *Quaderni del carcere.* Torino: G. Einaudi.

Gramsci, Antonio, and Benito Mussolini
  1997   *Contro la legge sulle associazioni segrete.* Rome: Manifestolibri.

Grasseni, Cristina
  2007   *Skilled Visions: Between Apprenticeship and Standards.* New York: Berghahn
          Books.

Greenhouse, Carol J., Elizabeth Mertz, and Kay B. Warren, eds.
  2002   *Ethnography in Unstable Places: Everyday Lives in Contexts of Dramatic
          Political Change.* Durham: Duke University Press.

Grewal, Inderpal
  2005   *Transnational America: Feminisms, Diasporas, Neoliberalisms.* Durham:
          Duke University Press.

Grewal, Inderpal, and Caren Kaplan, eds.
  1994   *Scattered Hegemonies: Postmodernity and Transnational Feminist Practices.*
          Minneapolis: University of Minnesota Press.

Guarino, Mario
  2001   *Fratello P2 1816: L'epopea piduista di Silvio Berlusconi.* Milan: Kaos.

Guha, Ranajit
  1997   *A Subaltern Studies Reader, 1986–1995.* Minneapolis: University of
          Minnesota Press.

Gupta, Akhil, and James Ferguson
  1997a   Eds. *Anthropological Locations: Boundaries and Grounds of a Field Science.*
          Berkeley: University of California Press.
  1997b   "Beyond Culture: Space, Identity, and the Politics of Difference." In
          Culture, Power, Place, ed. A. Gupta and J. Ferguson (Durham: Duke
          University Press).

Habermas, Jürgen
  1989   *The Structural Transformation of the Public Sphere: An Inquiry into a Category
          of Bourgeois Society.* Cambridge, Mass.: MIT Press.

Handler, Lisa
  1995   "In the Fraternal Sisterhood: Sororities as Gender Strategy." *Gender and
          Society* 9(2): 236–255.

Haraway, Donna Jeanne

1991   *Simians, Cyborgs, and Women: The Reinvention of Nature.* New York: Routledge.

Harding, Susan

1991   "Representing Fundamentalism: The Problem of the Repugnant Cultural Other." *Social Research: An International Quarterly* 58(3): 373–393.

2000   *The Book of Jerry Falwell: Fundamentalist Language and Politics.* Princeton: Princeton University Press.

Hardt, Michael, and Antonio Negri

2009   *Commonwealth.* Cambridge, Mass.: Belknap Press of Harvard University Press.

Harland-Jacobs, Jessica.

2007   *Builders of Empire: Freemasons and British Imperialism, 1717–1927.* Chapel Hill: University of North Carolina Press.

Herzfeld, Michael

1980   "Honour and Shame: Problems in the Comparative Analysis of Moral Systems." *Man* 15: 339–351.

1985   *The Poetics of Manhood: Contest and Identity in a Cretan Mountain Village.* Princeton: Princeton University Press.

1987   *Anthropology through the Looking-Glass: Critical Ethnography in the Margins of Europe.* Cambridge: Cambridge University Press.

1997   *Cultural Intimacy: Social Poetics in the Nation-State.* New York: Routledge.

2000   "Uncanny Success: Some Closing Remarks." In *Elites: Choice, Leadership and Succession*, ed. J. de Pina-Cabral and A. P. de Lima, 227–236. New York: Berg.

2001   *Anthropology: Theoretical Practice in Culture and Society.* Malden, Mass.: Blackwell Publishers.

2004   *The Body Impolitic: Artisans and Artifice in the Global Hierarchy of Value.* Chicago: University of Chicago Press.

2005   *Cultural Intimacy: Social Poetics in the Nation-State.* New York: Routledge.

2009   *Evicted from Eternity: The Restructuring of Modern Rome.* Chicago: University of Chicago Press.

Hobsbawm, E. J., and T. O. Ranger

1983   *The Invention of Tradition.* Cambridge: Cambridge University Press.

Holmes, Douglas

2000   *Integral Europe: Fast-Capitalism, Multiculturalism, Neofascism.* Princeton: Princeton University Press.

Hood, Christopher, and David Heald, eds.

2006   *Transparency: The Key to Better Governance?* Oxford: Oxford University Press.

hooks, bell

1981   *Ain't I a Woman: Black Women and Feminism.* Boston: South End Press.

1984   *Feminist Theory from Margin to Center.* Boston: South End Press.

Irigaray, Luce

1974   *Speculum de l'autre femme.* Paris: Éditions de Minuit.

Isastia, Anna Maria

2004   "Massoneria e fascismo: La grande repressione." In *La massoneria: La storia, gli uomini, le idee,* ed. Z. Ciuffoletti and S. Moravia, 179–237. Milan: Oscar Mondadori.

Jacob, Margaret C.

1991   *Living the Enlightenment: Freemasonry and Politics in Eighteenth-Century Europe.* New York: Oxford University Press.

2006   *The Radical Enlightenment: Pantheists, Freemasons, and Republicans.* Lafayette, La.: Cornerstone Books.

Jacquemet, Marco

1996   *Credibility in Court: Communicative Practices in the Camorra Trials.* Cambridge: Cambridge University Press.

Jakobsen, Janet R., and Ann Pellegrini, eds.

2008   *Secularisms.* Durham: Duke University Press.

Jones, Graham M.

2011   *Trade of the Tricks: Inside the Magician's Craft.* Berkeley: University of California Press.

Kahn, Susan Martha

2000   *Reproducing Jews: A Cultural Account of Assisted Conception in Israel.* Durham: Duke University Press.

Kant, Immanuel

2002   *Critique of Practical Reason.* Trans. W. S. Pluhar. Indianapolis: Hackett.

Kaplan, Caren

1996   *Questions of Travel: Postmodern Discourses of Displacement.* Durham: Duke University Press.

Kaplan, Caren, Norma Alarcón, and Minoo Moallem, eds.

1999   *Between Woman and Nation: Nationalisms, Transnational Feminisms, and the State.* Durham: Duke University Press.

Kertzer, David I.

1980   *Comrades and Christians: Religion and Political Struggle in Communist Italy.* Cambridge, U.K.: Cambridge University Press.

1988   *Ritual, Politics, and Power.* New Haven: Yale University Press.

1996   *Politics & Symbols: The Italian Communist Party and the Fall of Communism.* New Haven: Yale University Press.

Kleinman, Arthur

1999   "Experience and Its Moral Modes: Culture, Human Conditions, and Disorder." In *The Tanner Lectures on Human Values*, vol. 20, ed. G. B. Peterson. Salt Lake City: University of Utah Press.

Kleinman, Arthur, Veena Das, and Margaret M. Lock, eds.

1997   *Social Suffering*. Berkeley: University of California Press.

Kondo, Dorinne K.

1990   *Crafting Selves: Power, Gender, and Discourses of Identity in a Japanese Workplace*. Chicago: University of Chicago Press.

Koonz, Claudia

1987   *Mothers in the Fatherland: Women, the Family, and Nazi Politics*. New York: St. Martin's Press.

Kotef, Hagar

2009   "On Abstractness: First Wave Liberal Feminism and the Construction of the Abstract Woman." *Feminist Studies* 35(3): 495–522.

Koven, Seth, and Sonya Michel, eds.

1993   *Mothers of a New World: Maternalist Politics and the Origins of Welfare States*. New York: Routledge.

Krause, Elizabeth L.

2005   *A Crisis of Births: Population Politics and Family-Making in Italy*. Belmont, Calif. Thomson/Wadsworth.

Kundera, Milan

1991   *Immortality*. New York: Grove Weidenfeld.

Lave, Jean, and Etienne Wenger

1991   *Situated Learning: Legitimate Peripheral Participation*. Cambridge, U.K.: Cambridge University Press.

Leuci, Linda, and Giuseppe M. Vatri

2003   *La massoneria delle donne: Regolamenti e rituali (1730–1780)*. Torino: Età dell'acquario.

Lévi-Strauss, Claude, Rodney Needham, and James H. Bell

1969   *The Elementary Structures of Kinship*. Boston: Beacon Press.

Liechty, Mark

2003   *Suitably Modern: Making Middle-Class Culture in a New Consumer Society*. Princeton: Princeton University Press.

Little, Kenneth Lindsay

1951   *The Mende of Sierra Leone: A West African People in Transition*. London: Routledge.

Lonzi, Carla

1982 [1970]   *Sputiamo su Hegel: La donna clitoridea e la donna vaginale.* Milan: Gammalibri.

Lorde, Audre

1984   *Sister Outsider: Essays and Speeches.* Trumansburg, N.Y.: Crossing Press.

Luhrmann, T. M.

1989   *Persuasions of the Witch's Craft: Ritual Magic in Contemporary England.* Cambridge, Mass.: Harvard University Press.

Macciocchi, Maria Antonietta

1976   *La donna nera: Consenso femminile e fascismo.* Milan: Feltrinelli.

MacCormack, Carol P.

1980   "Proto-Social to Adult: A Sherbro Transformation." In *Nature, Culture, and Gender,* ed. C. P. MacCormack and M. Strathern, 95–118. Cambridge, U.K.: Cambridge University Press.

Macpherson, Jay

2008   "The Magic Flute and Freemasonry." *University of Toronto Quarterly* 76(4): 1072–1084.

Maher, Vanessa

1987   "Sewing the Seams of Society: Dressmakers and Seamstresses in Turin between the Wars." In *Gender and Kinship: Essays toward a Unified Analysis,* ed. J. F. Collier and S. J. Yanagisako, 132–159. Stanford: Stanford University Press.

Mahmood, Saba

2001   "Feminist Theory, Embodiment, and the Docile Agent: Some Reflections on the Egyptian Islamic Revival." *Cultural Anthropology* 16(2): 202–236.

2005   *Politics of Piety: The Islamic Revival and the Feminist Subject.* Princeton: Princeton University Press.

Mahmud, Lilith

2012a   "In the Name of Transparency: Gender, Terrorism, and Masonic Conspiracies in Italy." *Anthropological Quarterly* 85(4): 1177–1207.

2012b   "'The World Is a Forest of Symbols': Italian Freemasonry and the Practice of Discretion." *American Ethnologist* 39(2): 425–438.

2013   "The Profane Ethnographer: Fieldwork with a Secretive Organisation." In *Organisational Anthropology: Doing Ethnography in and among Complex Organisations,* ed. C. Garsten and A. Nyqvist, 189–207. London: Pluto Press.

Mainguy, Irène

2004   *Simbolica massonica del terzo millennio.* Trans. M. Faccia. Rome: Edizioni Mediterranee.

Maira, Sunaina

 2009   *Missing: Youth, Citizenship, and Empire after 9/11*. Durham: Duke University
         Press.

Malinowski, Bronislaw

 1984   *Argonauts of the Western Pacific: An Account of Native Enterprise and
         Adventure in the Archipelagoes of Melanesian New Guinea*. Prospect Heights,
         Ill.: Waveland Press.

Marcus, George E., ed.

 1999   *Paranoia within Reason: A Casebook on Conspiracy as Explanation*. Chicago:
         University of Chicago Press.

Marcus, George E., and Peter Dobkin Hall

 1992   *Lives in Trust: The Fortunes of Dynastic Families in Late Twentieth-Century
         America*. Boulder: Westview Press.

Marcus, George E., and Michael Powell

 2003   "From Conspiracy Theories in the Incipient New World Order of the
         1990s to Regimes of Transparency Now." *Anthropological Quarterly* 76(2):
         323–334.

Masco, Joseph

 2006   *The Nuclear Borderlands: The Manhattan Project in Post–Cold War New
         Mexico*. Princeton: Princeton University Press.

 2010   "Sensitive But Unclassified: Secrecy and the Counterterrorist State."
         Public Culture 22(3): 433–463.

Mauss, Marcel

 1925   *Essai sur le don: Forme et raison de l'échange dans les sociétés archaiques*.
         Paris: Alcan.

Mazzarella, William

 2006   "Internet X-Ray: E-Governance, Transparency, and the Politics of
         Immediation in India." *Public Culture* 18(3): 473–505.

Mazzocchi, Antonella

 1994   *La massoneria nella stampa italiana degli anni '80*. Florence:
         A. Pontecorboli.

Mbembe, Achille

 2001   *On the Postcolony*. Berkeley: University of California Press.

McDowell, Deborah E.

 1986   Introduction. In Nella Larsen, *Quicksand and Passing*, ix–xxxvii. New
         Brunswick, N.J.: Rutgers University Press.

McGoey, Linsey

 2012   "Strategic Unknowns: Towards a Sociology of Ignorance." *Economy and
         Society* 41(1): 1–16.

Merleau-Ponty, Maurice
2002   *Phenomenology of Perception.* London: Routlédge.

Merrill, Heather
2006   *An Alliance of Women: Immigration and the Politics of Race.* Minneapolis: University of Minnesota Press.

Merry, Sally Engle
2006   *Human Rights and Gender Violence: Translating International Law into Local Justice.* Chicago: University of Chicago Press.

Meynell, Kate
2005   *Women of the Lodge.* BBC News, June 28. http://news.bbc.co.uk/go/pr/fr/-/ 1/hi/magazine/4629813.stm. Accessed on July 29, 2005.

Mill, John Stuart
1989   "On Liberty" and Other Writings. Trans. S. Collini. Cambridge, U.K.: Cambridge University Press.

Mohanty, Chandra
1988   "Under Western Eyes: Feminist Scholarship and Colonial Discourse." *Feminist Review* 30: 60–88.
2003   *"Under Western Eyes* Revisited: Feminist Solidarity through Anticapitalist Struggle." *Signs* 28(2): 499–535.

Mola, Aldo Alessandro
1992   *Storia della massoneria italiana dalle origini ai nostri giorni.* Milan: Bompiani.
2008   *Gelli e la P2: Fra cronaca e storia.* Foggia: Bastogi.

Molé, Noelle
2010   "Precarious Subjects: Anticipating Neoliberalism in Northern Italy's Workplace." *American Anthropologist* 112(1): 38–53.

Moraga, Cherríe, and Gloria Anzaldúa
1981   *This Bridge Called My Back: Writings by Radical Women of Color.* Watertown, Mass.: Persephone Press.

Mosse, George L.
1988   *Nationalism and Sexuality: Middle-Class Morality and Sexual Norms in Modern Europe.* Madison: University of Wisconsin Press.

Muehlebach, Andrea
2012   *The Moral Neoliberal: Welfare and Citizenship in Italy.* Chicago: University of Chicago Press.

Murphy, William P.
1980   "Secret Knowledge as Property and Power in Kpelle Society." *Africa* 50(2): 193–207.

Nader, Laura

    1972   "Up the Anthropologist: Perspectives Gained from Studying Up." In *Reinventing Anthropology*, ed. D. Hymes, 285–311. New York: Pantheon Books.

Najmabadi, Afsaneh

    2006   "Gender and Secularism of Modernity: How Can a Muslim Woman Be French?" *Feminist Studies* 32(2): 239–255.

Narayan, Kirin

    1993   "How Native Is a 'Native' Anthropologist?" *American Anthropologist* 95: 671–686.

Needham, Rodney

    1972   *Belief, Language, and Experience.* Chicago: University of Chicago Press.

Négrier, Patrick

    2006   *Le rite des anciens devoirs: Old charges, 1390–1729.* Groslay: Ivoire-clair.

Ong, Aihwa

    1999   *Flexible Citizenship: The Cultural Logics of Transnationality.* Durham: Duke University Press.

Ortner, Sherry B.

    1996   *Making Gender: The Politics and Erotics of Culture.* Boston: Beacon Press.

    2003   *New Jersey Dreaming: Capital, Culture, and the Class of '58.* Durham: Duke University Press.

    2005   "Subjectivity and Cultural Critique." *Anthropological Theory* 5(1): 31–52.

    2006   *Anthropology and Social Theory: Culture, Power, and the Acting Subject.* Durham: Duke University Press.

Panourgiá, Neni

    2009   *Dangerous Citizens: The Greek Left and the Terror of the State.* New York: Fordham University Press.

Parker, Andrew

    1992   *Nationalisms & Sexualities.* New York: Routledge.

Paxson, Heather

    2004   *Making Modern Mothers: Ethics and Family Planning in Urban Greece.* Berkeley: University of California Press.

Però, Davide

    2007   *Inclusionary Rhetoric/Exclusionary Practices: Left-Wing Politics and Migrants in Italy.* New York: Berghahn Books.

Pile, Steve

    2011   "Skin, Race and Space: The Clash of Bodily Schemas in Frantz Fanon's *Black Skins, White Masks* and Nella Larsen's *Passing.*" *Cultural Geographies* 18(1): 25–41.

Pina-Cabral, João de, and Antónia Pedroso de Lima, eds.

2000   *Elites: Choice, Leadership and Succession.* New York: Berg.

Pinkus, Karen

1997   "Shades of Black in Advertising and Popular Culture." In *Revisioning Italy: National Identity and Global Culture*, ed. B. Allen and M. J. Russo, 134–155. Minneapolis: University of Minnesota Press.

Pitt-Rivers, Julian

1966   "Honour and Social Status." In *Honour and Shame: the Values of Medittera- nean Society*, ed. J. G. Peristiany. Chicago: University of Chicago Press.

Plesset, Sonja

2006   *Sheltering Women: Negotiating Gender and Violence in Northern Italy.* Stanford: Stanford University Press.

Povinelli, Elizabeth A.

2006   *The Empire of Love: Toward a Theory of Intimacy, Genealogy, and Carnality.* Durham: Duke University Press.

Rainey, Lawrence S.

2009   "Introduction: F. T. Marinetti and the Development of Futurism." In *Futurism: An Anthology*, ed. L. S. Rainey, C. Poggi, and L. Wittman, 1–42. New Haven: Yale University Press.

Ramaswamy, Sumathi

1997   "Virgin Mother, Beloved Other: The Erotics of Tamil Nationalism in Colonial and Post-Colonial India." *Thamyris* 4(1): 9–39.

Ratzinger, Joseph Cardinal

1983   *Declaration on Masonic Associations.* Vatican City: Office of the Sacred Congregation for the Doctrine of the Faith. http://www.vatican.va/roman_ curia/congregations/cfaith/documents/rc_con_cfaith_doc_19831126 _declaration-masonic_en.html, accessed on August 20, 2012.

Rossi, Gianni, and Francesco Lombrassa

1981   *In nome della "Loggia": Le prove di come la massoneria segreta ha tentato di impadronirsi dello Stato italiano; I retroscena della P2.* Rome: Napoleone.

Rubin, Gayle

1975   "The Traffic in Women: Notes on the Political Economy of Sex." In *Toward an Anthropology of Women*, ed. R. R. Reiter. New York: Monthly Review Press.

Saïd, Edward W.

2003   *Orientalism.* New York: Vintage Books.

Sapir, Edward

1960   "Culture, Genuine and Spurious." In *Culture, Language and Personality: Selected Essays*, ed. D. G. Mandelbaum. Berkeley: University of California Press.

Sargent, Lydia

    1981   *Women and Revolution: A Discussion of the Unhappy Marriage of Marxism and Feminism.* Boston: South End Press.

Schneider, David Murray

    1980   *American Kinship: A Cultural Account.* Chicago: University of Chicago Press.

Schneider, Jane, and Peter T. Schneider

    2002   "The Mafia and al-Qaeda: Violent and Secretive Organizations in Comparative and Historical Perspective." *American Anthropologist* 104(3): 776–782.

    2003   *Reversible Destiny: Mafia, Antimafia, and the Struggle for Palermo.* Berkeley: University of California Press.

Schor, Naomi, and Elizabeth Weed, eds.

    1994   *The Essential Difference.* Bloomington: Indiana University Press.

Schumann, William

    2007   "Transparency, Governmentality, and Negation: Democratic Practice and Open Government Policy in the National Assembly for Wales." *Anthropological Quarterly* 80(3): 837–862.

Scott, Joan Wallach

    2007   *The Politics of the Veil.* Princeton: Princeton University Press.

Sedgwick, Eve Kosofsky

    1985   *Between Men: English Literature and Male Homosocial Desire.* New York: Columbia University Press.

    1990   *Epistemology of the Closet.* Berkeley: University of California Press.

Shohat, Ella

    1992   "Dislocated Identities: Reflections of an Arab Jew." *Movement Research Journal* 5 (Fall/Winter).

Shore, Cris, and Stephen Nugent, eds.

    2002   *Elite Cultures: Anthropological Perspectives.* London: Routledge.

Silverstein, Paul

    2002   "An Excess of Truth: Violence, Conspiracy Theorizing and the Algerian Civil War." *Anthropological Quarterly* 75(4): 643–674.

Simmel, Georg

    1906   "The Sociology of Secrecy and of Secret Societies." *American Journal of Sociology* 11(4): 441–498.

Sommer, Doris

    1991   *Foundational Fictions: The National Romances of Latin America.* Berkeley: University of California Press.

Spivak, Gayatri Chakravorty

1988   "Can the Subaltern Speak?" In *Marxism and the Interpretation of Culture,*
        ed. C. Nelson and L. Grossberg, 271–313. Chicago: University of Illinois.

1993   *Outside in the Teaching Machine.* New York: Routledge.

Stacey, Judith

1988   "Can There Be a Feminist Ethnography?" *Women's Studies International*
        Forum 11(1): 21–27.

Steedly, Mary Margaret

1993   *Hanging Without a Rope: Narrative Experience in Colonial and Postcolonial*
        Karoland. Princeton: Princeton University Press.

1996   "What Is Culture? Does It Matter?" In *Field Work: Sites in Literary and*
        Cultural Studies, ed. M. Garber, P. Franklin, and R. Walkowitz, 18–25.
        New York: Routledge.

Stevenson, David

1988   *The Origins of Freemasonry: Scotland's Century, 1590–1710.* Cambridge, U.K.:
        Cambridge University Press.

Stoler, Ann Laura

1995   *Race and the Education of Desire: Foucault's History of Sexuality and the*
        Colonial Order of Things. Durham: Duke University Press.

Stone, Linda

1997   *Kinship and Gender: An Introduction.* Boulder, Colo.: Westview Press.

Strathern, Marilyn

1992   *Reproducing the Future: Essays on Anthropology, Kinship and the New*
        Reproductive Technologies. New York: Routledge.

2000   "The Tyranny of Transparency." *British Educational Research Journal* 26(3):
        309–321.

Tambiah, Stanley Jeyaraja

1990   *Magic, Science, Religion, and the Scope of Rationality.* Cambridge:
        Cambridge University Press.

Taussig, Michael T.

1986   *Shamanism, Colonialism, and the Wild Man: A Study in Terror and Healing.*
        Chicago: University of Chicago Press.

Tsoukas, Haridimos

1997   "The Tyranny of Light: The Temptations and the Paradoxes of the
        Information Society." *Futures* 29(9): 827–843.

Turner, Victor Witter

1967   *The Forest of Symbols: Aspects of Ndembu Ritual.* Ithaca, N.Y.: Cornell
        University Press.

1969   *The Ritual Process: Structure and Anti-Structure.* London: Routledge &
        K. Paul.

Urban, Hugh B.

2001   "The Adornment of Silence: Secrecy and Symbolic Power in American Freemasonry." *Journal of Religion & Society* 3: 1–29.

Vattimo, Gianni

1992   *The Transparent Society.* Baltimore: Johns Hopkins University Press.

Verdicchio, Pasquale

1997   *Bound by Distance: Rethinking Nationalism through the Italian Diaspora.* Madison: Fairleigh Dickinson University Press.

Vidich, Arthur J., and Joseph Bensman

2000   *Small Town in Mass Society: Class, Power, and Religion in a Rural Community.* Urbana: University of Illinois Press.

Vigni, Francesca, and Pier Domenico Vigni

1997   *Donna e massoneria in Italia: Dalle origini ad oggi.* Foggia: Bastogi.

Visweswaran, Kamala

1994   "Betrayal: An Analysis in Three Acts." In *Scattered Hegemonies: Postmodernity and Transnational Feminist Practices*, ed. I. Grewal and C. Kaplan, 90–109. Minneapolis: University of Minnesota Press.

1996   "Small Speeches, Subaltern Gender: Nationalist Ideology and Its Historiography." In *Subaltern Studies: Writings on South Asian History and Society*, vol. 9, ed. S. Amin and D. Chakrabarty, 83–125. Oxford: Oxford University Press.

1997   "Histories of Feminist Ethnography." *Annual Review of Anthropology* 26: 591–621.

West, Cornel

1999   *The Cornel West Reader.* New York: Basic Civitas Books.

West, Harry G., and Todd Sanders, eds.

2003   *Transparency and Conspiracy: Ethnographies of Suspicion in the New World Order.* Durham: Duke University Press.

Weston, Kath

1991   *Families We Choose: Lesbians, Gays, Kinship.* New York: Columbia University Press.

1998   "Virtual Anthropologist." In *Long Slow Burn: Sexuality and Social Science.* New York: Routledge.

2002   *Gender in Real Time: Power and Transience in a Visual Age.* New York: Routledge.

Williams, Raymond

1977   *Marxism and Literature.* Oxford: Oxford University Press.

Willis, Paul E.

1981   *Learning to Labor: How Working Class Kids Get Working Class Jobs.* New York: Columbia University Press.

Wollstonecraft, Mary
  2004   *A Vindication of the Rights of Woman*. New York: Barnes & Noble Books.

Yalman, Nur
  1967   *Under the Bo Tree: Studies in Caste, Kinship, and Marriage in the Interior of Ceylon*. Berkeley: University of California Press.

Yanagisako, Sylvia Junko
  2002   *Producing Culture and Capital: Family Firms in Italy*. Princeton: Princeton University Press.

Young, Iris Marion
  2000   *Inclusion and Democracy*. Oxford: Oxford University Press.

INDEX

Communists/Communism, 11, 38, 64, 98, 104, 158–159, 161–164, 205n14, 209n1

conservatism, 38, 97–103, 204n6, 205n10, 211n12

conspiracy theories: overview of, 7, 120, 125, 160–161, 184; discretion and, 30, 148; gender differences and, 18, 113, 171–173, 175, 211n12; media's stereo-typical images and, 6, 122; nation-state and, 159–161; P2 case and, 3–4, 11, 72, 113, 162–165, 210n3, 210nn6–7; persecution of Masons and, 30, 58, 72, 159–160; transparency and, 159–161, 178, 183, 185, 210n4, 211n14

Constitution, and Article 18, 11, 14, 44, 155, 191

Constitutions of the Free-Masons, The (Anderson's *Constitutions*) (Anderson, Vibert, and Freemasons), 7, 9–10, 67, 83, 112, 199n1

cooperatives, feminist, 97, 99

corruption, 58, 91–92, 159, 164, 171, 178, 183, 184, 204n3

cosmology, 38, 71, 99, 102, 128, 131, 153

cosmopolitanism, 16, 111, 129, 132, 136, 196, 205n9, 207n7

covert lodge, 162. *See also* P2 case (Propaganda 2)

cultura (high culture). *See* high culture (*cultura*)

cultural capital: *agape* dinners and, 150; distinction and, 124, 207n10, 211n13; gender differences and, 141–145, 208n16, 209nn19–20; nationalism and, 207n10; speculative Freemasonry and, 18, 124–125, 129–132, 136–142. *See also* distinction; high culture (*cultura*); social capital; symbolic capital

cultural intimacy, 90, 170, 178–179, 211n11

culture versus high culture, 143, 147, 209n18, 209n21

death: "death sentence" and, 61, 66, 69, 210n6; "Eternal Orient" and, 151–153; initiations and, 56, 60–61, 65–66, 69

De Certeau, Michel, 21

De Gouges, Olympe, 204n2

degrees of initiation, 12, 56–57, 200n6. *See also* initiations; *and specific degrees of initiation*

De Lauretis, Teresa, 205n12

democratic ideals: overview of, 7–8, 16–17; antidemocratic strategies and, 7, 58, 92–93, 153, 178, 183; persecution of Masons and, 191–193; secrecy and, 168, 193; terrorism and, 160–161; transparency and, 157, 161, 175–178

De Molay, Jacques, 119–120

Derrida, Jacques, 17, 83, 93–94, 196, 206n18

desire for power/joining, 170, 211n11

deviated Freemasonry (*Massoneria deviata*), 11, 113, 165, 193, 210n3, 210n6. *See also* conspiracy theories; P2 case (Propaganda 2); terrorism

DIGOS, 163, 172, 185

discretion: overview of, 17–19, 28, 43–44, 193–194; architectural sites and, 29–31; democratic ideals and, 168; distinction and, 133, 148, 194; ethnographers and, 19, 33, 39–40, 44–45, 91, 188–189; gender differences and, 194; gestures of recognition and, 29, 44, 90, 95, 187; high culture and, 44, 133, 136–138, 147–148; identity of Masons and, 29, 64, 180; initiations and, 65–66, 83; pedagogies and, 65–66, 128; practices of, 33, 51, 153, 180, 194; secrecy and,

discretion (*continued*)
28, 79, 197; secrecy versus, 43, 180;
self-cultivation and, 134; spaces of,
28–30, 33, 43–44, 138, 153–154; stealing with the eyes and, 121, 134–136,
208n13; subjectivity in context of,
63–64, 193, 202n4; transparency and,
157–158, 179–182

distinction: cultural capital and, 124,
207n10, 211n13; discretion and, 133,
148, 194; gender differences and, 143–
144, 194; high culture and, 130–136,
146–148, 208n14. *See also* elitism

divine universal love (*agape*), 77–78,
83–84, 197. *See also* friendship (*philia*);
love (*amore*)

dues for membership, 57–58, 124

Eco, Umberto, 121–122

education or erudition (*istruzione* or *erudi-*
zione), 130–133, 207n9, 208n12

egregore, 112, 114, 197

elitism: overview of, 8–9, 14–15; *agape*
dinners and, 154; fraternity and,
84, 91; secrecy and, 9, 14; spaces of
Freemasonry and, 44; subjectivity and,
58. *See also* distinction; high culture
(*cultura*)

Enlightenment: democratic ideals and, 16,
58, 67, 80–81; fraternity and, 84–85,
112, 195; history of Freemasonry and, 7,
10, 16; self-cultivation and, 134, 145

Entered Apprentice: initiations and, 52, 55,
57; Oath of, 55, 65, 141, 177, 179, 182,
196. *See also* Apprentice Freemasons

equality. *See* fraternity (*fratellanza* or
brotherhood/brotherly love); freedom
(liberty); gender differences; sexism

erudition or education (*erudizione* or *istru-*
zione), 130–133, 207n9

ES (Order of the Eastern Star). *See* Order
of the Eastern Star (ES)

esotericism: overview of, 13; *agape* dinners
and, 154; ES and, 68–69; high culture
and, 146, 148; initiations and, 7, 57;
profane and esoteric tension and, 39,
51–52, 129, 140–141; stealing with
the eyes and, 121, 135; subjectivity
and, 61. *See also* rituals; speculative
Freemasonry

Eternal Orient, 151–153

ethnographers/ethnographies. *See*
fieldwork

Evans-Pritchard, E. E., 10

Fanon, Frantz, 35

Fascism, 10–11, 38, 98, 143, 191–192,
205n14, 210n3. *See also* neo-Fascism

Faubion, James D., 217n10

Fellow Mason (Fellowship), 12, 57, 60–61,
126

feminism: conservatism and, 97–98,
205n10; cooperatives and, 97, 99;
fraternity and, 95, 97–106, 204nn4–6,
205nn10–12, 205n14, 206n15; Italian
compared with American or French,
98–99, 205nn11–12; the Left and, 98,
104, 205n11; Mason's view of, 100;
nationalism and, 203n1, 205n10;
postfeminism and, 101; the Right
and, 97–98; scholarship and, 19, 95,
189–190, 194–195, 204n4; sisterhood
and, 95, 204nn4–5

fieldwork, 1–6, 19, 189. *See also* native
ethnographers

Foucault, Michel, 176

founding fathers, 8, 85, 86

Francophone Masonic lodges, 69, 199n3

Franklin, Benjamin, 8, 85, 86

fratello (brother), 18, 79–82, 86, 94–95

fratello di sangue (blood brother), 95

fraternity (*fratellanza* or brotherhood/
    brotherly love): overview of, 16–18,
    58, 83–86, 114–116, 195–197, 206n19;
    abstraction of liberal subjects and,
    106–114, 206n18; agency and, 104,
    105; brother and, 18, 79–82, 86,
    94–95; Catholic Church and, 104;
    chain of union and, 112–113; char-
    ity and, 101, 108–109; class and, 92,
    95, 104, 107–108, 110, 115, 206n18;
    conservatism and, 97, 99–103, 204n6;
    corruption and, 91–92, 109; cosmology
    and, 99; cultural intimacy and, 211n11;
    discretion and, 45; *egregore* and, 112,
    114; elitism and, 84, 91; feminism and,
    95, 97–106, 204n4, 204n6; gender
    differences and, 70, 75–78, 80–81,
    107–110, 116, 141–142, 194; gestures of
    recognition and, 90, 187; homophobia
    and, 103; imagined communities and,
    93, 195, 211n11; kinship and, 91, 93,
    95–96; the Left and, 98, 103, 104; lib-
    eral humanism and, 18, 37, 81, 84–85,
    93, 105, 115–116, 195–196; lived experi-
    ences of, 86–93, 107; love and, 76–78,
    83–84, 114; Marxism and, 98–99,
    205n11; modernity and, 84–85, 91,
    94–95, 115, 202n9; nationalism and,
    84; nation-state and, 91–93, 211n11;
    neoliberalism and, 101–102; nepotism
    and, 91–92, 109, 204n3; persecution
    of Masons and, 113, 192; privilege and,
    91, 106–108, 195–197, 205n9; race
    and, 37, 90, 95, 195; the Right and, 95,
    98, 103–104; secrecy and, 17, 192, 197;
    self-cultivation and, 7, 10, 81; sexism
    and, 89–90, 195; sisterhood and, 83,
    93–96, 204n4, 204n6; social capital
    and, 93; subaltern subjects and, 105,

115, 195; subjectivity and, 109–110;
    transnationalism and, 96–97, 111–112,
    205n9; unmarked subject and, 80, 84,
    115. *See also* race

freedom (liberty): overview of, 7, 16–17,
    58; feminism and, 104–105; race and,
    37–38; self-cultivation and, 10; subjec-
    tivity and, 76, 80–81, 203n12; transpar-
    ency and, 180; universality and, 195;
    universality of, 110–111, 116. *See also*
    fraternity (*fratellanza* or brotherhood/
    brotherly love); race

Freemasonry (*Massoneria*), 6–12, 74–75,
    199n3, 200n4, 200n6, 202n8. *See also*
    fraternity (*fratellanza* or brotherhood/
    brotherly love); initiations; spaces of
    Freemasonry; speculative Freemasonry;
    women's lodges; *and specific lodges and
    Masonic Orders*

Freire, Paulo, 208n12

friendship (*philia*), 13, 58–59, 71–75,
    88–89. See also *agape* (divine universal
    love); love (*amore*); loved ones, and
    paths; treaties of friendship

Garibaldi, Giuseppe, 8, 31, 60, 72, 178,
    211n13

Gelli, Licio, 162, 210n6

gender differences: conservatism and,
    211n12; cultural capital and, 141–145,
    202n6, 209nn19–20; distinction
    and, 143–144, 194; fraternity and, 70,
    75–78, 80–81, 107–110, 116, 141–142,
    194; high culture and, 141–145, 194,
    209nn19–20; initiations and, 69–71,
    74; nationalism and, 18, 211n12;
    pedagogies and, 128, 143, 208n17;
    speculative Freemasonry and, 141–145,
    208n16, 209nn19–20; speculative labor
    and, 141–142, 148; subjectivity and,

Gran Loggia Massonica Femminile d'Italia. *See* Grand Women's Masonic Lodge of Italy (GLMFI)

Great Architect of the Universe, 10, 70, 123, 152

Grewal, Inderpal, 207n7

Habermas, Jürgen, 8, 193

habitus, 19, 29, 48, 130, 132

Handler, Lisa, 204n6

Head of the Order, 8, 49–50, 200n6. *See also* Maestra/o (Masters); Masonic Order

Herzfeld, Michael, 6, 129, 204n3, 211n11

hierarchy of values, 125, 129–131, 143

high culture (*cultura*): overview of, 147–148; culture versus, 143, 147, 209n18, 209n21; discretion and, 44, 133, 136–138, 147–148; distinction and, 130–136, 147–148, 208n14; gender differences and, 141–145, 209nn19–20; imagined communities and, 137, 143–144, 147, 207n5; legitimacy and, 140, 177, 208n15, 211n13; nation-state and, 207n5; pedagogies and, 127–133, 146, 207n5, 207nn8–10; performance of, 143–144; privilege and, 129, 140, 146; taste and, 103, 124, 133, 136–138, 140, 147, 196, 208n14. *See also* cultural capital; elitism; privilege

history of Freemasonry, 7–11, 77, 123–124

homophobia, 31, 103, 205n13

hooks, bell, 204n4, 206n16

humanism. *See* liberal humanism

identity category: of Masons, 27–28, 95; nationalism and, 34–36, 62; privilege and, 26, 35–36; rituals and, 62; secrecy

and, 29, 64, 67, 179–180; subjectivity and, 58, 61–62, 64, 67, 73–74, 79, 81, 158, 209n1

Illuminati, 200n4

imagined communities, 93, 137, 143, 195, 211n11

immigration, 22, 24, 35. *See also* race

initiations: overview of, 48, 52, 78–79; Ancient and Accepted Scottish Rite and, 57, 201n1; Apprentice Freemasons and, 63, 75–76; Chamber of Reflections and, 56; class and, 58, 67, 70; death and, 56, 60–61, 65–66, 69; degrees of initiation and, 12, 56–57, 200n6; Entered Apprentice and, 52, 55, 57; ES and, 69; esotericism and, 57; ethnographers and, 37, 41, 201n7; gender differences and, 69–71, 74, 203n6; love and, 75–78; membership dues and, 57–58; nationalism and, 201n1; paths to, 57–59, 61, 66–75, 202n8; philosopher's stone and, 56–57; political subjectivity and, 67, 75–78; Rites and, 57; ritual differences and, 74; subjectivity production and, 59–60; VITRIOL and, 56. *See also* rituals

intersubjectivity, 17, 57, 79, 86, 202n9. *See also* subjectivity

istruzione or *erudizione* (education or erudition), 130–133, 207n9

Jones, Graham, 207n9

Kaplan, Caren, 207n7

Kertzer, David, 209n1

kinship: blood relatives and, 34, 93, 95; fraternity and, 91, 93, 95–96, 204n3, 205n8; members and, 13, 74; nation-state and, 34; paths and, 58–59, 68–71; profane and, 64

Knights Templar, 12, 119–121, 135, 200n4
knowledge production, 127, 160–161, 188–189
Kondo, Dorinne K., 206n1
Kotef, Hagar, 107, 108, 111
Kundera, Milan, 146

labor, speculative, 124–125, 131, 140–141, 147–148, 196. *See also* operative Freemasonry; speculative Freemasonry
landmarks, 199n1
Larsen, Nella, 26
Lead Years (*Anni di Piombo*), 11, 28, 158–159, 162, 174–175, 210nn2–3
the Left (left-wing): feminism and, 98, 205n11; fraternity and, 98, 103, 104, 205n11, 205n14; persecution of Masons and, 11, 155–156, 191; race and, 24; terrorism and, 158–159; violence and, 201n8. *See also specific events and ideologies*
legitimacy: high culture and, 129, 140, 208n15, 211n13; lodges and, 13, 55, 111, 182, 200nn7–8; pedagogies and, 129; rituals and, 52, 112–113; women's lodges and, 76, 78, 80, 141–142, 148, 194
Lévi-Strauss, Claude, 77
liberal humanism: abstraction of liberal subjects and, 86, 106–114, 197, 206n16, 206n18; fraternity and, 18, 84–85, 93, 105, 115–116, 204n2; Occidentalism and, 81, 190, 196, 203n12; as paradox in modernity, 84–85; persecution of Masons and, 10–11, 190–192; race and, 37–38, 80; secrecy and, 4, 193; self-cultivation and, 7, 16–17, 80–81; sexism and, 16, 93–94, 143, 195, 203n10, 204n2; unmarked subject and, 80, 107

liberty (freedom). *See* fraternity (*fratellanza* or brotherhood); freedom (liberty); gender differences; race
lived experiences, of fraternity, 86–93
lodge/s, 7–8. *See also* fraternity (*fratellanza* or brotherhood/brotherly love); Freemasonry (*Massoneria*); initiations; Masonic Orders; spaces of Freemasonry; speculative Freemasonry; women's lodges; *and specific lodges and Masonic Orders*
Lonzi, Carla, 99
love (*amore*), 75–78, 83–84, 114, 203n1. See also *agape* (divine universal love); friendship (*philia*)
loved ones, and paths, 58–59, 71–75. *See also* friendship (*philia*)
Luhrmann, Tanya M., 206n3

Maestra/o (Masters), 12, 57, 143, 168. *See also* Grand Maestra/o (Grand Masters)
Mahmood, Saba, 105, 126, 206n2
Malinowski, Bronislaw, 1
Mambro, Francesca, 175, 210n3
Marcus, George E., 211n14
Marx, Karl, 123
Marxism, 98–99, 124, 190–191, 205n11
Masonic Orders: blue Freemasonry and, 12; Rites and, 12, 168–169, 200n6, 210n8; as secret societies, 158, 169. *See also* initiations; *and specific degrees and Masonic Orders; specific roles/positions and Orders*
Massoneria (Freemasonry), 6–12, 74–75, 199n3, 200n4, 200n6, 202n8. See also fraternity (*fratellanza* or brotherhood/ brotherly love); initiations; spaces of Freemasonry; speculative Freemasonry; women's lodges; *and specific lodges and Masonic Orders*

operative Freemasonry, 7, 11, 50, 123–125, 199n1. *See also* speculative Freemasonry

Opus Dei, 120–121, 160

Order of the Eastern Star (ES): overview of, 5, 12; charity and, 108–109; esotericism and, 68; feminism and, 103; fraternity and, 88–89; friendships among Freemasons and, 88–89; initiations and, 69; kinship and, 96; paths for women and, 68–69; philanthropy and, 68; rituals and, 68, 69; treaties of friendship and, 68, 75; Worthy Matron and, 5, 12, 108; Worthy Patron and, 5, 12, 88, 117

Ordine della Stella d'Oriente. *See* Order of the Eastern Star (ES)

Orient, the (in temples), 50, 52, 138, 151–153. *See also* death

Orientalism, 1, 81, 127–129, 132, 203n12, 206n15, 207n6

Ortner, Sherry B., 202n2

outing (coming out), 64, 156–157, 172, 176. *See also* queer studies and theory

P2 case (Propaganda 2), 3–4, 11, 65, 72, 113, 162–165, 167, 210n3, 210nn5–7

Parliament, 11, 100–102, 130, 144, 162–163, 192

passing (*passare*), 23, 25–26, 44–45

password, 18–19, 26, 140, 146

paths, 57–59, 61, 66–75, 202n8. *See also* initiations

pedagogies: overview of, 147–148; agency and, 108, 126, 206nn2–3; gender differences and, 128, 143, 208n17; high culture and, 127–133, 146, 207n5, 207nn8–10; legitimacy and, 129; modeling and, 134–136, 145, 208nn11–12; race and, 37–38; rule of silence and,

125–126, 206nn1–3; self-cultivation and, 63, 65; Socratic method and, 119; stealing with the eyes and, 121, 134–136, 208n13; *tavola/e* and, 50–51, 126–128, 207n4. *See also* speculative Freemasonry

persecution, of Masons, 9–11, 26, 42, 58, 64, 92, 113, 161–162, 179–180, 189–193, 201n8

philanthropy or charity, 68, 101, 108–109, 177, 196–197, 206n17

philia (friendships), 13, 58–59, 71–75, 74, 88–89. See also *agape* (divine universal love); love (*amore*); loved ones, and paths; treaties of friendship

philosopher's stone, 56–57

Pirandello, Luigi, 2

Poggi, Giuseppe, 29

political subjectivity, 16, 19, 67, 80, 84, 176, 180, 196, 203n1

politics: overview of, 3–4, 9–11, 113, 210n3; legitimacy and, 160–161; ritual symbols and, 152, 209n1; secrecy and, 7–9, 11; spaces of Freemasonry and, 38; women's role in, 98. *See also specific ideologies*

postcolonial subjects, 34–35, 197, 207n7

postcolonial theory, 80, 189–190, 194–195, 203n1, 206n15

postfeminism, 101

Powell, Michael, 211n14

Power, Margaret, 97–98

power/joining, desire for, 170, 211n11

privacy, 11, 31, 40, 42, 179–180, 200n1

privilege: overview of, 58, 190–191; fraternity and, 91, 106–108, 124, 194–197, 205n9; high culture and, 129, 140, 146, 148; men and, 145, 194, 195, 209n19; Occidentalism and, 146, 194–197, 207n7; passing and, 26, 35–36; profa-

nation of, 19, 192; spaces of Freemasonry and, 44; unmarked subject and,
101–102, 115, 145; women and, 77,
106–108, 145, 174–175, 195
profanation, 19, 187, 192
profane (*profana/o*): overview of, 26,
38–39, 200n2; discretion in the context
of, 28–30, 43–44, 65–66, 91, 138,
193–194; esotericism tension with,
51–52, 107, 125, 128, 150, 177, 179; ethnographies as, 5–6, 19, 37, 48, 76, 192,
197; gestures of recognition and, 90;
kinship and, 64, 95; queer community
compared with Freemasonry and, 26,
28–29, 64, 202n4, 209n1; rituals and,
39, 48–50, 56–57, 61, 86–87; spaces
of Freemasonry and, 28–29, 31–34,
43–45, 64; subjectivity in context of,
56–57, 88, 202n4; white agape and, 74,
117–118, 149. *See also* secularism
Propaganda 2 (P2 case), 3–4, 11, 65, 72,
113, 162–165, 167, 210n3, 210nn5–7
the public, 8, 11, 157, 162
public events, 31–34, 138–141, 177
publicity, 7–8, 181–182, 193
public relations, 176–177, 188, 211n13
public sphere, 8, 32, 153

queer studies and theory, 26, 28–29, 64,
202n4, 209n1

race: fraternity and, 90, 95, 195; immigration and, 22, 24, 203n12; pedagogies
and, 37–38; spaces of Freemasonry
and, 34, 35–38, 201nn4–5; unmarked
subject and, 115. *See also* fraternity
(*fratellanza* or brotherhood); freedom;
immigration; whiteness
Ratzinger, Joseph (Benedict XVI), 9
Rectified Scottish Rite, 201n1

Red Brigades, 158–159, 174–175, 210n3
red Freemasonry, 12. *See also* Rite
regolare. See legitimacy
religious beliefs, 9–10, 199n3. *See also*
Catholic Church
the Right (right-wing): overview of, 38,
201n8; feminism and, 97–98; fraternity
and, 95, 98, 103–104, 205n14; race
and, 24; terrorism and, 3, 11, 158–159,
201n8; transparency and, 158–159;
women's lodges and, 18, 86. *See also*
specific events and ideologies
Risorgimento, 9, 72
Rites, 12, 57, 71, 168–169, 200n6, 201n1,
210nn8–10
rituals: overview of, 7, 60–62; chain
of union and, 112–113; differences
in, 74; legitimacy and, 52, 112–113;
nationalism and, 152–153, 209n1;
nation-building and, 152–153, 209n1;
persecution of Masons and, 9–10;
ritual differences and, 74; secrecy and,
11, 17; social organization and, 12–13;
subjectivity and, 58; toasts at *agape*
dinners and, 151–153, 209n1; women's
lodges and, 68–69. *See also* esotericism; initiations
Rivolta Femminile (Feminine Revolt), 99
Rosicrucians, 12
rubare con gli occhi (stealing with the eyes),
121, 134–136, 135, 208n13. *See also*
gestures of recognition; pedagogies
rule of silence, 125–126, 206nn1–3

Santippe (Xanthippe), 142–143
Sapir, Edward, 147, 207n5
Scottish Rite, 57, 201n1
secrecy: overview of, 6–11, 17, 123, 155,
192–193, 200n4, 207n9; democratic ideals and, 7–8, 168, 178, 193;

cosmopolitanism and, 129, 132, 136, 205n9, 207n7; cultural capital and, 18, 124–125, 129–132, 136–142; gender differences and, 141–145, 208n16, 209nn19–20; high culture and, 136–148, 208nn14–16, 209n19; Marxism and, 123, 124; nationalism and, 132–133, 217n10; nation-building and, 130; nation-state and, 129, 130–131; operative Freemasonry versus, 7, 11, 123–125, 199n1; social capital and, 124–125; speculative labor and, 125, 131, 140–141, 147–148, 196. *See also* pedagogies; self-cultivation

speculative labor, 125, 131, 140–141, 147–148, 196. *See also* operative Freemasonry; speculative Freemasonry

Spivak, Gayatri Chakravorty, 205n12

Stacey, Judith, 204n5

stealing with the eyes (*rubare con gli occhi*), 121, 134–136, 208n13. *See also* gestures of recognition; pedagogies

Steedly, Mary, 145, 202n5, 212n2

stereotypical images, in media, 72–73, 92. *See also* persecution, of Masons

Stoler, Ann Laura, 203n11

structure of Freemasonry, 12, 200n6

subaltern subjects, 80, 105, 115, 190–191, 194–195, 206n15

subjectivity: overview of, 17–18, 57, 79–82, 202nn2–3, 202n9; brother and, 18, 79–82; discretion and, 63–64, 193, 202n4; elitism and, 58; esotericism and, 61; fraternity and, 109–110; freedom and, 76, 80–81; "Freemason within" and, 62–63, 79, 148; gender differences and, 15, 48–50; identity category and, 58, 61–62, 64, 67, 73–74, 79, 81, 158, 209n1; intersubjectivity and, 17, 79, 86, 202n9; mimicry and,

80–82, 203n10, 203n13; modernity and, 81, 203n11; Occidentalism and, 82, 203n12; paths and, 57–58, 61; production of, 59–62; profane in context of, 64–66, 202n4; rituals and, 58; secularism and, 81, 203n12; self-cultivation and, 17, 57–58, 61–63, 79–81; sexism and, 71, 203n13; subaltern subjects and, 80; traffic in women and, 77; transparency and, 157, 175–176; unmarked subject and, 80. *See also agape* (divine universal love); love (*amore*)

surveillance, 135, 156–157, 162–163, 171–172, 175, 178, 182–184, 191

symbolic capital, 37, 124–125, 133, 147. *See also* cultural capital; social capital

Symbolic Rite, 201n1

tablet or papers (*tavola/e*), 50–51, 126–128, 207n4

taste, 103, 124, 133, 136–138, 140, 147, 196, 208n14. *See also* high culture (*cultura*)

temples, 7, 41–42, 46–53, 51, 87, 138. *See also specific lodges, Masonic Orders, and rituals*

terrorism: overview of, 158–159; Bologna train station bombing and, 28, 159–160, 210n3; democratic ideals and, 160–161; Lead Years and, 11, 28, 158–159, 162, 174–175, 210nn2–3; the Right and, 3, 11, 158–159, 201n8; stereotypical images in media and, 72–73; Via dei Georgofili bombing and, 27–28, 113; women activists and, 174–175, 210n3

toasts ritual, 151–153, 209n1

traffic in women, 77

transnationalism, 96–97, 112, 203n1, 205n9

transparency: overview of, 11, 18, 37, 155–158, 183–185, 193–194; blacklists and, 155–157, 163–164, 170, 172, 174–175, 210n7; blame/suspicion narratives by Masons and, 42, 161–162, 164–170; conspiracy theories and, 159–161, 185, 210n4, 211n14; cultural intimacy and, 170, 178–179, 211n11; democratic ideals and, 157, 161, 175–178; desire for power/joining and, 170, 211n11; discretion and, 158, 179–182; gender differences and, 157–158, 163–164, 170–176, 211n12; modernity and, 178, 211n11; public relations and, 176–177, 188, 211n13; the Right and, 158–159; strategies of, 176–179, 211n13; subjectivity and, 157, 175–176; women's lodges and, 163–164, 172, 174–175, 182, 194

treaties of friendship, 13, 53, 68, 75, 111–113, 200n7. *See also* friendship (*philia*)

tropes of fieldwork, 1–6, 19

Tsoukas, Haridimos, 181

Tyler, 49, 107

United Grand Lodge of England (UGLE), 13, 111–113, 200n7

unmarked subject: abstraction of liberal subjects and, 106–107, 109–110; fraternity and, 80, 84, 115; liberal humanism and, 107; privilege and, 101–102, 115, 145; race and, 115; subjectivity and, 80; women and, 106; women's lodges and, 93, 95, 109. *See also* whiteness

unsympathetic subjects, 7, 191–192, 201n7, 205n10, 212n2

utopian projects, 19, 57, 116, 206n19

Vatican Sacred Congregation for the Doctrine of the Faith, 9

Via dei Georgofili bombing, 27–28, 113

violence, and representation of Freemasonry, 28, 30, 201n8. *See also* conspiracy theories; terrorism; *and specific events*

VITRIOL, 56

Warden, 107, 153

Weston, Kath, 144, 185

white *agape* dinners, 74, 117–118, 149. See also *agape* (divine universal love); *agape* dinners (*agapi*)

whiteness: abstraction of liberal subjects and, 106, 146, 206n16; democratic ideals and, 16; feminism and, 95, 99, 194–195, 204n4; high culture and, 146; identity category and, 25, 35; modernity and, 81, 85; nation-state and, 36; passing and, 26; privilege and, 175; symbolic capital and, 37. *See also* Occidentalism; race

Williams, Raymond, 15

women: politics and, 98; as privileged, 106–108, 145, 174–175, 195; terrorism and, 174–175, 210n3; traffic in, 77; unmarked subject and, 106

women's lodges: overview of, 7, 14–16; auxiliary lodges and, 5; blacklists and, 163–164, 172, 174–175; conspiracy theories and, 18; initiations and, 48, 52; legitimacy and, 78, 80, 141–142, 148, 194; paths for, 68–69; political subjectivity and, 67, 75–78; the Right and, 18, 86; rituals and, 68–69; self-cultivation and, 145, 209n20; social class and, 70; speculative labor and, 148; subjectivity and, 15, 49, 77; traffic in women and,

77; unmarked subject and, 93, 95, 109. *See also* Freemasonry; gender differences; men, as privileged; women; *and specific lodges and Masonic Orders*

work, speculative, 125, 131, 140–141, 147–148, 196. *See also* operative Freemasonry; speculative Freemasonry

Worshipful Maestro, 32, 50–51, 107, 128

Worthy Matron, 5, 12, 108

Worthy Patron, 5, 12, 88, 117

Xanthippe (Santippe), 142–143